D0171174

EYES
WIDE
OPEN

EYES
WIDE
OPEN

Overcoming Obstacles and
Recognizing Opportunities in a
World That Can't See Clearly

• • •

BY
ISAAC LIDSKY

A TARCHERPERIGEE BOOK

An imprint of Penguin Random House LLC
375 Hudson Street
New York, New York 10014

Most TarcherPerigee books are available at special quantity discounts for bulk purchase for sales promotions, premiums, fund-raising, and educational needs. Special books or book excerpts also can be created to fit specific needs. For details, write: SpecialMarkets@penguinrandomhouse.com.

ISBN 9780143129578

Printed in the United States of America
1   3   5   7   9   10   8   6   4   2

For The Kidskys, with hope you will see great blessings in your lives, and for Dorothy, the greatest in mine.

CONTENTS

CONTENTS

[W]orse than being blind is having sight but no vision.

—Helen Keller

EYES
WIDE
OPEN

CHAPTER 1

Seeing and Believing

What you don't know can't hurt you, but what you think you know certainly can.

When my wife, Dorothy, was a little girl, she was fascinated by her pet goldfish. Her father explained that fish swim by quickly wagging their tails to propel themselves through water. Without hesitation or doubt, Dorothy responded by informing him that fish swim backward by wagging their heads! In her mind, in her world, it was a fact as true as any other. Fish swim backward by wagging their heads.

Our lives are full of fish swimming backward. We make faulty leaps of logic. We make myriad assumptions. We prejudge. We harbor biases. We assume. We experience our beliefs and opinions as incontrovertible truths. We know that we are right and others are wrong. Fish swim by in reverse, frantically wagging their heads, and we do not notice them.

We are hardwired to do this. It is in our nature. As babies, we develop an understanding of our environment through countless observations of cause and effect. A baby drops her spoon on the ground. She is chastised by her mother, who bends to pick it up, washes it off in the sink, and then returns it to the breakfast tray. This scene plays out repeatedly for months or years, much to the mother's irritation. Along the way, the child learns about gravity, she begins to understand the concept that the floor is dirty, and she refines her understanding of how her actions can capture her mother's attention and impact her mother's emotions.

This is how we learn to survive, to interact with our world. We are creatures designed to find order in chaos, definition in ambiguity, certainty in a world of probabilities. We build up a vast database of experiences and design for ourselves rules and logic consistent with those experiences. We generalize, simplify, predict.

Our predisposition to reason from experience is a useful tendency, to put it mildly. It explains how our ancestors knew to run from a ferocious animal they had never before encountered, and how your child learns to say his first words. It also explains how a good salesman instinctually refines his pitch over time, learning to read responses and overcome common objections.

This tendency is also the source of great harm. How often do you miscommunicate with someone because you are making faulty assumptions about his motives or meaning? On what basis have you decided that your goals, hopes, or dreams are unattainable? Do you fear the worst, "borrowing trouble"? Do you strive for unattainable perfection and find disappointment in the inevitable result? How often do you stop to consider the profound difference between what you know and what you think you know?

Precocious little Dorothy's fish are amusing and innocent. Those that swim through our adult lives rarely are. In our careers and personal lives, in our relationships, and in our hearts and souls, our backward-swimming fish do us great harm. They exact a toll in missed opportunities and unrealized potential. They paralyze us with fear. They engender insecurity and distrust where we seek fulfillment and connection. They breed bias and prejudice.

In this book I will teach you to see the fish swimming backward through your life. I didn't notice mine until I slowly lost my sight to a progressive eye disease. But as I went blind I began to see them clearly. The deterioration of my sight cast them into focus. As I learned to recognize them, I embraced my blindness and gained a life richer in understanding, connection, and success. I call it living eyes wide open.

At work and at home, living eyes wide open has brought me immeasurable joy, fulfillment, and success. It is the philosophy that led me to leave behind my childhood acting career to attend college after starring as "Weasel" on NBC's sitcom *Saved by the Bell: The New Class*. I graduated from Harvard with an honors degree in mathematics and computer science at age nineteen, then founded an Internet advertising technology company. Living eyes wide open led me to leave that company when it was finally thriving, this time to attend Harvard Law School. After Harvard Law I spent three years litigating appeals in the federal courts as a U.S. Justice Department attorney before achieving my dream of serving as a U.S. Supreme

Court Law Clerk, working for Justices Sandra Day O'Connor and Ruth Bader Ginsburg. Then, in 2011 I saw eyes wide open the enormous potential in a struggling Orlando construction company. I put aside my legal career, figured out how to acquire the company, doubled down when the early days seemed to spell financial disaster, and turned it around, growing it tenfold in five years.

Living eyes wide open is also how I accepted my blinding disease, then embraced it. With eyes wide open I cherish my extraordinary wife, Dorothy, and our marriage. I celebrate our six-year-old triplets, our ninety-eight-day fight for their health, and their miraculous triumph against all odds. I celebrate their little sister, too. I see my life bursting with blessings, and I strive for the grace to honor these blessings.

People often ask how I have had so many diverse experiences at such a young age or accomplished so much so quickly. Invariably, they will then say something like: "And you did it all despite going blind. I can't imagine." Yet for me, going blind has not been a limitation on my life. In fact, it has helped me to achieve and to thrive. I've derived great lessons and blessings by going blind. I've gained vision by losing my sight.

Going blind is the blessing that showed me how to live my life eyes wide open. But anyone can choose to see what I see, even the sighted! That's why I wrote this book. I wrote it to teach you how and to inspire you to do so. In the chapters that follow, I'll share practical ways to open yourself to new learning, unexplored opportunities, and your true potential. I'll help you to confront both your fears and your perceived limitations. I'll show you how to embrace your work and your life, not resign to them. And I'll challenge you to be a leader in your own life and in the lives of those around you.

But before you can live eyes wide open, you need to better understand what happens when you open your eyes. Paradoxically, when it comes to fish that swim backward, your sight obscures your vision. The way you experience sight makes it harder to spot these fish.

Living with your eyes open and living eyes wide open are two very different things. In the difference lies the space those fish need to swim by undetected. They are hiding in plain view—more precisely, they are hiding in your sight. Understanding how is the place to start.

Virtual Reality

Do you see with your eyes? I'll bet you find this question strange and the answer obvious. You're likely thinking, *Of course I do.* You're wrong. Here's another odd question: What happens when you open your eyes? When you open your eyes you see the world around you, right? There's not much more to say about it, is there? Now you're very wrong. (If you're thinking, *This blind guy is crazy and I should stop reading his book*, stay with me for another few pages, please!)

As a kid growing up in Miami, I would have given the same wrong answers to these two questions. I can picture myself at the age of thirteen acting on the set of a television commercial at Filmworks, attending one of my dad's many hearings in the Miami-Dade County Courthouse, or taking classes in the theater program at

New World School of the Arts. I took my sight for granted, as most people do. It was not something I thought about. I saw just fine. I didn't even need glasses like the youngest of my older sisters, Ronit (pronounced "row," as you would a canoe, and "neat," as in "interesting").

That thirteen-year-old Isaac would answer our two questions impatiently and confidently, saying something like: "Yes, of course I see with my eyes. When I open my eyes I see what they are pointed at. I'm walking away now, sorry." Young Isaac was invincible. He did not know he had a disease called retinitis pigmentosa, or RP, that would dramatically change his answers to these questions as he slowly went blind. But I did have RP, I did go blind, and my answers did change.

To understand how, imagine the "Magic TV," the huge screen above center court at Orlando's Amway Center, where the Orlando Magic play. It's forty-two feet tall and forty-two feet wide, for a total area of 1,764 square feet. It has 9,470,400 pixels that collectively create the images you see, just like the pixels on your computer monitor.

The retina at the back of each of your eyes is like that Magic TV. It is a little smaller, approximately one thousand square millimeters, and it has a bit more pixels, approximately 125 million on each retina. (Put another way, the average human retina has 13.2 times more "pixels" than Amway's screen, even though that giant screen is 163,881 times bigger.) In terms of resolution, the retina is 2,163,068 times more powerful.

Instead of LED bulbs, the "pixels" of the retina are special cells called photoreceptor cells. They come in two varieties, known as "rods" and "cones" for their respective shapes. Just as the bulbs on the Jumbotron screen individually turn on or off to create an image in aggregate, each photoreceptor cell captures information about its tiny piece of the world. Each rod or cone cell is tuned to particular wavelengths, or colors, of light. (The more numerous rods respond to light of any color, while the cones, which are concentrated toward the center of the eye, each respond only to a particular color.) When a photoreceptor cell is hit by light that it is tuned to receive, it "fires," producing a bit of biological magic, a chemical reaction that generates a signal sent back to your brain. When you open your eyes, your 250 million photoreceptor cells fire feverishly to create your image of the world.

RP causes the photoreceptor cells to deteriorate, cease to function and ultimately die. Returning to the Magic TV, imagine that you are watching my life as a movie on that giant screen. Imagine further that the pixels on that screen slowly and randomly break. At first, you might not even notice, but as more and more pixels break you will start to spot holes in the image, dark regions on the screen. Over time those regions will grow in size and number. As still more pixels break, you will eventually struggle to decipher what you are watching. That struggle will grow more difficult and less successful as more pixels break. You will see less and less of my life as the movie plays on, until finally you'll see nothing at all.

That is what my sight was like as RP progressively broke the photoreceptor cells of my retina. It is impossible to say exactly when the deterioration of my sight started, and it is impossible to pinpoint a precise moment in time when I became blind as a result. I know, however, that as a young child I grew up with seemingly normal sight, through my teens my sight was clearly failing, and by my early twenties my dwindling sight was of diminishing use to me. I lived as a blind man by my twenty-fifth birthday.

One pleasant Saturday in the spring of 1997, I was walking through Harvard Square in Cambridge, Massachusetts, on my way to buy a late lunch. I was seventeen years old, a sophomore studying mathematics and computer science at Harvard College. My late lunch was technically a very late breakfast, as I had managed to roust myself from my bed only an hour earlier. The plan for breakfast was a cheeseburger sub from Pinocchio's Pizza & Subs on Winthrop Street—or "Nokes," as we called it. The plan was making my mouth water with eager anticipation.

I turned a corner and a giant tree branch came flying at my head. Luckily, I reacted quickly, diving to the side, landing in some bushes. Major, perhaps life-threatening head trauma was narrowly avoided, and I sustained only a few minor scrapes and bruises. I stood up, brushed off dirt and leaves, and heartily congratulated myself for preventing major injury with my impressive catlike speed and reflexes.

Then I looked around and realized the self-congratulation was unwarranted. There was no flying branch. There was a giant tree branch suspended over the sidewalk, well above my head, but it was firmly affixed to a towering tree. Neither the tree nor its branch had budged recently.

My lack of real physical injury notwithstanding, I felt substantial injury of the emotional kind. I was intensely embarrassed. I was frustrated by my failing eyes. I was angry that I was stuck with them.

Worst of all, I was forced once again to contemplate the big questions, the ones that were never far from my mind in those days, the questions of my fears. How bad is this going to get? How quickly? What will my life become as I go blind? I didn't feel hungry anymore. I felt scared, sad, and lonely. I walked back to my dorm room in Lowell House and crawled back into my bed.

In the months and years that followed, my retinas progressively deteriorated. My world blurred and morphed, the familiar and passive experience of sight becoming an arduous struggle to make sense of a bizarre carnival fun house hall of mirrors and illusions. This is when my answers to our two questions changed, how I learned: (1) You do not see with your eyes, you see with your brain. (2) The experience of sight is far more complex than perceiving what is around you. The flying tree branch I saw that day in Harvard Square came to symbolize these insights for me.

Your eyes capture a breathtaking amount of information, but that's only where sight begins. A full third of your brain is devoted to processing that information. Known as the "visual cortex," this third of your brain receives every second up to a billion signals from each of your retinas, two billion total. (The rest of your body can send your brain only an additional billion.) Your visual cortex creates from this torrent of two-dimensional data the three-dimensional experience we call sight, a truly miraculous feat. You see with your brain, not your eyes.

Consider an unremarkable scenario. You see your friend Carol across a crowded room at a cocktail party and walk over to her. You navigate myriad obstacles along the way without effort or thought. For example, you dodge a waiter's tray of hors d'oeuvres while mounting two small steps and hardly notice.

As you keep walking to Carol, you catalog countless details about your environment, consciously and unconsciously. You notice several stains on the carpet. You glance at the buffet table and see a large tray with a single shrimp lying lonely at its center. A woman steps into view and your eyes are drawn to her bright yellow hat. Curious, you take a closer look at the hat and conclude it is hideously ugly.

As you approach Carol, she stands with her back to you, engaged in a conversation. Eager to make a joke about the questionable headwear in the crowd, you tap her on the shoulder. A complete stranger turns to you, confused and slightly irritated. You respond with embarrassment, "I'm sorry, I thought you were someone else."

But that's not true. You didn't think she was someone else. You knew she was someone else. You knew she was Carol. You never questioned it. Indeed, you never even thought about it. In the world you experienced, you tapped Carol on the shoulder. She was there, in your brain, not your eyes.

Carol was as real as the backward-swimming, head-wagging fish in little Dorothy's world. Your brain created a reality that included her in just the same way little Dorothy's brain created a world with those curious fish. Your experience of sight and the physical reality of the world were two very different things. The former was an imperfect creation of your brain in response to the latter.

Now consider the true story of Marvin Anderson instead of the fictitious story about Carol. In the summer of 1982, a rape victim identified Anderson as her attacker, selecting his picture from a photo array and then identifying him in a lineup at the police station. Improperly suggestive procedures were employed by the police, making it more likely that the victim would choose Anderson. Still, she was certain he was the perpetrator of the violent assault, and at Anderson's trial she testified to that effect. In her reality, he was her attacker. She believed it. She knew it. Anderson was convicted on the basis of her certainty.

Anderson spent fifteen years in prison before he was paroled. After his parole, he spent another five years fighting to prove his innocence. Finally, in 2001 he gained access to DNA evidence that conclusively proved it. In 2002 he was granted a full pardon, twenty years after his arrest and conviction.

Marvin Anderson's image was a goldfish swimming backward through the victim's horrific recollections of her trauma. She saw him clearly, though he simply could not have been there. Unfortunately, his story is not unique. The Innocence Project reports that of all cases in which DNA evidence has conclusively exonerated the wrongly convicted, more than 70 percent of the time, false eyewitness testimony played a part in the conviction. That's a lot of false realities with great consequences.

Those realities involve far more than the mere perception of light by eyes. Each is the creation of a visual cortex. Greatly oversimplifying matters, coded in the visual cortex are a hierarchical set of increasingly complex filters or rules that you learn as a developing child.

For example, consider a baby sitting on the floor as a red ball rolls by. The pattern of information coming from her retinas that corresponds to the image of that object—a circle of firing red cone photoreceptor cells—is continuously sent to her visual cortex. The location of that pattern, however, shifts along her retinas as the ball rolls by. As she repeatedly encounters this phenomenon—a spatially shifting pattern of information—her visual cortex literally reshapes its wiring, creating a neural network that will "fire" in response to the phenomenon. Let's call that network a "motion detector."

Having a motion detector is necessary to see a moving object, but it is not sufficient. Our baby must also develop a higher-level understanding of the very concept of motion. She builds up that understanding through repeated experimentation. She rolls the ball back and forth, picks it up, puts it in her mouth, rolls it some more, picks it up again, realizes that it is the same ball before and after she has rolled it. Instinctively she begins to comprehend that the ball is a discrete object that can move in space.

Critically, a linkage is formed between her motion detector in her visual cortex and her higher-level cognitive understanding of motion. To experience seeing an object in motion she relies upon both—and her brain's ability to associate the two. She cannot see motion in any meaningful way if she does not understand it.

A striking illustration of this point was chronicled by anthropologist Colin Turnbull when he spent time with the Mbuti pygmies in the Ituri Forest of the Democratic Republic of Congo. The Ituri Forest is extremely dense. A life lived entirely within its borders would not afford you experience with vast open spaces or sight across long distances. Such was the life of Kenge, a twenty-two-year-old Pygmy. That is, until Turnbull showed up and enlisted Kenge to be his assistant and guide.

On an excursion they drove into a rare clearing. Two miles across the plain a herd of buffalo were grazing. Kenge had never had any experience perceiving such large objects at such a great distance. He thus did not see buffalo in the distance. His brain wasn't wired to produce that experience. Instead, he saw insects nearby. When he asked Turnbull to name the strange insects, Turnbull drove in their direction to demonstrate their size. The buffalo insects appeared larger and larger to Kenge as they grew closer, another new experience for him. Kenge grew uncomfortable and asked Turnbull if witchcraft was at work.

More dramatic examples are common in people who regain sight later in life—more precisely, people who regain eyesight, or functioning of their eyes. Robert Kurson brilliantly recounted the story of Michael May in his book *Crashing Through*. In 1957, when May was three years old, his corneas (the very front of the eye) were destroyed in a chemical explosion. Forty-three years later they were repaired by a pioneering stem cell treatment. The treatment restored normal function to his eyes, but it left him with far less than normal sight. For example, he does not experience depth perception in any meaningful way. Walk away from May and he perceives you shrinking in size. He can conceptually understand what is going on, but his visual cortex never developed the perceptual analog to that conceptual understanding.

Your experience of sight is inextricably intertwined with your conceptual understanding of the world. In our cocktail party example, this is how a pattern of firing photoreceptor cells in your retinas became the muscle movements necessary for you to climb those stairs—without so much as a single conscious thought on your part. You did far more than simply perceive those stairs with your eyes.

Beyond conceptual understanding, the experience of sight implicates your knowledge, memories, opinions, emotions, and mental attention. All of these things, and far more, are linked in your brain to your sight. The linkage works both ways. For example, your experience of sight can impact the way you feel, and the way you feel can impact what you see. Making matters even more complicated, these linkages most often play out subconsciously—you are unaware of them.

Are you growing doubtful? Return to our false Carol sighting. If you had just spoken to Carol and knew she was out of town, would you still have seen her? Did you falsely spot Carol because you unconsciously recognized the stranger's dress as one that Carol owns?

What about that yellow hat? Suppose that the woman wearing it is a dear friend of yours who is courageously battling cancer. She recently began a course of chemotherapy and as a result has lost her hair. Do you still see a hideously ugly hat, or does it now look beautiful to you, a bold image of strength? Similarly, what would the hat look like if earlier in the day you had seen a photograph of your favorite celebrity wearing it? Could the magazine photo change your perception of the hat—even if you don't consciously make the connection?

Consider your mood and your memories. If you begrudgingly arrived at the party ravenously hungry and you think shellfish of all varieties are disgusting, what happened when you saw that one meager shrimp on that vast tray? Did it worsen your mood? If you were feeling miffed to be at a lousy party with lousy food and not enough of it to boot, what details did you take in about your surroundings—consciously and unconsciously? Did the stains on the floor jump out at you and stick in your mind all night? Were you more inclined to see shabbiness and tune out cocktail party chic?

Instead imagine that years ago you met the love of your life when your hands accidentally touched as you both reached for the last shrimp on a tray at a New Year's party. You and your beloved adore shrimp. Near midnight that New Year's Eve a little boy dressed in an adorable suit raced by the two of you and jostled your glass, spilling your wine on your pants. Your future spouse produced a napkin and tended to the stain. Embarrassed, you averted your eyes and stared down at the floor, focusing on the stain your spilled wine made on the carpet. The crowd began to count down the New Year, and your heart skipped a beat.

What do you see now when you look around the room after studying that final shrimp loaded with potential? Do you see a quaint and charming room? Do those stains on the floor remind you of the little boy and reinforce your impression that this is a special place to host a party? Are you in a beautiful place, physically and mentally? What are you likely to remember about your evening?

Finally, consider all of the things you didn't notice that night. Is it possible that Carol was there after all, only a dozen steps away, and you somehow missed her entirely? A famous 1999 Harvard research study performed by Christopher Chabris and Daniel Simons color-fully demonstrates this point. Chabris and Simons showed their re-search subjects a video of six people passing basketballs around, three wearing white shirts and three wearing black shirts. The study participants were told to count the number of passes made by the players in white shirts, a task that required a high degree of concentration and focus.

The video contained a rather substantial wrinkle, a man in a gorilla costume. In the middle of the video, the gorilla walked to the center of the screen, thumped his chest, and then left. The gorilla's appearance lasted a full nine seconds, hard to miss.

But it wasn't hard to miss. Half of the research subjects failed entirely to notice the gorilla. For them, the gorilla was invisible. Engrossed in the counting task at hand, they missed it entirely. In their reality, the gorilla never existed.

Sight is much more than meets the eye. It is our thoughts, our memories, our emotions, our judgments, our experiences, our instincts. All of these aspects of who you are literally color what you see. And what you see shapes the contours of these diverse aspects of your life.

Numerous research studies have demonstrated as much. For example, estimates of a man's walking speed vary according to whether research subjects are primed to think about fast animals like cheetahs or slow animals like turtles. Similarly, interpretations of an ambiguous figure that can be seen as a woman's face or as a man playing a saxophone depend on whether people have been recently primed with the concepts of "flirtation" or "music." A hill appears more steep after the perceiver jogs vigorously for an hour, and the distance to a goal seems longer if the perceiver has strapped on a heavy backpack.

Additionally, sight is at work in these feedback loops even when your eyes are closed! Your visual cortex is hard at work as a mental air traffic controller when you are dreaming. When you experience memories you are playing them back through your visual cortex. Think about an elephant and, you guessed it, your elephant detectors in your visual cortex will fire.

More abstractly, we construct mental images of ideas or concepts. For example, we talk about the "image of success." What does that mean? Does your mind invoke the concept of success when you perceive an expensive car, a laughing child, both, neither? Conversely, when you imagine yourself achieving great success, do certain images come to mind?

Finally, what is it that you see, anyway? I said earlier that the photoreceptor cells of our eyes are tuned to respond to light. The full truth is more complicated. That light comprises a small sliver of electromagnetic radiation, a sliver we call "visible light." Electromagnetic radiation is characterized by the relationship between its wavelength and frequency, and it spans a vast spectrum that corresponds to a range of values for those properties. Our photoreceptor cells respond to electromagnetic radiation with a wavelength that falls in a particular, narrow range of values.

How tiny is that sliver? .00000000001 percent. As David Eagleman explains in his riveting TED Talk "Can we create new senses for humans?" we perceive only one ten trillionth of the electromagnetic radiation that floods our world. That's not much. And there's a lot of interesting information in the invisible spectrum, such as radio waves, microwaves, infrared, ultraviolet, X-rays, and gamma rays.

Is there anything magical about our microscopic sliver? No. Indeed, other animal species can see electromagnetic radiation outside the "visible spectrum." That is, they see electromagnetic radiation invisible to us humans. Change the tuning of your photoreceptor cells, even slightly, and you see a different world. Imagine a world in which you could see radio waves and microwaves, or X-rays and gamma rays. What does reality look like in that world? Which world is "right"?

Speaking of "right," is that even the goal? Is the human experience of sight optimized to render the information we perceive with accuracy? That may seem like an odd question, but Donald D. Hoffman, a professor of cognitive science at the University of California, Irvine, has spent three decades thinking about it. His conclusions are eye-opening. He summarizes them in his TED Talk "Do we see reality as it is?" which I encourage you to watch.

Hoffman posits that the purpose of our visual system is not to accurately portray some objective reality (if there is such a thing), but instead to create an experience that furthers the evolutionary goals of survival and reproduction. Put another way, our minds are less concerned with getting it "right" than they are with getting it "useful." The very point of sight, he argues, is to augment information, not represent it. In a recent interview published in *The Atlantic*, he explained: "Evolution has shaped us with perceptions that allow us to survive. They guide adaptive behaviors. But part of that involves hiding from us the stuff we don't need to know. And that's pretty much all of reality, whatever reality might be."

Hoffman uses the desktop interface for computers as a metaphor: "Suppose there's a blue rectangular icon [of a file] on the lower right corner of your computer's desktop—does that mean that the file itself is blue and rectangular and lives in the lower right corner of your computer? Of course not. But those are the only things that can be asserted about anything on the desktop—it has color, position, and shape. Those are the only categories available to you, and yet none of them are true about the file itself or anything in the computer.... You could not form a true description of the innards of the computer if your entire view of reality was confined to the desktop. And yet the desktop is useful. That blue rectangular icon guides my behavior, and it hides a complex reality that I don't need to know. That's the key idea."

Sight is profoundly complex. Your eyes siphon a miniscule stream of data from a vast ocean of electromagnetic information. Your brain processes and abstracts that data, creating a functional "desktop." That desktop experience both shapes and is shaped by who you are and the totality of your circumstances in any moment. Sight is a virtual reality.

It doesn't feel that way, however. Sight feels effortless and passive. It is immediate. You open your eyes and perceive the world around you. The experience is complete, consistent, convincing beyond doubt. Your reality is what you see. You believe it. Seeing is believing, and sight is truth.

This is a fundamental contradiction, and it lies at the core of eyes wide open. It is in your very nature to construct a virtual reality in your mind and simultaneously to experience that reality as objective truth. Think about the implications. What you see is a complex mental construction of your own making, but you experience it passively as a direct representation of the world around you. You create and perpetuate your own reality, your own truth.

A New Vision

As my sight eroded, making sense of the fractured, incomplete snippets of information my retinas captured became an arduous, frustrating task. I furtively scanned the space around me, tilting my head at different angles, squinting my eyes to focus, then opening them wide, consciously trying to piece together clues with which I could assemble a view of the world. Objects would magically become clear and come into existence for me once my mind had enough information to achieve recognition.

But "recognition," I was frequently reminded, was really my mind making its best guess. Objects often morphed upon further investigation. The salesperson I was relieved to spot in a store was really a mannequin. I realized the pattern of stripes on the floor was in fact a descending stairway as I stumbled down the first few steps. Reaching down to wash my hands in an unfamiliar restroom, I suddenly saw it was a urinal I was touching, not a sink, when my fingers felt its true shape. An image emerged from an indecipherable photograph, clear as day, when Dorothy described the content depicted. And on Winthrop Street, there was no flying tree branch after all.

I was reminded daily that my sight was a virtual reality. It wasn't a very good one, and I was forced to play an active role in decoding it. The experience gave me rich insight into the inner workings of the visual machine. More practically, it meant I could not rely upon my eyes.

Remarkably, as sight lost its previously unchallenged centrality in my world, other pathways of perception emerged. One night in 2006, Dorothy and I dined at a new restaurant in Washington, DC, with some friends. By this time I had very little useful sight and I was already using a walking cane for the blind. None of the four of us had ever been to the restaurant, and we were excited to try it. After waiting about twenty minutes (despite having made a reservation), we were finally shown to our table.

Just after we sat, our friend remarked that she had to go to the restroom and she asked if any of us knew where it was. Dorothy responded that she wasn't certain, but that it looked like the restrooms would be off the corner at the far side of the room. Visually, that was Dorothy's guess at where they should be.

"No, that is not where they are," I blurted out. Without thinking I continued: "Remember when we made that right turn about halfway down the bar and then walked down that narrow hallway and made another right turn to enter this room? If you had made a left turn instead of that second right the bathrooms would be down the stairs."

We were all a little surprised, myself included. I was also thrilled, as I realized in that moment the extent to which I was developing a new, nonvisual processing system for interacting with the world.

When the hostess walked us along the bar, I could literally hear its shape from the pattern of conversations and other noises—drinks being put down, drinks being mixed, snacks being crunched. And it smelled like a bar. No mistaking it. I could feel and hear the narrow hallway we turned into. At the end of that hallway, I could hear to my left the sound of sandals slapping against steps as a patron climbed up the stairs. I turned my head slightly to the left and smelled her perfume. And also the smell of dampness—moisture in the air rising up from a poorly ventilated space at the bottom of the stairs. We turned right, then I heard a distant toilet flush behind me before we again turned right, into the large room in which we were seated.

As I thought about this chain of events, what struck me was not the amount of information I could gain from my nonvisual senses. I had been devoting a lot of attention to that endeavor for years. What struck me was how natural the process had become, and how rich the experience could be.

I had synthesized information, drawn logical inferences, constructed a mental image of my space, and committed the details of that image to memory—all without thought or effort. It had been years since I had experienced perception so naturally or effortlessly. Sight had long ago ceased to be such an experience. Now I had the experience again, but without sight.

I was seeing my world without sight. And as far as spotting the bathroom goes, I saw far better than my sighted companions! They heard, smelled, and felt all the same things that I did as we walked to the table. But they had no idea where the bathroom was.

This is how I started to think about living eyes wide open. It was at first a physical necessity for me, a strategy to compensate for my deteriorating sight and ultimately my blindness. It was about the practicalities of interacting with the world as I came to understand the true nature of my sight by losing it, and as I gained heightened abilities of perception employing my other senses.

Living eyes wide open became far more. My insight into sight was the proverbial peek behind the curtains that exposed the wizard. Once I knew he was there I began to see his hand at work in other aspects of my life. The virtual realities of our minds that we experience as truth do not end with sight, or with perception more generally. That is where they begin. I saw this with blindness.

I saw everywhere the difference between universal truth and the virtual reality of the mind. I learned to see my many backward-swimming fish. With this ability I gained control over my life, freedom from self-destruction and self-limitation, the empowerment to shape my own destiny, the choice to live life eyes wide open.

Eyes wide open became my powerful philosophy and active daily strategy. It is how I live and lead with deeper awareness, understanding, connection, and success—at work and at home. In the chapters that follow I'll explain it to you. We'll explore life eyes wide open in various contexts, with examples from my life.

The next two chapters will teach you how to view your challenges eyes wide open. Chapter 2 will tackle fear in moments of crisis or extreme change, while Chapter 3 will deliver strategies for ongoing, sustained progress in the face of struggle. You'll learn to take ownership of your mental images and shape your reality with discrete, practical solutions.

In Chapter 4 you'll learn to see the thin, elusive line between acceptance and surrender, between strength and weakness, between confidence and vulnerability. I'll teach you to productively focus your viewpoint when it comes to your purported weaknesses and to integrate the views of those around you, leveraging both to build strength.

In Chapter 5 we'll tackle your perception of luck and how you view events in your life through the lens of being lucky and unlucky.

The eyes wide open view is highly nuanced, casting luck as a complex and continuous force in your life that you can shape.

Chapter 6 will introduce a rigorous framework for assessing your "value" and "success," eyes wide open. Again we'll bring nuance to bear, this time on the question of whether you're achieving your goals in your career and at home.

In Chapter 7 I'll teach you to listen ears wide open, to expand what you hear, to better understand what people are trying to tell you.

Finally, Chapter 8 presents the eyes wide open view of life. Give yourself permission to see with your heart and choose who you are and how you want to live each moment. Take ownership and seek inspiration to create your own narrative.

Between chapters we'll take Fishing Trips. In each we'll trawl a personal story from my life and hook a backward-swimming fish or two. These Fishing Trips are meant to illustrate broadly the eyes wide open concepts explored in the chapters, and also to provide a brief diversion from the dense material the chapters contain (though the chapters have plenty of personal stories, too).

I encourage you to read this book start to finish, but you don't have to do so. I've written the chapters and Fishing Trips so that each stands alone. Skip around if particular subjects are of interest (or not). If you're in the mood for stories, hit the Fishing Trips. When you're ready for heavier lifting, explore the ideas presented in the chapters. I hope you will find all of the material interesting and useful, and that you'll come back to revisit this book, in whole or in part, whenever you feel your vision narrow.

Living eyes wide open is an ongoing journey. It is a learned discipline that takes effort and attention. I work hard at it every day. For me, it is well worth the effort.

I want to know what you think. As you read this book, please visit lidsky.com/eyeswideopen to share your stories and insights, provide feedback, submit your questions, or tell me how eyes wide open has made an impact at home or at work. There's wisdom in community. I invite you to join mine. I hope you will.

Fishing Trip I: Action, Lights, Camera!

Summer 1993

If you flipped through a teen magazine in the summer of 1993, chances are you saw an article about me. I use the term "article" loosely. The glossy pages revealed my favorite color or animal, broke the story of the latest pool party I attended, described my thirteen-year-old dream date, or shared other mundane inanity. It wasn't journalism. It wasn't literature. Often, it was barely English. Still, month after month I was there in full-color photos in all the "Teen X" publications (*Teen Machine, Teen Life, Teen Screen, Teen World, Teen Beat, Teen Bag,* etc.) and their more imaginatively named brethren *(Bop, Tiger Beat, 16 Magazine, Big Bopper, J-14,* etc.).

I was famous, a celebrity, and I did the things a famous celebrity does. I made public appearances at high-profile events for charities. I took VIP tours of theme parks in the name of publicity and didn't have any fun. I visited the corporate offices of the athletic apparel company that "sponsored" me and helped myself to their newest products, most of which were not yet available to the public and none of which I paid for. I was recognized by strangers in stores and restaurants, malls and airports. I signed autographs. I received fan mail.

Why?

In 1989 the Disney Channel television series *Good Morning, Miss Bliss* was revamped and relaunched on NBC as *Saved by the Bell*. The new version was a huge success. *Saved by the Bell* quickly became the highest-rated Saturday-morning television show ever. Its regular characters, the principal of the fictitious Bayside High School and six of the school's students, became popular culture icons. The actors who played those characters gained fame and fortune.

Over four years, more than sixty episodes of *Saved by the Bell* and two movie spin-offs were produced. Alas, teenagers grow up and stop looking like teenagers, even in Hollywood. (Especially in Hollywood.) This presented both a problem and an opportunity for NBC in 1993: what to do about graduation day at Bayside High for *Saved by the Bell*'s actors?

NBC's solution was twofold, a doubling down. First, it created a new prime-time show, *Saved by the Bell: The College Years*. After graduation, most of Bayside's buddies conveniently wound up on this sitcom university campus, on essentially the same show with a different name and time slot. (But Saturday-morning antics do not play well in prime time, so *The College Years* failed out in its first semester.) Second, NBC decided to rinse and repeat with the Saturday-morning time slot, creating *Saved by the Bell: The New Class*.

The New Class was more remake than sequel. It had the same Bayside High School sets, same principal, same number of series regular students—six total, three boys and three girls. While each of the characters had a new name, each was strikingly similar to a character from the original show. The new scripts were strikingly similar to the old ones, too. If it ain't broke, don't fix it.

In 1993 the *Saved by the Bell* franchise was anything but broken. It was wildly popular, with millions of fans. Many of these fans were excited that *The New Class* was in the works. They were impatient for its debut. They were eager to meet its cast. NBC was eager to take advantage of this eagerness, so it launched a nationwide search for Bayside's incoming freshmen, chronicled by *Entertainment Tonight*, a teen magazine of television journalism. That's where I come in.

At this point I was neither famous nor a celebrity, but I was an experienced actor. It was a family affair. When my oldest sister, Ilana, was a little girl, she told our mother that she wanted to be on television. My mom researched acting opportunities in Miami and discovered that a lot of television commercials were filmed in our hometown, especially in the winter, when New York ad agencies used any excuse to migrate south for a few days of warm weather and beaches. My mom signed Ilana up with a handful of agents, and Ilana quickly began to book acting gigs. My other two older sisters, Daria and Ronit, were soon acting as well.

My mother had already become a pro in town when I was born. I starred in a commercial for diapers when I was six months old, and by the time I started preschool my mom wasn't the only pro. I had weekly auditions and acted in a commercial or two each month.

I thought everyone did. One day a neighborhood friend invited me to play at his house after preschool. But I knew there was an audition that afternoon, and I reminded him about it. He was confused by my response. His confusion confused me. I did not understand why he did not understand auditions and commercials and acting. When he insisted that he was going to play after school, I cried in frustration. Eventually I learned that my childhood acting career was uncommon—and that it demanded a monumental commitment from my mother.

A two-pro team, we spent countless hours together at auditions, on sets, and traveling to and from both. By the time NBC was recruiting *The New Class*'s six star students, I had acted in more than 100 commercials, probably more than 150, though we didn't keep count. Beyond TV ads, I had some lucky breaks, like the starring role in *Boy*, a short film written and directed by Jerry Lewis. I had far more disappointments, however—big television and film roles that I didn't land. My work was steady and unglamorous. I was an actor, but not a celebrity. I was not famous.

I thus had no illusions when I showed up at the Miami casting for *The New Class* to read for the part of Barton "Weasel" Wyzell. Don't get me wrong—it was exciting. I was a *Saved by the Bell* fan, and I indulged the fantasy of starring on the show. Weasel was the nerdy character, the reincarnation of the original show's "Screech." It was great fun to imagine myself, in the inevitable logic of the franchise, as "The New Screech." But I understood it was just that: good fun, a fantasy. I knew how long were the odds of success in this nationwide search. I had faced long odds many times, could recall plenty of unrealized fantasies. A couple days after the audition I had forgotten about the whole thing.

My agent called a few weeks later and reminded me. She told me that NBC wanted me to audition for the show's producers in Los Angeles. I had made such a journey once before without success, a bid for a leading role in a pilot for a television series that was never produced. (A classic Hollywood failure, failing to land a pilot that fails.) Still, the news was exhilarating. Me, The New Screech? The odds weren't so long anymore. I could think of little else. Time crawled.

Then the day came. My mother and I endured a long flight across the country; suffered an endless cab ride to our hotel, victims of LA's interminable traffic; and finally tried to get some sleep, an exercise in futility. Early the next morning, we made our way to the studio, where we were led to a large conference room. Fifteen to twenty kids were led to that conference room that morning, each with a parent, thirty to forty of us in total, crowded, anxious, hopeful. We were left to make our own introductions, to speculate together about the plan for the day, to divine our own fates, to agonize, to sweat.

With aggressive, self-interested curiosity disguised as polite conversation, we uncovered one another's key characteristics. Right away we established that five or six of us kids were there to audition for the part of Weasel, but each of the five remaining series regular roles had only two or three contenders present. None of us knew, however, whether there were other rooms somewhere with other auditioning actors, or auditions scheduled for other days, or both. I decided to focus on our procedural uncertainty instead of the anomalous oversupply of aspiring Weasels, though it is unclear which was more disheartening.

With a little bit more time we pieced together each other's professional qualifications. The boy from Colorado had only a few high school plays to his credit. The girl from Northern California had bagged an ABC pilot and some voice-over work for a Nickelodeon cartoon. One kid was represented by an A-list manager and agent. Another had no representation at all. On the whole it seemed I had far more acting experience than most of my compatriots.

But was this good or bad? *Saved by the Bell* lore highlighted the inexperience of the show's cast. They came together without much practice acting, bonded on the set, and together found fame and success. The on-screen effectiveness of the original cast's authentic amateur chemistry—a quasi-precursor to "reality" television—was a theme in the publicized narrative of the nationwide search for *The New Class*. Did I have too much experience to re-create the original experiment? Another troubling question without an answer.

There would be plenty of time to ponder. Poorly camouflaged interrogations petered out as we exhausted pertinent inquiries of each other, replaced by idle chitchat, feeble and forced. Before long we collectively gave up and made an unspoken agreement to just keep to ourselves. Then we waited.

They came for us kids one at a time. The door opened, a name was called, a kid hopped up and hustled out, the door closed. Ten or fifteen minutes later the kid came back, giddy, mortified, thrilled, devastated, or catatonic, huddling and whispering with his parent, clinging to a paper-thin poker face that hid nothing. The messenger returned a few minutes later.

The fourth or fifth summons was for me. I was ushered through a maze of hallways to another large room, this one filled with a couple dozen important people arranged in tiered rows of seating. I was led to the front, and one of the important people (the show's director as it turned out) called out one of Weasel's lines in one of the scenes I had been told to prepare. "Take it from there, please, Isaac," he said. I did. We hit two or three other scenes before some signal I did not notice alerted my usher somehow, and she led me back to my mom and our cohorts in the large conference room without explanation. Then I waited behind my transparent mask.

A couple hours into the morning there was a conspicuous addition to the routine. The messenger appeared and summoned one of the aspiring stars. But this time she told his mother to come along, too. We were stunned. What could this mean? Moments later the mother shuffled back into the room to collect her purse. "They said we should head back to the hotel and wait to hear about next steps," she mumbled to no one in particular, a woman broken. Everyone heard her. Everyone pretended not to. From then on, whenever a parent was called with his child, he took everything out of the room with him. Parent-child pairs did not return. There were no good-byes.

It went on this way for hours. At some point they brought deli sandwiches in for lunch. Self-initiated excursions out of the conference room for bathroom breaks increased in frequency with the intensity of our boredom. Otherwise, the pattern continued. Kids ushered to the room of important people and back again in no apparent order. Kids and parents sent home. I was ushered back three or four times as the day wore on and the conference room crowd dwindled. The rest of the time I waited and wondered.

In the afternoon it seemed a new pattern was emerging. When

only a single candidate remained for a particular role, he was no longer called out of our conference room—neither to visit with the important people nor to head home with his parent. This pattern sparked suspicion, ignited a flame of optimism, fueled an uncontainable blaze of hope. Had the sole remaining actor auditioning for a particular role been chosen by the important people to play that role on *The New Class*? Could it be? We wanted to believe it, to know that this would all end today, to think that it might end with our dream come true.

As the pattern held and the room slowly cleared out, I wanted desperately to be the sole remaining Weasel, a desire so intense it hurt. For a while there were still three of us. Then only two. Two Weasels, one of every other series regular character on the show, seven parents living for their children, one conference room, one very long day that wasn't over yet. I sat for an eternity suspended in quantum probability, half heartbroken, half elated, heart pounding, barely breathing, thirteen-year-old washout failure Hollywood superstar frozen in a moment, waiting for the grim reaper's coin toss. Finally, she came to summon her last victim, and when she took him despite his tears I remained. Six of us remained, praying the only plausible rationalization for the day's torture would soon be revealed, confirmation we'd scored a television sitcom guaranteed its progenitor's huge audience the moment it was conceived. We did not dare to speak.

When the executive producer of the show burst into the room, flanked by bright lights from *Entertainment Tonight* film cameras and popping flashes from NBC's publicity photographers, silent vigil gave way to ecstatic celebration in an instant. "I guess you've figured it out," he said. "Congratulations, you're the cast of *Saved by the Bell: The New Class*." Less than ten minutes later we were escorted to the front of an auditorium, where we sat for our first press conference, facing representatives from more than two hundred media outlets. Publicity was the first order of business.

Business boomed. After a quick trip home to Miami for a few days, I returned to NBC's Burbank studios to get to work with my new colleagues. On day one we shot publicity photos with NBC's in-house PR team. The next day was more of the same. And the next. For an entire week we took pictures to promote the show. Pictures on dozens of sets, wearing scores of outfits, in hundreds of cast permutations. So many pictures that my cheeks hurt when I smiled.

Then we made the rounds at the teen magazines. Each required its own photographs with its own photographers, more hours spent posing for cameras. Some of the magazines actually conducted interviews, too, but most didn't. Most of them wanted me to fill out a questionnaire instead.

These questionnaires were long, rambling, and bizarre, covering every conceivable teenage biographical datum, every "favorite" I might have, every pet I ever had, every crush I ever had, every breakup I ever had, every job I ever had, my top three funny stories, top three scary stories, top three sad stories, and on and on and on. Trudging through the third or fourth of these interrogatory tomes I finally gave voice to my naïve curiosity and asked the magazine's representative to explain why so much information was required at our first meeting. She chuckled and informed me that this would likely be our only meeting.

My answers to the questionnaire would provide her employer

ample material to dole out in dribs and drabs for dozens of issues to come, she explained. All that really mattered, she continued, was that a picture of me appear in some form in every issue so that the "readers" who cared about my character would find something new to look at every month—and would think that I had been interviewed. As long as I had a television show, of course. A bunch of pictures and a lengthy questionnaire will suffice, thank you very much. Best of luck to you for a bright future. Good-bye.

A few weeks later the public appearances began. Celebrity guest at a fund raiser. Celebrity contestant on a game show. Celebrity visitor to a theme park. Free press, lots of it. There were private appearances as well, like the mandatory "cast pool party" with the anonymous organizer and more photographers than attendees. The precise nature of that party was never clear, but the photographs looked great in the magazines. Most important, it sure seemed that *The New Class* was bonding rather nicely, though we'd yet to spend time together unphotographed.

In this way we were made famous. We were made celebrities. We were made the characters in a real-life narrative as artificial as a Saturday-morning television show. We were plucked from our lives and inserted into a virtual reality carefully crafted to perpetuate itself.

It worked. It worked so well, in fact, that even some of my new classmates believed it was real. Our overnight fans certainly did. They talked about us, wrote to us, asked for our autographs. They believed we were the best of friends. They believed we were celebrities. They cheered for us.

Why?

Even in 1993 there were people who were famous for being famous. And if the person who wins an enormous lottery payout is drenched in fame for fifteen minutes, the spectacle of our thespian jackpot merited similar attention. But this was different. In the summer of 1993 we were famous sitcom actors who had never acted on a sitcom. By design. Before we had filmed the first minute of our first episode, strangers applauded our "work" and told us that they loved our show. It felt fraudulent, all of it.

This thought was steady and unglamorous in my mind. It proved prophetic, too. I never bonded with my new best friends. No off-screen chemistry catalyzed the alchemy of television gold. At best *The New Class* forged bronze. Many of the important people weren't so important after all. Too few were kind or caring. (Our director was one of these few, and it was a privilege to work with him.) No matter, we were famous.

My acting career survived a single season of *The New Class*. If you flipped through a teen magazine in the summer of 1994, you did not see me in its pages. In 1995 I left Los Angeles to begin my college studies a couple weeks after my sixteenth birthday, skipping my senior year of high school, impatient to move on with real life. The fan mail, public recognition, and autograph requests slowed rapidly, then trickled for a few years before ceasing altogether.

Today, folks continue to find my brief and ancient stint as The New Screech interesting or amusing. Old friends tease me without mercy. New friends want to hear all about it. I don't mind. I find it all amusing, too. It was another life, another world, another reality. It doesn't feel real. It never did.

CHAPTER 2

Heroes and Villains

The only thing we have to fear is fear itself.

—Franklin Delano Roosevelt

Worry becomes anxiety trending toward panic. I am lost. Blind, without a phone, wandering a deserted street, armed only with my cane, and lost. That tortuous Washington, DC, intersection threw me off, the spaghettilike jumble of streets, a perpendicular intersection superimposed on a curving road, adorned by another street slashing across at a random angle. I took a wrong turn exiting the maze of streets and sidewalks. Was that seven blocks ago or eight? How many turns have I made since then? I've lost track. My heart races. I am all alone and don't know where I am.

I thought I could handle it. An early effort at blind independence, this walk was supposed to build confidence in my mobility skills. I left my house about an hour ago full of hope and optimism, forgetting my phone. There was a bounce in my step. Now I feel like a failure and a fool, panic rising. I'm frozen where I stand, muscles tense, jaw clenched.

Fear choreographs a troupe of obstructive emotions, making a circus of my thoughts. Embarrassment and shame soar acrobatically, sadness commands center ring with a pathetic clown act, pride falls violently from a precarious perch and is rushed away. Mentally, I am drawn in. My world narrows, my focus zooms in tight. I think only awful thoughts, exaggerating my immediate predicament and cataloging implications for my life and future that are as dreadful as they are false. I am hopeless and helpless and will never regain my independence. Everything else is shut out. Fear is the master of ceremonies. It is masterful.

I find the curb with my cane's tip, sit down, take several deep breaths, and concentrate on mentally zooming out. I begin with two simple questions: What, precisely, is my problem? What, precisely, can I do about it? Eyes wide open, I think it through.

It is around eleven on a beautiful spring Sunday morning. There is nowhere I need to be right now and nothing I need to be doing. My goal for the morning was humble and inconsequential, a stroll to procure coffee on my own. It took me fifteen minutes to walk from my Capitol Hill home to Eastern Market, where I bought a double espresso and enjoyed it while sitting in the sun listening to the newspaper on my new Victor Reader Stream, a handheld media player for the blind and visually impaired. I got lost on the way back. I can't be more than ten minutes away from my house.

I'm on a small, empty residential street without pedestrians to rely upon for help, but it is safe. It is lined with row houses. Most of them contain their residents at the moment, it occurs to me, scenes of tranquility and Sunday-morning laziness. I can knock on a door or two, find a neighbor, ask to borrow a phone, call Dorothy to report my address, and wait for her to pick me up. I don't have much of a problem after all.

It really is an exceptionally beautiful day, and I'm enjoying the weather again. I'm in no rush to ask Dorothy to rescue me, so I sit a while longer. I realize I don't need to call her yet. Instead, once I roust a neighbor, I'll ask for directions, not a phone, and I'll make my own way. If I get lost again I can always knock on another door and call Dorothy then.

The weather is a delight. I'd rather not disturb a neighbor and suffer an awkward doorstep conversation, so I stay seated and think a bit more. My nemesis, the jumbled-up intersection, is always busy with cars and pedestrians. I'd easily find someone there who could help me recalibrate my route. Moments ago I swore I'd never again go near that absurdity of asphalt. Now I want to find my way back to it.

It is a silly excuse for an intersection, but it is always noisy. Always loud. I hop up and head back in the direction I came from, listening intently. After two or three blocks, I begin to hear the noise. My tormentor has become my guide. I follow my ears, pleased that I will ask a fellow pedestrian for help instead of knocking on a random door.

Along the way I review my mental map of the intersection. There are only two logical mistakes I could have made, one far more likely than the other. As I reach the scene of the epic disaster, I decide to test my hypothesis. I retrace my steps, taking the path dictated by my mental reenactment. It feels right—and I can always turn around and find a helpful pedestrian if it is not. No problem at all.

My pace has quickened and the bounce is back in my step as I reach a familiar landmark, a large crack in the sidewalk, confirmation that I'm back on track. A huge smile lights up my face. I feel like a hero, like Indiana Jones. I'm home in five minutes. I have loved that jumble of roads on Capitol Hill ever since.

I often think of it and my coffee run on that beautiful day. In a matter of minutes, my world turned upside down and back upright again, better than before. Unjustified as it was, my fear was no less real. I was terrified, consumed by ugly thoughts, helpless. I saw agonizing defeat and a dire emergency.

When I expanded my view and focused on the external realities of the situation, however, seeing beyond the distortions of my internal emotions, I confronted a minor practical problem. There was a simple solution, and with thought and proactivity, successively better ones emerged. Ultimately, I found great confidence in my ability to work through a challenge that had initially seemed so disastrous, and I gained new skills. Getting lost did far more for my independence than an uneventful trip would have. It turned out to be a good thing.

My experience that day illustrates the eyes wide open approach to the challenges we face in our lives, big and small, at work and at home. In this chapter and the next we will examine how we can overcome obstacles with this practical approach. This chapter tackles the first step: zoom out and refocus. How do we see a way forward when fear narrows and darkens our view? How do we accurately see ourselves empowered to transcend and thrive when that is not how we feel? In the next chapter we will zoom back in, ready to develop the perspective to initiate and sustain progress in the face of ongoing struggle.

First, we must understand our fear.

Fear's Tunnel

The oldest and strongest emotion of mankind is fear, and the oldest and strongest kind of fear is fear of the unknown.

—H. P. Lovecraft, *Supernatural Horror in Literature*

His fear narrowed his vision so that he couldn't see anything except what he stood to lose.

—Joe Hill, *Horns*

Fear is a powerfully destructive force in our lives. We confront it in times of crisis, extreme change, or great challenge. We tend to fear pain and failure. We are wired to fear the unknown.

As explored in Chapter 1, you understand the world, learn to interact with it, and even perceive "reality" by building up and referencing a vast database of experiences, rules, and logic. The unknown is the domain that lies outside your database. By definition, you have no experience with the unknown and no rules or logic with which to understand it. That is why the unknown can be so problematic.

Fear is familiarity's imposter. It passes off what you dread for what you know, offers the worst in place of the ambiguous, serves up anxiety in the absence of comfort, substitutes assumption for reason. Under the warped logic of fear, anything is better than the uncertain. Fear fills the void at all costs.

Like that of three-card monte, fear's sleight of hand is masked by diversion. Fear narrows your focus and tunnels your vision. It draws you into a pinhole view of the world deep from within. It commands your full attention.

In this way, your fear of the unknown is self-fulfilling. When you confront the unknown, you face the greatest need to look outside yourself, to see beyond your mental database, to broaden your perspective and to think most critically. But fear produces the opposite effect. It beats a retreat deep inside your mind, shrinking and distorting your view. It drowns your capacity for critical thought with a flood of disruptive emotions. You glimpse the world down a long, dark tunnel, cowering cramped in a cold cave, your back to the rough wall.

Similarly, fear often emerges when you face a compelling opportunity to take action, to evolve, to make progress, to overcome, to transcend. But fear can be paralyzing. Its inertia is massive. Like its sibling denial and its cousin pride, fear clings to the status quo. Fear thrives in the fictitious minutiae of the mental images it inspires. It immerses you in those images, lulls you into inaction, and invites you to passively watch its prophecies fulfill themselves.

I first experienced pure, unrestrained fear when I learned I was going blind. When it all began I didn't see what any of it had to do with me. I was thirteen. I felt like an innocent bystander swept into someone else's medical saga. Specifically, my seventeen-year-old sister Daria's medical saga.

Daria was clumsy. Nothing major; she bumped into things. It was part of her sunny, absentminded personality. Occasionally, she'd take a nasty fall, suffer an awkward collision, or narrowly avoid more substantial injury. But for the most part, they were run-of-the-mill incidents. It was just Daria. It was cute, often funny.

Then it ceased to be funny. The incidents increased in frequency and severity, causing Daria physical and emotional pain. It became a source of great concern for our parents, an "issue" for the family. The problem seemed to have something to do with her eyesight. It was no longer cute.

My parents decided something had to be done when Daria misjudged a large intersection alone at the wheel one night and made a left turn into oncoming traffic. Mercifully, nobody was hurt. But my family was terrified by the near brush with tragedy. A checkup at our neighborhood ophthalmologist's office was in order.

I was roped in for the visit along with Daria and my two other older sisters, Ilana and Ronit. No big deal; the four of us had routine checkups every year or two. They were quick and easy. Ronit might get a new prescription for her glasses or the latest contact lens gear. Otherwise, the visits were uneventful.

This one turned into a big deal, however. At the end of the visit our longtime family ophthalmologist made no diagnosis and offered no solution. Instead he told my mother that she should take us to see a retinal specialist. All of us. Something he saw in our eyes shook him. In Daria's eyes? What was it? Why all of us? There was nothing wrong with my eyes.

That's how Daria's saga swept me up and dumped me in my mom's car several days later, for an interminable early morning ride to the Bascom Palmer Eye Institute at the University of Miami. Daria's saga would end well, I knew, like all our emergencies, scares, and traumas over the years, like those of other families. If Daria had a problem, there would be a solution. It was that simple. Some more drama, then things would return to normal for Daria and the family.

That left one unanswered question: what did this retina specialist have to do with me? I should still be asleep back home, not cramped in the car for the long ride to his office. I was irritated. I was thirteen.

My mood did not improve that morning when soon after our arrival at Dr. W's office it became clear that we were in for far more than a routine checkup. This would be neither quick nor easy. We began with the "normal" exams you expect from an eye doctor— "Better one or better two?"—but they took twice as long and the numerous staff were so serious you'd think they were assembling a bomb.

Later I was brought before The Dot Machine. Its technical description, automated perimetry, sounds benign. But do not be fooled. By any name The Dot Machine is an instrument of torture. Slow, freakish, game-show-like torture.

Imagine a giant bowl about three feet in diameter, standing up on its edge so that you're looking straight into it. Now pull up a chair and sit in front of that bowl. It is important that your face remains precisely centered in the bowl, so you'll need to rest your chin on a small, hard piece of plastic and lean your head forward until your forehead rests against another small, hard piece of plastic.

Try to get comfortable, as you're going to be in this position for all eternity.

Grab the buzzer on the side of The Dot Machine and the game-show fun begins. The rules are simple—that is, the rule is simple. If you see a Dot flash in the bowl, press the buzzer. Voila. Nothing to it, right? Doesn't sound so bad? Just wait.

The Dot Machine can produce an infinite number of Dots. And it will, while you sit there, your face pressed against its plastic, one eye covered by a patch on a flimsy elastic string, a dime-store pirate. Dots of different colors, Dots of different intensities, Dots of different sizes. Dots against a brightly lit background, Dots in the dark. The Dot Machine will flash every permutation of Dot at every point inside your field of vision, and at many more points outside of it. All the while, it will track your every buzz, knowingly, critically.

We'll have to do this with each eye, of course, one at a time. Then we'll dilate your eyes and give it another whirl. Don't worry, The Dot Machine will helpfully break forever up into Dot sequences that last between three minutes and five months. You'll have a chance to rest between sequences while you listen to The Dot Machine's whirring gears and rotors cook up the next batch of Dots.

Unless "we have to repeat a few points from that last sequence because the results are unclear." (That means that The Dot Machine decided that your buzzes didn't make any sense.) In that case you won't hear anything, because you haven't really made any progress. There will be only 423 sequences today. Unless Dr. W wants us to do a few more when he reviews the results. He will want us to do more.

Just relax, you're doing fine. By that I mean you are slowly going insane. Dot after Dot after Dot after Dot like the drip, drip, drip of water torture. Wait, was that really a Dot or your mind playing tricks on you? Never mind, no Dot about it, you just saw a Dot for sure! What a relief, you're back in the game.

Did you buzz? No, you didn't—you completely forgot to buzz. How is that possible? How could you forget to buzz for an undeniable, clear-as-day Dot? Is it too late to buzz? It is too late. Let that one go. Focus.

Did you just fall asleep? Wow, you literally just fell asleep. For how long? Your forehead isn't touching the plastic, slacker, tighten up. Oops, you just buzzed and there isn't even a hint of a Dot around. This can't be going well.

Don't chase the Dot with your eye, look straight at the center mark. Don't chase the Dot with your eye, look straight at the center mark. Don't chase the Dot with your eye, look straight at the center mark. You are not looking at the center mark.

Loud beep from The Dot Machine and the sequence is over. Then it taunts you with silence. Gratuitously long pause before the examiner reports: "We have to repeat a few points from that last sequence." Oh, really? Big surprise.

The monotony of the Dots is so complete and relentless that any interruption is welcome. I was thus relieved when I was called away from The Dot Machine because "it was time for my ERG." I had no idea what an ERG was, but I soon learned.

The electroretinogram is a diagnostic test that measures the electrical activity generated by retinal cells in response to a stimulus. It measures this activity with electrodes that are embedded in a bulky contact lens. Those contact lenses are put in your eyes. They are difficult to insert, very uncomfortable, and fall out easily, especially when you blink. You're not supposed to blink. But you'll want to blink, because the stimulus is an intensely bright light flashed directly into your eyes. In a nutshell, hold still and open those eyes nice and wide while we shine lightning at your face. I was relieved when the ERG was over and I could return to The Dot Machine.

The day wore on in this fashion. Long stretches of Dots broken up by other exams, trips to the bathroom, a quick hospital cafeteria lunch. It was seven or eight hours before The Dot Machine finally fell silent for good. We did not need to repeat any points. Dr. W had no more sequences to run. There were no other tests to complete. Blessedly, I was done. I joined my mother and sisters in the waiting room, and we put it to its intended use.

We waited a long time, exhausted, impatient, and cranky. We would soon feel much worse. Our final "before" moments ticked away wasted. Eventually, we were escorted to Dr. W's spacious office for his verdict.

He breezed in behind us, walked to his bookshelf, removed a textbook, placed it facing us on his desk, and flipped pages until he came to a series of photographs. Ugly photographs, depicting diseased human tissue. They looked like ghoulish glamour shots of the lungs of a lifetime cigarette smoker, the ones my teachers showed us in elementary school to scare us off the cancer sticks. That is how I remember them, at least. I will never forget what came next.

"Those are pictures of the retinas of patients with a disease called retinitis pigmentosa," he said. He was cold and casual. "Retinitis pigmentosa causes progressive vision loss and ultimately blindness. Ilana, Daria, and Isaac have RP. They will slowly lose their sight and go blind. Nobody can tell you how long it will take. There are no treatments or cures. We don't know much about the disease. Good luck."

In a sense, Dr. W's staff did assemble a bomb that day. A diagnostic bomb he detonated without warning or compassion. Its explosive force tore through my family. Then there was "after." After is when I first experienced pure, unrestrained fear.

Writing this book twenty-four years later, I can offer only an approximation of that fear to the best of my recollection. Today, being blind does not scare me. It hasn't scared me for more than a decade. I must remind myself that this aspect of my existence, which is like any other as far as I am concerned, stands out for others like a baby on a battlefield—and is terrifying to them. I have to remind myself that years ago I, too, was terrified.

Of course I can remember the fear. I don't mean to suggest otherwise. But I remember it the same way you might remember cowering in your bed at night as a child, frightened of the monster under your bed. You now understand there never was a monster, that your fear was irrational, self-imposed, the product of your imagination. You can recall feeling terror back then, but when you lay down tonight, you will not be afraid, not of nighttime monsters, at least.

That's how I feel about blindness. It is the monster that didn't really exist. I'll do my best to remember and describe the nights I lay awake as a child alone and afraid. You'll have to keep in mind, however, that there was nothing under my bed.

Odds are that you find this hard to believe. I understand every detail and every practicality of blindness. I'm an expert at being blind. It is familiar, comfortable, normal, routine. Still, you likely don't believe me when I tell you it isn't that bad. I'm the exasperated parent, stomping my foot and repeating, "There are no monsters, go to bed!"

That is the point. Most people have little or no experience with blindness, but nonetheless harbor a visceral fear of it. I had such a fear when we left Dr. W's office that day. I was thirteen, but I felt a lot older.

Blindness is my death sentence, I thought. *It will end my life as I know it.* End independence and confidence. End strength and leadership. End achievement. Blind, I will cease to be special, funny, successful. I will be helpless, pathetic, weak.

I will live trapped in my mind. Blindness will disconnect me from the world. I will be unable to perceive my surroundings, unable to relate to other people. I will remember my life with sight, though. Those memories will torment me as I live alone in the dark.

It will be an insignificant, sad life, like the cliché of the small-town high school's star quarterback who never made it out. After graduation he makes ends meet with a series of meaningless jobs, eats a lot of pizza and drinks a lot of beer, has some fun every once in a while, and leaves his hometown for the occasional wedding or funeral. He pulls out the scrapbook his mom kept on the shelf under his trophies and peruses the articles from the local paper. For a few years they cheered him up, but now they make him feel worse. He'll never get rid of that scrapbook, though. He dreads his class reunions, but he'll never miss one.

I am living a dream—child prodigy and sitcom star—but I know in advance that I am experiencing the best my life will ever offer. This foresight is a cruel persecution. The anticipation of my decline is not the worst part. The worst part is that the unwelcomed prophecy has stolen even the triumph before my fall. There is no more joy when I take the stage, no pride when the crowd cheers. In my achievements and blessings I see that which I know I will lose. I experience them in preemptive mourning.

I mourn the things I'll never have, too, like a wife, a partner in life. I will be alone. How can I capture a woman's affections while in a process of total ruin? Can I expect someone to fall in love with me as my every attractive quality is fading away? And if she does, what next? I sweep her off her feet, we ride off into the future, and I become her burden, at best a shell of my former self. Like me, she will remember. She will resent me, pity me, abandon me, mother me, mourn me, or blame me. She will not admire me or respect me. She will not love me. How could she? I will neither admire nor respect myself. I will not love myself.

My prospects will not improve once I am blind. A woman who falls in love with a blind man commits her heart to charity, sacrifices romance for service. I will preserve a last scrap of pride and reject this selfless gift. I pray for the will to keep this promise, the courage to defend this barren ground to my death.

I will never be a father. It is for the better. No child deserves that. Besides, I'll no doubt remain a child myself, dependent on my parents. Whom will I turn to when they are gone?

Through my teenage years, this was my reality of blindness. Psychologists have a great term for it: awfulizing. As defined by the online Psychology Dictionary, awfulizing is "an irrational and dramatic thought pattern, characterized by the tendency to overestimate the potential seriousness or negative consequences of events, situations, or perceived threats." Put simply, to awfulize is to make something its most awful in your mind. Like Carol at the cocktail party, awfulizing is a mental construction. Like Dorothy's backward-swimming fish, it is the product of imagination. Like both, however, we experience as reality that which we awfulize. It is our manufactured truth.

I awfulized blindness. I did not know the first thing about it. I had no experience with it. I had not thought much about it. On this blank canvas of ignorance, my fear painted with a palette of anxiety, insecurity, and doom. The horrific scene it created captivated my attention, drew me in, consumed my thoughts, overpowered me.

It felt so real that it became real. I could not look away. I saw my destination, my future, my fate in that scene, and I did not question it. Blindness was my death sentence. It was only a matter of time.

Destiny Outsourced

Fear's work does not end with the baseless reality it concocts in your mind. That is where fear's work begins. To perpetuate its reality, fear must lull you into playing your part. When you look beyond fear's canvas, when you recognize with peace the uncertain and the unknown, when you seek greater understanding, when you take control, you break fear's spell. The concept is simple, but it is difficult to accomplish. It is difficult to break the spell because fear is the ultimate enabler.

The accomplices in fear's elaborate con are your villains and your heroes. Fear conjures a world in which these villains and heroes command responsibility for your fate like the gods of Greek mythology acting from Mt. Olympus on high. *Blame your villains,* fear whispers in your ear. The fault lies with those around you. The problem is your awful circumstances. *Worship your heroes,* fear admonishes. They have the power to solve your problems, to make you happy. They can save you.

The drama is epic and endless, shifting and complex. You sit back and struggle to take it all in, to keep it all straight, to see how it will shake out. Samuel Taylor Coleridge wrote of the poet's need to create "persons and characters supernatural, or at least romantic ... so as to transfer from our inward nature a human interest and a semblance of truth sufficient to procure for these shadows of imagination that willing suspension of disbelief." He could have been writing about fear. With supernatural villains and heroes, fear procures for the awful shadows of your imagination your willing suspension of disbelief.

That's the con. The details are unimportant. The drama is smoke and mirrors, a diversion. What matters is that you have accepted the reality fear has created for you. You are a cooperative participant in that unfounded reality. You do not question the premise. You play nice. You abdicate responsibility. You blame and credit others. You outsource your destiny.

I was an easy mark for my fear because my diagnosis was the prophecy of a distant fate. Dr. W said it could take decades for me to lose my sight. With luck, I might not confront blindness until my thirties, forties, or even fifties. I clung to that fact. My struggle with blindness felt an eternity away, a far future.

Blindness was a can I could kick well down the road. There

were no immediate challenges to confront, no obvious action items, no present implications. Nothing had to be done, so I did nothing. I did not take control, question my assumptions, connect with and learn from others, or seek greater understanding. I waited. I was a sitting duck.

Fear took careful aim. My villain was the monster under my bed, Blindness. Not blindness, as in sightlessness, but Blindness, the amorphous bogeyman, the animating terror of my fears. Like the bogeyman invented by parents to scare good behavior into their children, Blindness had no set form or appearance in my mind. Blindness was a nonspecific force of destruction I could not see or define. I could feel it, though, like the rapid drop in barometric pressure before a powerful storm, like the rain you can smell and taste before the first drop falls. Blindness was foreboding doom. I could pray for time before the rain came, and I did, but come it would.

I was trapped in this awful world of gloom and haze by the promise of rescue. My heroes, brilliant research scientists, would deliver a treatment or a cure for me. I was certain of it. Because they would soon rescue me, I did not need to confront Blindness. I did not need to rescue myself. I was paralyzed by hope.

That was fear's con. The drama, villain and heroes in conflict, drew my focus to the stage. The unconvincing details of the set faded away, as did the audience around me, the theater. There was only the play. I watched, my disbelief willingly suspended. I believed in Blindness. I believed in Science.

I was Science's active, enthusiastic fan. Shortly after the diagnosis, my parents set out to understand the state of the research efforts to develop treatments and cures, and they devoted themselves to the support of that research. To this day, they want more than anything in the world an answer for their children, a solution.

To that end, my parents identified and then befriended dozens of brilliant researchers laboring in the field. They embraced these scientists with gratitude, awe, and love. And they championed the research, working to raise charitable funding. In this fiscal endeavor, my parents turned to friends and family for support. They found a community of immense generosity and selflessness, one that grew larger through the years and achieved remarkable fund-raising successes.

I joined my parents in their mission. I served as a spokesperson in the media, at fund-raisers, and in governmental lobbying efforts. I later founded a nonprofit organization called Hope for Vision to coordinate our philanthropic activities with those of other communities nationwide. For five years I ran Hope for Vision. My parents and I celebrated and supported the researchers. Like my parents, I will forever feel profound gratitude for the many angels who helped us raise funds and awareness. I'm proud of my parents, proud of Hope for Vision, and glad to have played my part in the scientific mission.

Looking back, however, I realize that my crusade for the cure played into the hands of my fear. It was cover for the outsourcing of my destiny. I felt I was taking control, taking charge, swinging at the proverbial curveball life pitched at me. I was not.

Do not misunderstand me. My efforts were productive. As I've said, I'm proud of my contribution to the development of the research, however humble that contribution has been. And believe me when I say that I remain very eager for a cure! I do not regret the efforts I undertook with my family to hasten the development of that cure.

I do regret, however, that I confused fighting for a cure with confronting my fears. The embodiment of hope and optimism, I played the leading role in my fear's epic drama. I projected outward courage and bravery in my charge for research dollars. I would surely be rewarded with a Hollywood ending, saved in the nick of time. Disaster averted, problem solved. It felt good to play the part.

Psychologists have a term for this, too: denial. I thought I was taking a stand when I was really running away. My fight for a cure fueled the flames of my fears. I was reinforcing the awful narrative— Blindness as death—by committing myself to its defeat at the hands of Science.

I did not question the premise, fear's premise. I cheered frantically for my heroes. I bet it all on their victory. Blindness grew uglier, more awful. It had to be vanquished. It just had to be. Blindness is death. Fight. Survive.

While I fought, while I ran, my retinas deteriorated.

In the first few years, Blindness manifested itself in my physical world through minor annoyances and occasional nuisances. Trouble recognizing faces in a dark restaurant. An acquaintance's outstretched hand missed and ignored unshaken. Blindness was taunting me. *I'm coming for you*, it said, and my fears took on a mounting urgency. I started to hear the tick of a clock counting down. Not always, not loudly. But with each visit from Blindness I heard it clearly.

The nuisances and annoyances grew more frequent and more substantial over the next few years, as did my frustrations. Bumps and bruises, like Daria's. Missed fire hydrants, torn pants, bloodied shins. Awkward interactions with others. Tension and confusion, theirs and mine. Blindness no longer visited. It had moved in. It was always there. The clock ticks were loud and constant. I pled and bargained for time: *If my sight will just stay the way it is today, I will make do, I will not complain, I will be grateful. Just please, no worse. Please God, not Blindness.*

Then sight itself became a battle with the villain Blindness, a tug-of-war for my eyes with perception as the prize. Shattered, fragmented, transitory images I had to piece together. Mental gymnastics to unscramble the kaleidoscope. It was difficult and exhausting to see. The view was rarely worth the effort. But fear insisted I pull on the rope with all of my might, treasure the shards of the broken images I still had, work harder to understand and integrate the clues, restore the masterpiece of sight that time and Blindness had ravaged in my eyes. Fight for sight. Don't let go. Fight for time. Don't dare let go. Fight for the cure. Science will save me. Fight for the cure. Science will save me.

I had outsourced my destiny. I accepted the Blindness of my fears and ran from it. I embraced my hero, Science, and prayed it would rescue me in time. For years I lived a race against Blindness, a race against that clock, a race for the cure. I was convinced I would win that race.

But it didn't take decades for me to lose my sight. It took about a decade. In my teens and early twenties, The Dot Machine chronicled with precision the rapid demise of my retinas. I played the Dots twice a year, then once, then every other year, then less frequently. The games grew shorter. The Dots take less time when you can see fewer of them, a minor consolation.

Too minor, so I finally swore off the game. I did not need The Dot Machine to tell me that Blindness was on my heels. Science's cure was miles back, crawling. Rescue was decades away. The equation flipped. Blindness now, a cure in my thirties, forties, or fifties. I am not going to win this race. Science will not save me.

My fears foretold my awful fate. There would be no last-minute pardon from the governor. No stay of execution from the Supreme Court. It was time to accept my death sentence, to face it like a man, to lay still in bed, to wait for the monster underneath to attack.

Looking Under the Bed

The child lies awake in agony, wrestling with herself. A part of her, the brave part, knows there is no monster. *Just look under the bed*, that part says. *It will all be over.*

If you move, the monster will awaken and attack, her fear responds. *Do not move. Whatever you do, do not move.*

She is fighting with fear for control of her reality. Something deep inside has made her uncomfortable, scared. A subconscious exchange of innocence for wisdom. Ambiguous intuitions bubbling in the mental cauldron that roils with her amateur efforts to master life's cookbook. Whatever it is, something that she does not understand has made her uneasy.

Always quick with an explanation, fear creates the monster under her bed. Fear tunnels her vision on that awful monster and begs her to lie still and do nothing. Mystery solved. Avoid, divert, enable.

What if there really is a monster? fear asks. It is a knockout blow. It is a cheap trick.

The real question, the one fear cannot abide, is: *what if there is no monster?* That is the question the brave part of her is willing to confront, though it means uncertainty, implicates the unknown.

The brave part takes responsibility for her reality. She broadens her view, zooms out, and her blind spots are exposed. If there is no monster, why am I afraid? Why do I feel the way I do? Retreating into fear's tunnel obscures these blind spots. The brave part seeks to understand them, or at least to accept them. The brave part counsels action and craves growth. *Just look under the bed*, it says. *Be proactive. Help yourself.*

As a parent you encourage the brave part of your child. You search for a flashlight, get on your hands and knees, and peer under the bed when your child is simply too scared to do it. You are her hero for the moment. When she gets a little older, she joins you on the floor, able to confront her fears as long as you're close by. Eventually you'll remain in her doorway, insisting gently that she look for herself. You are teaching her a lesson about fear. You are teaching her to zoom out and refocus, to take control.

It is simple when you're dealing with monsters under your child's bed. It can be far more difficult to accomplish when you confront your own adult fears. More difficult to accomplish, but just as simple in concept. Even when your monster is Blindness.

I'd love to report that I threw off the covers unaided, hopped out of my bed, and exposed as a fraud the Blindness of my fears. That is not how it happened, however. The truth is far less impressive. It would be more accurate to say that I awoke from a delirious, sleep deprivation–induced doze to discover that my girlfriend's mother was hard at work under my bed designing a monster detection and defense system. You can imagine my surprise.

My mother-in-law, Brenda, was an occupational therapist. For years she served as the Director of Occupational Therapy at the Lucerne Spinal Injury Center, a top-ranked facility that received patients from all over the world. Brenda's typical patient was a woman who was thrown by a horse, broke her neck, and became a quadriplegic. After the surgeries, the consultations with doctors and nurses, and the mourning with friends and family, this woman would meet Brenda.

Brenda helped with the rest of the patient's life. Brenda assessed the patient's capabilities and surveyed the myriad tools and technologies available. She developed concrete solutions for specific problems. Maybe she would rig up a homemade attachment to help make a wheelchair joystick more accessible. Or she would introduce tools to enable her patient to feed herself. Grooming and hygiene. Reading a book. Getting in and out of bed. Take the problems one at a time, reduce them to their smallest, most discrete form, and work a solution. That is Brenda's perspective.

When Dorothy and I were dating, without either of us knowing anything about it, Brenda began to research solutions for the blind and partially sighted. She came across an expert in Boston named Chris, began corresponding with her, and set up a meeting during an upcoming trip to visit Dorothy. As the visit neared, Brenda invited Dorothy to come along. I caught wind of their plan and invited myself. Off we went, all three of us. It changed my life.

We've barely entered Chris's office when she asks me if I use a walking cane for the visually impaired. Her question turns my world upside down.

"Uh, no, I, well, I see too well to use a cane. I, uh, you see, I'm not blind yet, uh, I have some useful sight and, uh, it is too soon, I mean, too early for a cane," I respond. I am confused. Isn't Chris supposed to be the expert here? Of course I don't use a cane. It has never occurred to me to use a cane. Not yet.

"Do you bump into things?" she asks.

Do I bump into things? Really? We are supposed to be talking about Blindness. I'm here to figure out what I'm going to do then, when my life is awful and different and depressing. I'm not here to talk about now. Now is fine. I can handle now. Now is not the problem. Blindness is my problem.

"Yeah, I bump into things all the time," I say, trying to hide my impatience.

"Do you ever hurt yourself?" she asks.

Is this lady serious? I've been watching my sight fade away for years, literally. I'm constantly tormented by the knowledge that my life as I know it is ending. She wants to talk about bumps and bruises? Fine, I'll talk about bumps and bruises. I'll show her how meaningless they are to me compared to Blindness.

"You could say that," I reply, pulling up the leg of my jeans to reveal my shin. The bruise is one of my worst, and a few days after the injury it is looking its ugliest. I play it down. "A fire hydrant gave me this one," I say. No big deal, happens all the time.

"You know," Chris says, "if you learned to use a cane you wouldn't hurt yourself. It would be a lot safer."

The point is obvious. Brilliantly, completely, irrefutably obvious. The implications are enormous. There is something I can do to help myself. Right now. A cane won't fend off Blindness, but it can fend off fire hydrants. I'm speechless.

"People don't realize that you are low vision, right?" Chris asks. She does not wait for a response. "I'm sure that can be very frustrating and awkward. You know, if you carry a cane—even if you don't really use it—most people will see it and realize you have vision problems. That could be helpful."

Another blow. It lands hard. *That could be helpful? That could be absolutely amazing,* I think. *People will realize that I have vision problems. It won't mean a thing to Blindness, but it will make my day a lot easier.* I want to hug Chris.

She does not let up. "What about the computer?" she asks.

She is in my head. It has become painful to use my computer. I have to jack up the size of the text, use a high-contrast color scheme, and put my face right up to the monitor. I've managed to swap the default Windows pointer for a giant one that is neon green, but I lose track of even the new one. I spend a lot of time hunting down that green cursor and methodically following it across the screen. Blindness doesn't care whether I can use my computer or not, but I care deeply.

Chris has a solution for this problem, too. The visually impaired can use special screen-reading software to interact with the computer, she explains. Screen readers speak to you, reading text and narrating the various options and menus within a program. You use your ears instead of your eyes. You use keyboard commands instead of the mouse and cursor. She shows me. It takes time, effort, and patience to learn to use a screen reader, Chris warns me. But once you've mastered it, you don't need your eyes to use your computer. It is that simple.

Chris has many more simple solutions. A technique called "sighted guide" that Dorothy and I can use to walk together naturally and safely, gadgets for labeling things around the house, a method to keep track of different bills, strategies to organize my clothing to match outfits, resources for audiobooks and other digital content like newspapers. I am eager to hear about it all. I am excited to put it all to use in my life. I am impressed by the elegant simplicity.

Still, I cannot shake the feeling that we are ignoring the elephant in the room. We talked about canes and computers, about the mundane and the practical. But Blindness has escaped confrontation. We have said nothing about my dark future.

Then I have an epiphany, a revelation.

There is no Blindness, only fire hydrants, those who are unaware of my challenge, disappearing computer pointers on the screen, an open landscape of practicalities stretching to the horizon.

The scene on fear's canvas is a fiction, a mirage. You will never face fear's execution day. But tomorrow you will face your life, and the next day, and every day thereafter, until you have none left. Those days unlived are reality's blank canvas, and you are the only creator.

The palette of your fears is limited and ugly: anxiety, insecurity, doom, and loss. But you have a million more colors. Countless hues of strength, an endless rainbow of adaptations, growth bright and beautiful. You paint one stroke at a time, one day at a time, breathe a single breath after your last, a single breath before your next. You will never control tomorrow, but you can always choose whether to act today, and how.

With empowerment comes responsibility. There are no villains, no heroes, no gods on Mt. Olympus. No monster under the bed. Those shadows of imagination are excuses, rationalizations, justifications, stall tactics, cop-outs. Without them we are accountable. That is why our fears manifest these figments in defense, and it is why we cling to them. It is why we must let them go.

I chose to let go of Blindness in Chris's office. I stepped out of fear's tunnel into the wide unknown, shifting my focus from the foreground to the horizon. After fear's narrow, contrived, myopic scene, reality's expansive landscape of potential was exhilarating. My awfulized assumptions about Blindness had felt like immutable truths, inescapable reality. In Chris's office they were exposed as fear's self-limiting fictions, fish swimming backward through my mind. My destiny was again my own, my future unbounded. I could stop running.

The terrain ahead was undefined and uncharted. Fear's superficial struggle with Blindness was awful, but it was simple, too. Reality was far more complex. Chris forced me to contemplate the myriad discrete, specific challenges I would face—physical challenges, practical challenges, emotional challenges. I had a lot to learn and a lot to figure out.

It was my responsibility to do so. I accepted the obligation to help myself, to achieve my potential, and I committed to hold myself accountable at all costs. I took ownership of my fate. It weighed heavy on my shoulders.

I left Chris's office in a swirl of emotions. The heroes and villains I had come to know so well had vanished, and I felt an odd sense of loss. I was embarrassed to have run for so long from my illusory villain. Thinking about the years I'd wasted borrowing imaginary troubles and the agonies I had needlessly inflicted upon myself, I felt a deep sadness. I was impatient to master the tools and techniques Chris had introduced and to discover others. I felt great joy. I felt immense gratitude. I felt profound relief. I was giddy and somber at the same time, both energized and exhausted, inspired and overwhelmed, confident and apprehensive. It was confusing.

Lying in bed that night, I was at peace with my confusion. I did not have the answers yet, but for the first time I had zoomed out far enough to focus on the right questions. It was a good start. I was many things, felt many emotions. But I was not afraid. It was indeed a good start.

Fishing Trip 2: Man Plans, God Laughs

April 13, 2010

The story begins with events that are as common as they are miraculous. Man and woman fall in love, commit to live their lives together, and endeavor to start a family. They are blessed with a pregnancy without medical intervention, and two months later visit a doctor's office to ensure that the heart of their child-to-be is healthy and growing strong. At this point in the narrative, about one out of every ten thousand such couples (.01 percent) is let in on a cosmic surprise: triplets. Not one, not two, but three children on the way.

That's what happened to Dorothy and me the morning of Tuesday, April 13, 2010. We were living in London, about eight months into a planned one-year stint abroad, when Adil, our regular mini-cab driver, took us to Ultrasound Diagnostic Services on Harley

Street for Dorothy's early pregnancy scan. In the waiting room Dorothy noticed a sign that set out UDS's pricing policy for a multiple pregnancy: no additional charge for the first scan, but for every scan thereafter the parents-to-be must pay the fee for each child.

For a couple weeks I had been teasing Dorothy, insisting that she was pregnant with quadruplets. When she mentioned the sign I made a joke on that theme, protesting that her future visits would represent a financial burden unless we negotiated a bulk discount for our foursome. As things turned out, it was only 25 percent joke.

Lying on the examination table, Dorothy spotted two dark circles on the technician's screen. "Is that what I think it is?" she asked.

"Yes, you've twins," the technician confirmed with British understatement.

Dorothy turned to me, seated by her side opposite the screen. We hugged, cheeks pressed together, mumbling into each other's ears, overwhelmed by the news. In a flash I imagined our two growing children as newborn babies, as toddlers playing together, in high school, in college, inseparable in each context, the closest of friends. It struck me that the special bond between siblings who are joint venturers in birth and in life is an exceptional blessing, and I was overcome with happiness that our twins would be so blessed. These thoughts had just begun to take form when the technician broke in, her manner un-British in its abruptness.

"Wait! There's another one," she said, panic in her voice.

"Another what?" I reflexively blurted out, though clarification was wholly unnecessary.

Our baby had become twins moments earlier, and those twins were now triplets. Deep in the primal wiring of my mind, I detected an alarming trend, triggering an ancient animal instinct, fight or flight. On high alert, the part of my brain responsible for verbal communication took over before other, more sensible parts of my brain could catch up. That's the only way I can explain my next question.

"Are you going to find a fourth?" I asked. My tone was more terror than inquiry. In my defense, the circumstances were somewhat taxing and emotions were running pretty high. Still, the question wasn't helpful.

Dorothy began to cry. Fiercely independent, she had envisioned herself a self-sufficient mother doing it all without help, with her (single) child in tow. While my mouth worked through the news, Dorothy was realizing that she would want help to care for our triplets. She was realizing that they would not be easily integrated into her active lifestyle or our frequent travels. She was realizing that we would have to change our Plan. It felt to her a great loss.

We were fond of our Plan. Negotiated and refined with years of marriage, it was built upon the premise that Dorothy and I would at some identifiable time be officially "ready" to have a child. After months of debate, in December we had mutually invoked the Ready Clause, abandoned our birth control measures, and initiated our conception protocol, which we optimized with data from daily home fertility tests. The protocol brought quick success, conception in February. Pregnancy tests administered twice daily for a week in March confirmed as much.

Our Plan incorporated a second child contingency, as Dorothy and I suspected we would want to give our first a sibling. It was a remote contingency, however. Other critical clauses in our Plan would likely render that gift unfeasible, we recognized, like the "Isaac is a fancy lawyer," "Dorothy is a fancy dealer of art," and "we like to travel a lot" provisions. Could we really implement our overarching Plan with a second child? Did we want to do so?

When we learned Dorothy was pregnant these questions became the subject of frequent speculation, our favorite topic of conversation. Are there personality traits correlated with single children? Educational outcomes? Career paths? If we decide to have a second child, how many years should we wait? Does a daughter or a son benefit more from a sibling? We spent hours discussing these things. Thoughtful, mature adults, we had provided for some confined uncertainty in our Plan. We'd enjoyed carefully exploring that tidy uncertainty together.

Public notice of Dorothy's pregnancy was a different matter. On that score our Plan brooked no ambiguity. Pursuant to one of the concessions she had extracted from me when we triggered the Ready Clause, we were unequivocally prohibited from disclosing Dorothy's pregnancy until its thirteenth week. Not even family could be informed until we came upon this milestone, I had reluctantly conceded.

I adhered to the spirit of this prohibition but not its strict terms. My family and friends remained in the dark, no simple feat for me. (I like to share things. Everything.) It was agonizing to keep secret the only thing I could think about. I felt I would burst. To release some of the pressure and prevent catastrophic rupture, I told a couple people confined to our "London lives," figuring there was no risk the information would spread further. This is how Rob, my personal trainer, and Adil, our beloved minicab driver, became the third and fourth to know that Dorothy was pregnant. I spent hours discussing the second child question with Rob and Adil, too.

On the possibility of triplets, Dorothy's and my Plan was silent. Multiple pregnancy was an oversight, an unknown unknown, incompleteness in the potentialities enumerated, a special case that eluded the algorithm. We did not consider that Dorothy might naturally conceive fraternal twins—a boy and a girl—or that the boy twin might thereafter spontaneously split into two genetically identical boys. It was a miss. A big one. In the exam room our Plan crashed.

As we walked out of UDS I did not understand the implications. The more sensible parts of my brain were still far behind. Word of "the triplet parents" had spread, and UDS staff and patients gathered to cheer for Dorothy and me as we made our exit. Giddy, I could not stop laughing.

It is difficult to believe in retrospect, but I was worrying about our Plan's onerous notice provisions. The technician confirmed what we already knew, that Dorothy was in her ninth week of pregnancy. Having just learned that my child was in fact three children, I could not imagine waiting three weeks to tell the world. I could barely imagine waiting three minutes.

I hoped I might extract special dispensation from Dorothy in light of the day's developments. Our Plan obviously needed a hard reboot and some major adjustments. I could argue to Dorothy that we should accordingly put the public notice provisions back on the table. As we hailed one of London's spacious black cabs, I considered how best to advance that argument.

Dorothy called home and told her mother about the triplets

before the cab pulled away from the curb. I was stunned. Dorothy was way ahead of me (no surprise), and as I listened to her end of the conversation, I caught up. The sensible parts of my brain finally kicked in. I began to understand the implications.

Dorothy's pregnancy would be arduous and would carry risks not merely greater in relative terms but great in actual measure, for her and for our children alike. We would want her to see doctors expert in high-risk pregnancy and a maternal fetal medicine specialist. And a nutritionist could help her to maintain the astronomical calorie intake those doctors would recommend. These complexities of her medical care and the now suboptimal timing of our scheduled departure from London both meant we should move back to the States as soon as possible. Health-care considerations would be the primary priority in choosing our destination.

Assuming all went well, we would have to care and provide for three children. Three infants. At the same time. The magnitude of that challenge dawned late and bright for me in the back of our cab. If it takes a village to nurture a child, our triplets would require a metropolis. And as for my part, while I had been confident in my ability to care for our child, juggling three seemed an altogether different enterprise, especially without sight.

My frolic in the sun and surf of triplet fatherhood turned struggle against a riptide of anxiety. I was swept miles from the shore. Treading in waters deep and unsettled, I grasped for a lifeline, sought rescue by the Plan, prayed for salvation in certainty, in control. But there was only ocean, vast, empty, uncontrollable. *Man plans, God laughs*, the saying goes. I bobbed in a sea of divine hysteria.

Our Plan was a false idol, our sacrifices at its altar vain. I could see that now. With our rituals we had conjured illusions of control. Our faith, however, was the bliss of ignorance. There was no Plan. There never had been. There never would be. Uncertainty is untidy. It cannot be confined. We are never in control.

The cab pulled up in front of our flat at Stanley Gardens in Notting Hill. I thought about the long months ahead for Dorothy and me, for our families, for our children, all three of them. Already devoted to our trio with every molecule of my being, I was afraid for them. Futile or not, I would fight for these three. I had at least that certainty. For them I'd gladly flail against the tide and drown exhausted. That choice, at least, was in my control.

The intensity of my love for them was yet another common miracle, it struck me, part of some Plan not my own. I found beauty and grace in the thought. For now, though, my plan was blessedly simple. I hurried inside to call my parents—and everyone else I knew.

CHAPTER 3

The Critic and the Strong Man

Success is not final; failure is not fatal: it is the courage to continue that counts.

—Winston Churchill

A Chip and a Chair

Dorothy and I are hoping that our year-old triplets will keep sleeping as we scoop them from their cribs and load them into our Chevy Suburban. It is five a.m., painfully early. Lily Louise, Phineas, and Thaddeus, whom we call the "Tripskys," need their sleep. Dorothy and I need some peace and quiet. It is not a happy morning, and we have a lot on our minds.

Mercifully, the Tripskys sleep soundly as we pull away from the house. It is not our house. We've been renting it for less than four months now. It is a cookie-cutter house in a gated community that has hundreds of them. The community is in Windermere, a suburb of Orlando.

We pull onto Florida's turnpike, heading south, and I escape the endless hum of Tripsky lullabies by torturing myself again with a forensic reconstruction of the decisions that brought us to this early morning excursion. A year ago I was a lawyer in Manhattan. I was a very successful lawyer with an elite résumé and a bright, lucrative future working for a big international law firm as an appellate litigator. This somehow seemed problematic at the time, a subject I'll cover in detail in Chapter 6. The bottom line: my first decision was to stop practicing law.

I loved living in New York as a bachelor fresh out of college. A bite to eat at FireBird Russian caviar and champagne lounge, karaoke in Koreatown, a few glasses of the latest magical cocktail served up by the mixologist du jour at that great new bar in the Village, then home to order Ethiopian food for delivery at three in the morning. What more could you want? My studio apartment was expansive for my needs. Life was fun and easy. That was then.

Nine years later Dorothy's and my two-bedroom apartment felt small even before the Tripskys moved in. It felt microscopic when they arrived. The noise and hustle of the city was an affront to the one thing we truly wanted: sleep. Ventures slightly more practical than late-night culinary escapades were vastly more difficult. Groceries. Visits to the pediatrician. Finding a cab, walking the dog, finding space for the diapers and bottles and bibs and bouncy seats. It was all very arduous. Second decision: move out of Manhattan.

Having rejected both my profession and place of residence, I sought expert advice from a career coach. Over several weeks she led me through a series of psychological profiling and self-exploration exercises. The results were unequivocal. All indicators pointed in one direction. I should seek employment as a chief executive officer. The data demonstrated that I am ill-suited to work for anyone but myself.

This seemed like useless information. No company had expressed interest in retaining my leadership. My résumé offered no reason to think that any company would be open to the suggestion. I was born to do a job nobody would reasonably hire me to do.

I was explaining as much to my close friend and Harvard College roommate Zac when he made an audacious suggestion: he and I could buy a small business that I could run. Nobody would reasonably hire me as a chief executive officer, but Zac and I could unreasonably do so. As my wife's eight-year-old cousin Olivia later put it, Zac and I could buy me a job.

There was reason to think the idea was not entirely meritless. Zac had spent the twelve years since our 1999 graduation working in the finance industry. He had become expert in assessing market opportunities, business plans, and management teams. True, he had previously analyzed multibillion-dollar enterprises, not small companies, but business is business, we figured. Zac was very good at his job and he had a sizeable chunk of savings stashed away. He was willing to put both his money and his time on the line to help me reinvent myself, though he would keep his lucrative day job.

The timing seemed right. As 2010 was nearing its end, the U.S. economy was in a state of misery and numerous industries were stagnating at once-in-a-lifetime lows. Opportunity was banging on the door. I was without home or career to bog me down. How could Zac and I possibly pass up this moment? Third decision: buy a company with Zac.

Thus began my five-month search for a company to acquire.

Through daily Internet searches, cold calls to business brokers, and many conversations with patient friends and family, I came across thousands of potential target companies from which I culled several dozen genuine prospects. Zac and I spent a couple days in a suburb outside Boston and nearly bought a manufacturer of products for the prevention and treatment of lice. In San Diego it was a company that retrofitted industrial lighting fixtures. In Northern Virginia we visited one of the nation's leading providers of high-end trade show exhibits. There was a custom manufacturer of high-end stone fireplaces in Maine and an asphalt maintenance contractor in Colorado. And more.

Along the way, I read several finance textbooks to improve my conceptual knowledge. I read the biographies and memoirs of daring entrepreneurs to inspire me and to steady my courage. Meanwhile, I kept up with my share of triplet care—feedings, diaper changes, endless bottles, baths in the tiny sink in our tiny kitchen. There was little sleep and much delirium. As the weeks wore on without a promising deal, Dorothy and I began to formulate plan B.

Then I came across Orlando Decorative Concrete, Inc. Though you wouldn't guess it from the company's unfortunate name, Orlando Decorative Concrete was a residential "slab and block" subcontractor. Home builders hired Orlando Decorative to build the foundations (the slabs) and concrete block walls (the block) of new homes. Its customers consisted primarily of large national home builders who sold production homes—companies like Meritage Homes, Ryland Homes, and D.R. Horton. In the heyday of the early 2000s, Orlando Decorative built the slabs and block walls for thousands of those new homes.

When I found Orlando Decorative in April 2011, that heyday was in the distant past. More than thirty-five thousand new homes were built in Orlando in 2005. Then the housing and financial markets melted down. By 2009 that number fell below five thousand. Orlando Decorative and its customers were struggling.

Zac and I saw a phenomenal opportunity. With Orlando Decorative we could buy our way into a decimated industry that was bound to recover. If we could transform Orlando Decorative into an industry-leading construction services company that could scale up rapidly to handle growing demand, we reasoned, we would earn a tremendous amount of business when the housing market in Orlando inevitably recovered. An urgent need for a new kind of construction company was bound to emerge. We would build that company and call it ODC Construction. Fourth decision: buy Orlando Decorative Concrete and create ODC Construction.

Zac and I did not want to risk anyone else's money in this gambit. ODC Construction would be ours, for better or for worse. This meant that we would have to pay for it on our own, too. The bank demanded both Zac's and my personal guarantees to provide a loan, as well as those of our wives. The company's principal vendors would all require similar guarantees. The four of us repeatedly signed on the dotted line, and as a result, our families' theoretical liability in the deal grew well beyond our purchase price, by millions.

Despite Zac's investment and the bank loan, funding the purchase still required me to put up the entirety of Dorothy's and my savings. Committed to abandon my successful career and move my family to Orlando to buy a company in an industry I knew nothing about, I would need to invest our every penny for the privilege. Fifth decision: risk it all.

When we bought it three months earlier, we knew Orlando Decorative was struggling, but we did not realize how badly. The financial data I had meticulously analyzed suggested the company was treading water. Its owner assured us he was selling the company for purely personal reasons and that business was improving.

After the acquisition, the ground beneath us crumbled. The company's financials were the proverbial garbage spit out when an accounting system is fed garbage in. The books were a complete mess. ODC was hemorrhaging cash. Three months in, we had just about maxed out our working capital credit line. Our company was not treading water, but sinking like a stone. Our theoretical multimillion-dollar liabilities had become very real.

I confronted dark fears, awful images of my family's financial ruin, villains I wanted to blame, heroes I wanted to rely upon for rescue. Eyes wide open, I zoomed out and refocused on the reality beyond fear's tunnel. We covered that idea in the last chapter. This chapter is about what came next, after fear.

The market opportunity we'd found so attractive had not changed. In fact, now on the inside of the industry, we found the opportunity even more compelling. Our strategy was sound. The problem was that the company we had purchased to implement that strategy was not. Far from it.

In poker they say that all you need is a chip and a chair to build a fortune. We had planned to build upon a "lifestyle company," an unsophisticated sole proprietorship humming along with mediocre results. Instead we'd bought ourselves a turnaround business, a distressed company in need of an immediate and comprehensive overhaul. Still, it was a seat at the table. We had a chair. It was a wobbly, three-legged stool of splintering, rotten wood instead of the cozy armchair we had paid for, but it was a seat at the table nonetheless.

But we didn't have any chips. Worse, most of the chips we had lost were not our own. We owed a lot of people a lot of money. It seemed we would walk away from the game beaten and broke.

The Critic and the Strong Man

It is not the critic who counts; not the man who points out how the strong man stumbles, or where the doer of deeds could have done them better. The credit belongs to the man who is actually in the arena, whose face is marred by dust and sweat and blood; who strives valiantly; who errs, who comes short again and again, because there is no effort without error and shortcoming; but who does actually strive to do the deeds; who knows great enthusiasms, the great devotions; who spends himself in a worthy cause; who at the best knows in the end the triumph of high achievement, and who at the worst, if he fails, at least fails while daring greatly, so that his place shall never be with those cold and timid souls who neither know victory nor defeat.

—Theodore Roosevelt

We defeat ourselves by conjuring not only the awful, but also the ideal. As we saw in the last chapter, the former is the province of our fears. Under fear's spell we zoom in tight, retreat to a world within, and awfulize.

The ideal is the domain of the critic, who purports to show us the view from without. The critic tells us to disengage, zoom out, idealize, and judge. The critic's idealized standards are the unattainable, the impossible, and the perfect. Our critics can be as immobilizing as our fears.

We face real criticism and real critics. We receive "constructive criticism" from those we know and love. In a sense, parents constantly critique their children. It is one way to teach them. We also receive feedback from friends, teachers, role models, colleagues, and spouses. Those who are actively engaged in our lives share their opinions, insights, and judgments about our pursuits. These are not the critics of Teddy Roosevelt's inspirational poem.

Roosevelt's "cold and timid souls" are those who criticize to tear down, not build up. His critics do not join in to advance active pursuits with insights or knowledge. They have no stake in the fight. They judge from afar, cataloging shortcomings. Their defining characteristic is that they "neither know victory nor defeat." They never try. They never strive. They do not enter the arena. They are experts without experience.

You harbor an internal critic, an oppressive voice that sits in judgment inside your mind. It is important to distinguish that critic from self-criticism more broadly. This chapter is largely about that distinction.

Self-awareness and self-assessment are crucial to growth and progress. The strong man criticizes, too. *I can do better, I can try harder*, he will say. He is right. As Roosevelt put it, "there is no effort without error and shortcoming." We learn from our errors and short-comings only if we can recognize and understand them.

The critic's message is different. *You will never be good enough*, he says. *Don't bother trying.* Like misery, the critic loves company. *Come sit with me on the sideline*, he says, *and we'll point out where the strong men stumble.*

The critic in your head intimidates and overwhelms you with the ideal. He proselytizes faith in the potential of perfection. His dogma draws you in with a superficial optimism, a hint at the divine in man, a promise of inspiration. He tells you perfection can always be achieved in theory, and there is a warmth in the idea. You want to believe it. But the critic knows you will never be perfect in reality. You know it, too. There is coldness in this truth.

Being the best is insufficient for perfection. But it is necessary. The critic polices this mandate with constant comparison. He compares results, learned skills, natural talents, physical attributes, anything that can be measured. He will compare you to people you know and love, those you've never met, fictional characters, figures from any era. He is as creative and flexible in his efforts of comparison as he is rigid in his absolute evaluation. No stretch is too far to draw implications when it comes to comparable merit, especially when you compare unfavorably.

Like fear, the critic warps your reality. He pulls you out of the moment, zooming out, and the task at hand shrinks away below, swallowed by the vastness of the overarching enterprise. With altitude, relative scale is inescapable. What remains to be done is vast compared to that which you have achieved. You require far more resources than those already marshaled. Sparse patches of detail, of certainty, float in empty spaces, vague notions, and known unknowns. Success is an island fortress, hazy and remote. The critic is obsessed with that fortress, the outcome, the destination, the final product. Again and again he draws your attention to it across the sea. *You are on a fool's errand,* he says. *This is hopeless.* At best the critic engenders complacence or apathy. Surrender in the guise of acceptance, resignation cloaked as maturity. At best, your doubt and regret will not linger.

Often fear lurks behind the critic, filling the empty spaces of unknown with the most awful possibilities. Fear of failure. Fear of success. Fear of the uncertainty that is as abundant as your challenge is difficult, as pervasive as your struggle is worthwhile. The critic offers you the easy way out. *Why bother? Face the facts. Be realistic. This isn't worth it.*

The voice of the critic is often loudest before you've begun. This is when he can do his greatest damage. You have yet to commit to your goal. You have made no investment in your aspirations. You have risked nothing in pursuit of your plans. For this and this alone the critic will commend you. Your inaction is a proxy for his own, his commendation a rationalization of past cowardice. The odds never justify the critic's wager because you are guaranteed to fall short of perfection, as is every human endeavor. The critic's is a fraudulent faith of failure foreordained.

The strong man values effort, struggle, momentum, growth. He finds none of these things in perfection and thus has no use for it, in concept or in application. To the strong man, perfection is a vacuum, like death. There is no progress in the void of perfection, no motion, no life.

For the strong man, the "best" is a fallacy. He assesses the quality of the effort expended, not the results obtained. He understands that external comparison is meaningless in this context. There is no unit of measure for grit or determination. Language is insufficient to classify with any precision our struggles, let alone to compare them. You cannot quantify the heart you put into the fight or the meaning you ascribe to it. Those are feelings, inherently personal, of no comparative value.

They are the feelings the strong man lives for and the gauge by which he holds himself internally accountable. For the strong man, achieving some theoretical maximum on that gauge would be like suffering the sterile death of perfection. His gauge has no maximum. He might achieve his personal best thus far. But he will never achieve his personal best. He can always improve, can always grow. He yearns for better, always better, but knows no best.

The strong man is rooted to the ground. His reality is the moment; his focus, crisp. He studies the proximate terrain with care, glancing at the distance casually and infrequently. His obsession is momentum, progress. Confronting the cliff to be scaled he sees toeholds, paths of ascent, the leverage of his tools and gear. He is aware of the summit, of course. But his world is now, this reach. Stretch, grip, pull.

What next? he asks. It is his mantra. *Just keep moving.* Failure is a fertile soil for knowledge. Strength is made of muscles tearing. Today's mistake is tomorrow's innovation. We discover vistas of great beauty when we are lost, and somehow we find our way, as long as we keep moving. The strong man knows all of these things. His knowledge is fear's antidote. The strong man lives with the peace of conviction and the humility of awareness. *This is quite a journey*, he thinks.

The strong man savors the first step. He is impatient for it, craves it. As long as he strives valiantly, with his first step he has won. He will thrive in the arena, marred by dust and sweat and blood, daring greatly. The strong man welcomes the triumph of achievement to nurture his great enthusiasms and devotions. But he leaves the measure of that achievement to his critics.

They will not disappoint. Your critics—the real ones and the one in your head alike—seek you out. They volunteer their unsolicited opinions and advice. They promote their purported expertise about you to anyone who will listen. Critics are loud and aggressive, vexations to the spirit.

The strong man leads by example and teaches by sharing his experiences. He speaks his truth quietly and clearly. He does not offer advice. He inspires. The world is full of strong men, though they often go unnoticed. You will find them in your life if you look for them. When you do find one, study him, learn from his example, relate his experiences to your own. Be inspired.

We are born strong men and women. That is who you are in your natural state, at your core, in your soul. It is in your genetics, your biology, your chemistry. It is a law of your physics. It is the profound truth embodied in Nietzsche's famous line, "What doesn't kill you makes you stronger." Every action fuels the strong man's fire. Every experience yields knowledge, insight, wisdom. As future fades to past, you live the constant improvement of the present, the moment. Strength tested begets greater strength.

There is a corollary, a consequent law of human physics.

Strength unexercised will atrophy. Inaction makes us weaker. In stasis our capacities lessen. With every betrayal of your potential you diminish that potential.

Therein lies the greatest evil of that voice in your head, the critic. Every time you listen to him, he gains credibility. He keeps you off the stage with the promise of bad reviews, and without practice you forget how to dance and lose the joy in it. It is also the tragedy of your fears, the unintended harm of good intentions misdirected. You feel fear to keep you safe. It is nature's warning of imminent danger, the instinct of fight or flight. But every flight takes some of the fight out, makes you more vulnerable, moves the odds against you if ever you do choose to take a stand.

We are born strong men and women. Our fears and our critics conspire to make us weak. Fear by shrinking reality to our most awful assumptions, the critic with a view so broad that we see only the timelessness and magnitude of towering endeavor. They are commanding foes. But we choose our own scale, make our own realities. We find our strength in the moment if we dare to look.

Your inner strong man may be weak, but he is always there. He has always been there. He carries the insights of your experiences, the lessons of your past. He will nourish your growth if you choose to grow, guide your improvement if you choose to be better. Listen to him and he will speak for you. Trust him and you will become him. You were born strong.

I felt strong when we launched ODC Construction. Friends and family alike questioned my judgment. Did I really want to throw away my elite New York legal career to buy and run a small construction subcontractor in Orlando? There were critics, too. I could hear them whispering behind my back. They said nasty things.

Still, I felt strong and optimistic. It was a calculated risk, a bold move, a return to my entrepreneurial spirit. My motivation was solid, my intentions good. I was executing a plan to improve my family's quality of life and find greater satisfaction in my career. Nothing ventured, nothing gained.

Don't get me wrong, the critic in my head had plenty to say. As I read about heroic business success stories, he proclaimed that I would never compare. I sought to derive common principles. He cataloged differences. As I worked through the endless details of the acquisition, he distracted me with unanswerable big-picture questions. Would I still be running this construction company in ten years? Would I ever earn as much in business as I would have in law, and if so, when? How soon and how quickly would the housing market recover? Was this really what I wanted to do with my life?

At times I was discouraged or overwhelmed. More than once I wondered whether I had lost my mind. There were moments in which I wanted to abandon the enterprise, to back out. The critic offered comfortable and compelling rationalizations in those moments. But I felt grounded and strong, kept my focus sharp, took one step at a time, maintained momentum. I kept the critic at bay.

I had experience with wholesale reinvention to draw upon, my transition from sight to blindness. As I shared in the last chapter, that transition began with the realizations that enabled me to overcome my fears eyes wide open. It began in Chris's office.

It took years to complete, however. As Chris had warned, mastering screen-reading software took time and effort. There is no quick or easy way to learn how to use a blind man's cane to navigate the world. I learned to leverage my other senses, but that adaptation was deliberate, methodical, and gradual. In short, the hard work began when I left Chris's office.

With hard work comes strength; with practice, mastery. In the years after Brenda brought Chris into my world, I practiced their proactive approach: Identify discrete challenges. Seek creative solutions. Never sacrifice the good in search of the perfect. To get from A to Z, focus on getting from A to B. You're likely to change course long before Z anyway. There is no silver bullet, no shortcut. One foot forward, then the next. Think ahead, but don't borrow trouble. Make plans in postulation, not prediction. Build momentum, always momentum, above all else momentum.

With repetition this practical approach became routine, and with my progress, its promise was reinforced. As I embraced my blindness and thrived, I grew stronger through the years.

When I determined to reinvent myself personally and professionally as a business owner and CEO, the critic in my mind was no match for my strength. I knew what to do. Focus on the next step. Close the deal, hit the ground running, manage the company. Do the deeds that need to be done. I felt strong when we launched ODC Construction.

Then we discovered that ODC was in a nosedive, and the critic in my head pounced, loud, obnoxious, constant, and convincing. *Of course this is an epic failure*, he said. *How could it have turned out any other way?* The critic recast the strength I had felt as foolhardiness and cited my earlier confidence as evidence of extreme negligence. Over and over again I cataloged every stumble, analyzed how every deed could have been done better. I compared myself to my peers, my stewardship of my family's well-being to theirs. I did not fare well in the comparison. *You were a fool to enter this arena. You never stood a chance.*

While panning my performance, the critic often referenced Dorothy's love and support. She never doubted that I would provide for our family. Decision by insane decision, she was there for me. We talked them through, she embraced my logic, and she supported me unequivocally. It was fine by her if her fancy lawyer husband wanted to reinvent himself as a construction guy. She was even willing to move back to Orlando, though she had never wanted to return to live in her hometown.

Her reward? I turned our lives upside down. In New York we had dreamed I would build a business empire. Last week I told her I would likely file a personal bankruptcy. I had rambled on about my metaphysical discontent working for a top-tier international law firm. These days I was telling Dorothy that after a bankruptcy, I might not be able to find employment with a local Orlando legal outfit. We had giddily swapped a two-bedroom apartment for a four-bedroom home. We were now contemplating moving in with her parents. The critic recycled these painful details in his disapproving rants.

Then there was that short call from Zac. "It took me twelve years of work to create financial security for my family," he said. "In three months, you've ruined it." Zac was right. It hurt because it was true. The critic loved to tell that story, too.

I did not feel strong. I was depressed. I pretended all was well at work, knowing that dozens of people would likely lose their liveli-hoods on my account. I hid in my office when panic attacks struck.

At home I felt tremendous guilt as a husband and father. *Lidsky mortgages his family's future in the name of selfish vanity*, read the critic's review. I was letting down my wife and year-old triplets. I wanted to give up and sleep all day.

In this desire my critic was my ally. His brutality justified my surrender, a mirage of "tough love" to rationalize the escape I sought. *You cannot fix this*, he said. *Admit that you've failed and walk away. You cannot fix this, but you can end it.* I wanted to believe it.

Dorothy refused. As ODC unraveled, she was sympathetic, empathetic, understanding. She was also quite firm on one point: I simply had to fix it. I had great talents, she reminded me. We would not have embarked upon this crazy venture but for these talents of mine. Dorothy now insisted that I rescue my company and our family. She insisted that I could do so, and that I would. Fix it. That was her mantra. Fix it, fix it, fix it. I wanted to believe it. She was the reason I got out of bed.

The critic in my head fought to rationalize surrender. The strong woman by my side inspired me to fight. But in the early days of our crisis, their debate felt academic. ODC was out of money. We would not last long. A couple weeks, three at most. At best I was triaging a dying patient. *This will all be over soon*, the critic said. I found comfort in this cold conclusion, and because it was comforting I felt shame.

"Please be good to yourself, tatele," my mother pleaded. It was two days ago. I had called her to confess the epic error of my entrepreneurial escapade, to explain that Dorothy and I were going to lose everything. She used a Yiddish term of endearment, "tatele," or "little boy." She heard the pain in my voice. She wanted to save me.

"Tatele, I have some money saved up," she continued. "I have $350,000 in cash. Take it. It is yours. I know you can fix this. Please take it."

My parents are Jews who were born in Cuba. (This makes us Cuban Jews, known as "Jewbans.") Both of my grandfathers had to start from scratch twice in their lives due to political upheaval. In his experiences with banks and governments, my mother's father witnessed firsthand the importance of saving for the proverbial rainy day. History had taught him that the safest way to save is to save hard cash. My mother listened to his stories and learned his lesson well. $350,000 well.

Now she was offering me that money, another strong woman convinced I could fix my company. As my shock subsided, realization dawned. The debate at the center of my life was no longer theoretical. I could not continue to ignore it. I faced a choice, real and difficult. *Do I take the money and try to save ODC?*

I did not feel strong, but I was inspired by the strength and support of my wife and mother. I did not feel strong, but I was devoted to a worthy cause. I did not feel strong, but I knew I had strength within. I fought to find that strength in the moment.

Actually Striving

Critic: Absolutely not. $350,000 is not enough. Will that buy you a couple months? A few? You can't even answer that question with precision—how can you consider taking the money?

STRONG MAN: With my mom's money, ODC can pay these bills right away and get some breathing room. These other bills will have to wait.

CRITIC: You don't even know if you'll have profitable contracts at the end of the day, let alone enough of them to cover your expenses. This is madness.

STRONG MAN: Walk away from Customer X. Customer X is taking advantage of us. Talk to Customer Y, plead for higher pricing. We can prove we are worth it, and I bet Customer Y will agree. I don't know where our other customers will shake out. We'll have to talk to them and see.

CRITIC: Who are you to turn around a failing business? You have no idea what you are doing. You've proven that point already.

STRONG MAN: I understand my company and my industry far better now than I did when we first started. I am learning.

CRITIC: You were a fool. You bought a toxic company.

STRONG MAN: This is my company now, my team, my vision.

CRITIC: You are marred by dust and sweat and blood. You will fail.

STRONG MAN: I am marred by dust and sweat and blood, but I have not failed yet.

CRITIC: You will err again; you will come short.

STRONG MAN: I will actually strive.

For two days I wrestle with the decision whether to take the money, an endless ping-pong match of pros and cons, an infinite loop of flip-flops.

I see the overwhelming, expansive totality of the challenge ahead and the magnitude of my blunder just behind. I hear a methodical drumbeat that weighs heavy, mesmerizes, and immobilizes, like sinking into the warm depths of anesthesia. Face the facts, know when you are beaten, do the mature thing, turn down the money. Be a good son, guard your mother's best interests. Lick your wounds. Retrench. Pick your next battle. This is the critic's view and the critic's drumbeat. *Let go*, he says. *Sink gently*. It is an enticing choice.

Deep down, I have a sense that this is not right, however, a suspicion, an uncomfortable déjà vu. I think about Dr. W's office and Dot Machines for the first time in years. I think about Chris. *Tomorrow you will face your life, and the next day, and every day thereafter, until you have none left. Those days unlived are reality's blank canvas, and you are the only creator*, I think.

But this is different. This is not irrational fear, monsters under the bed, villains or heroes. This is spreadsheets, numbers, facts. Faulty investment analysis, bad data, objective mistakes. This is a $350,000 wager on hunch and determination, gut and perseverance. *You are not a good bet. Let go*, the critic says.

Is this different? *You paint one stroke at a time, one day at a time, breathe a single breath after your last, a single breath before your next. You will never control tomorrow, but you can always choose whether to act today, and how.* Yes, this is different. I have to think about tomorrow to make economic decisions today. What is the expected value of the business? What is the probability of survival? Perform an analysis of the costs and the benefits. Estimate the return on investment. I have a responsibility to mitigate my losses.

I have a responsibility to my company and my team. I have a

responsibility to my wife and my children. I have a responsibility to myself. I see it clearly, eyes wide open, right now, right here in this moment. I am the only bet. That is reality. That is all there is. What next?

This is no different. I must again accept my obligation to help myself, to achieve my potential. I must again hold myself accountable at all costs. I own my fate. It begins with two simple questions: What, precisely, is the problem? What, precisely, can I do about it?

It is the strong man I hear last. I recognize him. His eyes saw through Blindness. They saw toeholds, paths of ascent, the leverage of tools and gear. They are my eyes. It is my vision. I am a strong man.

•   •   •

I feel the Suburban decelerate as Dorothy exits the turnpike. I am exhausted. I do not feel strong, but I know that I am strong. I know that strength lies in striving, that life is striving. I choose to be strong. With that choice I have silenced my critic, for this moment, at least.

We have reached our turnpike rest stop rendezvous, a parking lot halfway between our home in Windermere and my mother's in Miami. Dorothy spots my mother's car and we pull into the empty spot next to it. I step out of the Suburban and into a tight hug.

My mother reaches into her car and pulls out a small duffel bag. She hands it to me, then hugs me again. "Please be good to yourself, tatele," she says. "I know you can fix this." Dorothy rolls down the windows. My mom peers in and blows kisses to the Tripskys. She is back in her car and on her way south again in a matter of minutes. Dorothy rolls up the windows. I stand next to our car holding a duffel bag filled with $350,000 in cash. Formerly my mother's life savings, it is now my shot at redemption. I am in the arena. What next?

What came next was years of hard work. There was no magical Hollywood moment in which it all turned around for us. No silver bullet, no quick fix. There were a lot of ups and downs, many difficult decisions to make, minor victories, setbacks, painful conversations. What came next was the actual striving, the doing of the deeds.

Above all else I labored to focus, to be strong, to keep my eyes wide open, to retain control of my reality. This was every day's top priority. It was a necessity. When my critic resurfaced and resumed his hypnotic drumbeat again, urging me to stare off in surrender at that remote island of success, I had to silence him, fix my focus firm. When my fears crept in and backed me into that narrow, awful tunnel, I had to again step forward, break free.

In the early weeks and months, this was a fragile equilibrium. It demanded active, careful minding. It was a burdensome requisite, well worth the effort but tiring nonetheless. It eventually became easier, came more naturally, gained stability. Strength tested begets strength.

I was not alone. I was blessed to lead a team of strong men and women. They pledged their hearts, minds, and souls to the fight, and together we strove for excellence. We insisted upon it. We demanded it of one another. We came short again and again, but we did not pause, we did not linger. Always we strove.

I found a brother by my side in the trenches and drew inspiration from his strength. A part-time consultant for Orlando Decorative when Zac and I bought the business, he was described to us as a "sales guy" without commitment or resolve. It was the description of his critics, and it bore the hallmarks of their warped reality.

Tony Hartsgrove is a strong man. He is brilliant, he is a natural operator, and he is willing to work as hard as anyone I've ever known. As we discovered the extent of our troubles, it was Tony who rolled up his sleeves and stood next to me, ready to dig out at any cost. For months we spent every waking moment at the office together. We became forensic accountants, spin doctors, masters of the speed chess tactics of the turnaround. In the early days, neither of us could eat, so we lost weight together. Neither of us could sleep, so we spoke at all hours of the night. We strove.

With time, saving ODC Construction ceased to be a burden. It became a privilege, a blessing, a joy. Eyes wide open I learned to see resources, opportunities, progress, growth. I found fulfillment in the struggle, the process, the journey. It even became fun.

There is a state of consciousness known as "flow" in the field of psychology. Named by pioneering happiness researcher Mihály Csíkszentmihályi, who was the first to study it with rigor, flow can be described in various clinical ways, such as "complete absorption in a task" and "completely focused motivation." More simply, it is referred to as "being in the zone." Csíkszentmihályi has described flow in far more compelling terms, as "the secret of happiness," and experience that "makes life meaningful."

As explained by Pursuit-of-Happiness.org, flow emerges in "moments in which your mind becomes entirely absorbed in [an] activity so that you 'forget yourself' and begin to act effortlessly, with a heightened sense of awareness of the here and now." Among other factors, to achieve flow you must have clear goals, immediate feedback, and a good balance between your challenge and your skills. In flow, your actions and your awareness are merged, distractions are excluded from your consciousness, and you have no worry of failure. Your self-consciousness disappears and you lose track of time. As a result, your activity becomes an end in itself.

Flow is the product of focus and intention. You can consciously pay attention to only so much information in any moment. For example, it is difficult to listen to two conversations at the same time, and most of us would find it impossible to listen to three or more. Your mental attention only has so much bandwidth. When you're in a state of flow, the entirety of that bandwidth is consumed by the task at hand, the moment.

Flow has been studied extensively, and volumes have been written about it. Researchers have applied the concept to the business world, elite sports, creativity, teamwork, and other arenas. They have labored to define and measure it.

I am not an expert in flow, or in any aspect of psychology for that matter. Far from it. But when we found our stride turning ODC around, I was in the zone. Of that I'm certain. And Csíkszentmihályi is right—the experience brought meaning to my life.

The notion of a deeper meaning inherent in flow resonates with religious themes found in Hinduism, Buddhism, and Taoism. Analogous ideas can be found in ancient philosophy. And flow is at the core of the discipline of mindfulness—Csíkszentmihályi himself has written that "the similarities between Yoga and flow are extremely strong," for example.

For me, living eyes wide open is a form of flow. It is a commitment to the reality of the moment unadorned by fears or critics. It is the strong man's focus on progress, effort. It is the organic accountability that flourishes when you know that you own your own reality. It is integrity, the alignment of your ideals with your actions. It is spiritual. It is actually striving, simple and pure.

This is the meaning I found in my efforts to rescue my company and fight for my family. The gift of that meaning, the grace of it, was mine immediately and irrevocably, independent of the outcome. At the worst, if I had failed, at least I would have failed while striving.

We did not fail, however. We are blessed to know the triumph of high achievement. In 2011 ODC construction booked about $11 million in revenue and lost a pile of money doing it. In 2016 the company was highly profitable, with about $150 million in sales. Our corporate team has grown from a dozen people to a hundred, and our full-time labor force has grown from fewer than one hundred to more than three hundred. We've added three locations in Florida, and on any given day, thousands of people build success with ODC Construction throughout the state. We start work on about four hundred new homes every month. The numbers are a by-product of greater accomplishments. We built something excellent, a company we are proud of, one that nurtures and invests in its employees while delivering world-class construction management services throughout Florida.

What next?

Fishing Trip 3: 98 Days, Part I

August 17, 2010, to September 14, 2010

And say, What is thy mother? A lioness: she lay down among lions, she nourished her whelps. . . . And she brought up one of her whelps: it became a young lion.

—Ezekiel 19:2–3

Dorothy's pregnancy was arduous. Her morning sickness, intense and misnamed, tormented her day and night. She was exhausted but could not sleep, a graduate student struggling to concentrate, a host body tall and thin making room at the long, narrow bar for a rowdy party of three. She loathed bathrooms because she spent so much time in them. She resented her treasured wardrobe because she could not wear it. She had little desire to eat but a pressing and persistent need to do so. After all, she had four to feed.

Eating was a daily battle. We moved to Manhattan at the end of May and made the rounds with a medical dream team—a high-risk obstetrics group, maternal fetal medicine specialist, and nutritionist. These experts repeatedly stressed the importance of sufficient caloric intake. Specifically, they urged Dorothy to consume at least four thousand calories daily. Though it made her miserable, Dorothy hit their mark every day. The goal was about a million calories before the triplets' birth.

From conception, the average human singleton pregnancy lasts thirty-eight weeks, a measure known as fetal age. Gestational age pins the start of "pregnancy" to the beginning of the mother's preceding menstrual cycle, on average two weeks earlier. Doctors usually employ gestational age because it references an event of origin more routinely observed without ambiguity than is conception. That's why we colloquially say pregnancy lasts forty weeks, even though the mother isn't pregnant for the first two.

For triplets, thirty-four weeks (from conception) is deemed sufficient. To state the obvious, space becomes scarce. Nature has compensated, though. Multiples develop more rapidly than their solo counterparts do. At a fetal age of thirty-four weeks, triplets' organs have matured and physical growth in size is pretty much the only thing going on in the womb. Accordingly, the prevailing view of science is that the risks posed by confinement outweigh the benefits from that point forward. The destination has not quite been reached, but it is best to boot the expanding clowns out of the clown car. They are safer walking the rest of the way.

Four thousand calories per day for thirty-four weeks comes out to 952,000 calories. We hoped the triplets would have a full thirty-four weeks to develop in Dorothy's womb. Hence, we hoped Dorothy would ingest about a million calories before their birth. We prayed she would.

Positive triplet outcomes are correlated with pregnancy duration and birth weight. That's a fancy way to say that you want your triplets to be born as late as possible and as big as possible. The earlier they show up and the smaller they are on their one true birthday, the greater the odds your triplets will face medical complications, at birth or later in life.

Most triplet pregnancies don't make it "full" term, however. In 93 percent, birth occurs by fetal age thirty-five weeks and in 41 percent by thirty weeks. The average triplet weighs less than 5.5 pounds at birth, and 37 percent weigh less than 3.3 pounds. By comparison, fewer than 1.5 percent of singletons are born before thirty weeks, and only 1 percent weigh less than 3.3 pounds. The infant mortality rate for triplets is about ten times what it is for singletons. The math is inescapable. Triplet pregnancies are risky for triplets. They tend to be born early and small, facing a panoply of potential consequences, minor, major, and everything in between.

Because it is effective to improve preterm birth and fetal growth, some doctors advise reduction when a triplet pregnancy presents. That's a fancy way to say they recommend termination of one or two of the triplet fetuses to improve the odds for the other(s). Triplets are born later and bigger when you get rid of one or two of them. That is, they face less risk if they're made twins or singletons. That's more inescapable math.

Our medical experts explained this to Dorothy and me, without recommendation at first, merely presenting reduction as an option. Though we'd never condemn, or even judge, parents who make a different decision (a point I will stress), for Dorothy and me the choice was no choice at all. Our crafted Plan debunked, we found faith in the natural plan not of our making. God had given us triplets, and we would fight for all of them. It was that simple for us.

It became more complex. Baby C was smaller than Babies A and B, and growing more slowly. Each week Dorothy and I visited the high-risk group for ultrasounds, and each week the gap in size between Baby C and his siblings grew wider. The doctors' concerns grew with that gap.

Some of the doctors saw it as a compelling reason to "reduce" Baby C. A tendency to abort any fetus can only strengthen as its prognosis worsens. Grim logic, but in the case of multiples it gets worse. As Baby C's prospects deteriorated, the statistical cost Baby C imposed upon Babies A and B mounted, as a mathematical proposition, at least. In the eyes of some of the doctors, that cost had grown unjustifiable, necessitating medical intervention. Some of them shared this assessment with Dorothy and me. Information about reduction became forceful advice to reduce. Our parental choice was reckless, they implied, our deliberation ignorant sentimentality.

Dorothy and I saw matters differently. We would love and care for Baby C if we were so blessed, whatever that might look like, and in our estimation each of our triplets had an equal claim to our protection. As to the doctors, we suffered the condescension of the few quietly, choosing to focus upon intentions we presumed positive. We appreciated those who informed without judgment. We adored those who supported our decision. We did not waver.

The reduction debate faced a deadline, a legal one, not medical. Consistent with U.S. Supreme Court precedent, the State of New York codified the last day of a pregnancy upon which doctors within its borders can lawfully perform the procedure. In light of this deadline, Dorothy and I reluctantly agreed to advance an appointment for some extensive testing, from a few days after the deadline to a few days before it.

"Gather the best information available to you while you still have options so you can proactively make an informed decision instead of having the choice made for you by default." That was the argument presented to Dorothy and me, a good one. We accepted it. Then we made our informed decision with the best available information. Reduction became a criminal act and matters grew simple again.

Not for long. Postdeadline we had one or two routine checkups (inasmuch as a triplet pregnancy checkup can ever be routine). Then came the first doctor's visit I did not attend, Dorothy's checkup on August 17, 2010. That morning I set out for the funeral of a good friend's mother, but I never made it.

I was in a car with several other funeral attendees, in moderate traffic on the Long Island Expressway, when Dorothy called from the hospital. She was hysterical. Baby C was in trouble. Exactly how or why was unclear, but it seemed there was a decision to be made. Dorothy asked me to hurry to her side. Her request was unnecessary. I was desperate to be there.

I did not want to divert all of the car's occupants from the funeral, however. I wanted to be alone in the back of a cab, traveling to the hospital at life-threatening speed on the phone with Dorothy. So I shouted at the driver to pull over and let me out right there on the side of the LIE. It took some convincing, but I eventually agreed to wait for the next exit instead, where we quickly found a gypsy cab that I commandeered. As in a movie, I offered every bill in my wallet in exchange for speed. As in a movie, it worked. I made it to Dorothy in record time.

"Baby C is very sick," the doctor told us.

"What is the problem?" I asked.

"Absent umbilical arterial end diastolic flow," the doctor said. "It is very serious."

"What does that mean?" I asked.

"Baby C's heart is sick," the doctor answered.

Thus began the conversational sparring. It was confusing, exasperating, and agonizing. Dorothy and I wanted precisely to understand the nature of the medical concern for Baby C. We needed to. Yet the doctor's answers seemed evasive, simplistic, or conclusory, not explanatory. *Just trust me, I'm the expert* was the strong message we received. Extracting the doctor's molars would have been easier.

When your heart muscle contracts, expelling a burst of blood, the flow of blood through your arteries is fastest and your blood pressure is greatest. When your heart expands and refills, taking in the blood it will next expel, blood flow through your arteries is slowest and your blood pressure bottoms out. Blood pressure and velocity rise and fall in a constant cycle. That's why your doctor reports two numbers when taking your blood pressure. Systolic blood pressure is the highest value in the cycle—when the heart muscle has just contracted—and diastolic blood pressure is the lowest—when the heart is resting and refilling.

The human fetus manages its own blood flow, an extraordinary responsibility. The fetal heart pumps blood out of the tiny body, through the umbilical cord, through the placenta, and back again. Umbilical arteries carry deoxygenated and nutrient-depleted fetal blood to the placenta. The umbilical vein carries freshly oxygenated and nutrient-rich blood back. The placenta works the biological magic in the middle, serving as a two-way filter, using mom's blood to supply inputs to baby and to carry off baby's outputs.

As in our arteries, blood pressure in an umbilical artery cycles from highest (systolic) to lowest (diastolic) with every precious fetal heartbeat. As in our arteries, the flow of blood through an umbilical artery speeds and slows with this cycle. Slows, but does not stop. The flow of blood is constant, only its pressure and velocity change. That's how it works when all is well, at least.

"Growth restriction" in a fetus often indicates uteroplacental insufficiency. In essence more "dense," the dysfunctional placenta demands greater pressure to sustain blood flow through its filters. The heart of a fetus with such a placenta must work harder. It grows in the womb under abnormal stress.

Baby C was bearing this abnormal stress. The doctors realized as much because he had absent umbilical arterial end diastolic flow. That's a fancy way of saying that at the point of lowest pressure in the blood flow cycle, the blood in his umbilical arteries stopped flowing altogether. The end diastolic flow through the arteries of his umbilical cord was "absent." Not good. Neither Baby C nor his heart was "sick," but Baby C was struggling with a deficient placenta.

The real problem, when we finally got down to it, was that Baby C might not be able to sustain this struggle much longer. Absent flow most often precedes "reverse flow." Picture a wave of water flowing through a tunnel, encountering a wall and bouncing back upon itself. That's reverse flow. With reverse umbilical arterial end diastolic flow, the blood the fetus has just pumped out through the umbilical cord bounces back off the placenta and returns from whence it came. If reverse flow reaches the heart, entering where blood should exit, the results are catastrophic. Baby C was perched on the precipice of such catastrophe.

"Flow will reverse in two to six days," the doctor said, confident in the prediction.

Dorothy's and my understanding still lacked precision at this point. (Precision would require a lot of research and conversations with knowledgeable friends and family.) Still, we understood enough to be devastated by the prognosis. We hugged and cried. Worse news followed.

The doctor recommended against surgical intervention to save Baby C's life. The limitations of modern medicine, the doctor explained, would not permit a rescue of Baby C without also delivering his two siblings. Even before their birth, our triplets were one for all and all for one. Whether at the will of nature or the surgeon's hand, they would enter the world together.

In medical parlance, the fetuses were "viable." The gestational age of Dorothy's pregnancy was twenty-five weeks and three days. She had carried our triplets for 23.4 weeks at this point, about 75 percent of the shortened thirty-four-week target triplet fetal age, or 67 percent of the average singleton's fetal age at birth. Our children would likely survive if surgically delivered. But survival is a modest goal.

Their lungs were far from fully developed, and they would need help to breathe, most likely through intubation—the insertion into the lungs of a tube through which a machine pumps air. The immature arteries in their brains were so fragile as to pose a substantial risk of cerebral hemorrhage at delivery. Their hearts might require surgical intervention to accomplish the critical anatomical transition that occurs naturally during a full-term birth—or more extensive repair. Their retinas were immature, and the prolonged exposure to oxygen that would accompany their months-long stay in the neonatal intensive care unit (NICU) could lead to permanent vision loss or blindness.

They might not be able to process food delivered to the stomach—at best through a feeding tube for months to come—and attempts could lead to serious disease of the gut. They would be highly susceptible to infection, without the defense of mature immune systems. Their razor-thin skin would be translucent and would bruise easily. They would face myriad developmental challenges, beginning with breathing unaided and learning to eat from a bottle; continuing with "normal" milestones like muscle control, the development of speech, and learning to crawl and walk; and persisting through their adolescence and beyond. Science could not predict the quality of life they would experience, nor for how long, and we might not know for years to come. Baby C weighed less than a pound.

Dorothy and I were by now expert in the grim, zero-sum logic of multiple pregnancy. We knew we were about to hear it recited once again. That didn't make it any easier. "Intervention will impose unreasonable risks upon two of your children for an unjustifiably small chance to rescue the third," the doctor said. There it was again, the math, plain and simple.

The contours of our tortuous dilemma took shape in my mind. In the next two to six days, Baby C would face grave danger. When that danger manifested, only an emergency delivery of all three triplets could save Baby C's life. The odds of success saving Baby C in this scenario were long. It was guaranteed, however, that delivering the triplets at such an early fetal age posed enormous risks for all three of them. Profound consequences were all but certain. In sum, Dorothy and I seemed destined to make an urgent, excruciating, intolerable decision. In the next six days.

"One option," the doctor said, "is to go home, take it easy, and come back at thirty weeks." The reference was to gestational age, not that it mattered. "Let nature take its course and we'll see where we stand then. That's what I recommend."

I've never experienced the feeling of drowning, but it can't be worse than that moment. Panic before comprehension, terror, desperation, thrashing futile and violent, angry grief, sadness absolute. For my children I'd gladly flail against the tide and drown exhausted.

"Can we constantly monitor Baby C—stay on top of this and see where things go?" I asked. Before receiving the doctor's shocking recommendation, I had assumed we would do just that.

"No. The only way to measure this is with one of the dopplers in our ultrasound unit. That's an exam, not monitoring," the doctor said.

"How frequently can we do the exam?" I asked. I was expecting something like "two or three times a day" as an answer and hoping for better.

"You could come back in a couple weeks to repeat the exam," the doctor said.

"Two weeks?!" I was begging. Medical intervention, so recently urged upon us without welcome, was nowhere to be found.

"I guess we could do it in a week," the doctor said, not a fan of the idea. "We really wouldn't do a doppler more than once a week."

Comprehension caught up with panic. This was advocacy and

opposition, not opinion or advice. Dorothy and I were speaking with self-appointed counsel for Baby C's siblings. Having already written off Baby C, counsel was determined to defeat Baby C's parents by doing nothing whatsoever, leaving him to contend with nature on his own.

To my family's lasting fortune, I was expert in advocacy. I recognized it in our doctor and ceased to beg, bracing myself to advocate instead. There was a vulnerability in the doctor's stance. I exploited it with relish, using powerful logic all too familiar.

"Look," I said, "we understand your position on intervention here, Doctor. All we want to do is gather the best information available to us while we still have options. We want to proactively make an informed decision when we have to do so, instead of having the choice made for us by default." Because I simply had to, I added: "We also want to do our best for Baby C as his parents."

The debate continued a little while longer. I grew more passionate, more aggressive, and in the end the doctor capitulated. Dorothy was admitted to the hospital a few hours later and placed on strict bed rest to minimize stress for Baby C. We scheduled another doppler exam to reassess the situation in two days' time.

Brenda (Dorothy's mother) arrived from Florida late that afternoon, summoned by my call hours earlier. In the evening the three of us met members of the hospital's NICU team. A NICU doctor came to Dorothy's room and spent almost an hour speaking with us. Then he took us to visit the NICU, pushing Dorothy in a wheelchair, where we met other doctors and several nurses. Finally, we were guided on a thorough tour of the facility, our many questions answered with care and precision.

I cannot overstate the impact on our lives. As far as the NICU team was concerned, our triplets were their patients, all three of them. "You hold on to them as long as you possibly can," one doctor told Dorothy. "But don't worry. We're here waiting for them. We'll take care of them when they get here." They were candid and concerned, no strangers to the math, vigilantly realistic. But at the same time they stood committed to care for our children. All three of our children, without question. We loved them for it.

We were still terrified when we returned to Dorothy's room, but for the first time we were hopeful, too. Our resolve was unchanged, for the simple reason that it could grow no stronger. Our immense guilt in that resolve, however, was greatly diminished. Unburdened we declared our conviction to fight for our three, indivisibly and without limitation. We had made that promise already, but kept it hidden in shame. Now we repeated it openly, without apology or hesitation.

We celebrated it. Over and over again that night we retold the stories the NICU team had shared hours before, stories of children born earlier than ours, children who thrived, children who returned to visit decades after their birth, happy, healthy, whole. We rehearsed the NICU creed: every day of pregnancy is a blessing, tomorrow is better than today, and when it is today, we're here and we're ready. Stories and creeds cannot change the math. But they can lift the heart. Our hearts were lifted to the sky.

Did it really matter? One could argue that the decrease in Dorothy's anxiety, like her bed rest, reduced the stress imposed upon the babies she carried. At the level of hormones and biology and chemistry and energy and tension, the peace she found in the affirmation we were doing our best for our children produced an objective medical benefit for the triplets. That makes good sense to me.

I also like to think that Baby C heard and understood, heard the stories and the creed, understood our promise and his burden. I like to think this lifted Baby C's heart, a heart that wasn't sick, just working very hard. Not literal hearing or understanding, but in some cosmic way we might someday comprehend but will never control.

Either way, or both, it mattered. Two days later Baby C's heart was still going strong. And four days after that. End diastolic flow did not reverse in Baby C's umbilical arteries in two to six days. It never did.

For twenty-six days, lionhearted Baby C carried his burden without a stumble. Brenda, Dorothy, and I settled into a routine. Dorothy was never left alone. Brenda and I took turns sleeping in the cot in Dorothy's hospital room, two nights for me, one for Brenda, or thereabouts. I worked there, too, leaving for meetings when necessary. Brenda handled laundry, food, and other essentials. Dorothy was a lioness lain down to bring up her whelps, and she was fierce.

It was a difficult time, a new cycle driving life. Pressure released every two or three days at Baby C's doppler exam, the world expanding with gratitude and relief. Then the endless wait for the next exam, pressure mounting, the world collapsed into a tunnel, sleepless nights imagining a wave of water flowing forcefully, encountering a wall and bouncing back upon itself.

On the twenty-seventh day, the doppler assessment indicated mounting strain. Dorothy and I made our decision. Not urgent, excruciating, or intolerable, but proactive, informed, and straightforward. Baby C had carried our family for four weeks, a gift miraculous in its proportions. Delivery still posed great challenges and ominous risks for the triplets. But the four extra weeks of fetal development meant a world of difference for their prognosis. The math was inescapable.

It was time to relieve the pressure on Baby C. We made our decision with the peace of conviction and the humility of awareness. We celebrated it. After all, it was our triplets' birthday we were planning.

On the twenty-eighth day, September 14, 2010, they were born, at 2:21, 2:22, and 2:24. It was not an emergency surgery. It was carefully choreographed and masterful—approximately thirty medical personnel divided among four teams, one for Dorothy and one for each of her whelps. Those whelps weighed less than 7.5 pounds combined. Brought out to become a lion, Baby C weighed 1.5 pounds. The NICU team was there, ready for our children. All three of our children. We loved them for it.

Had nature been left to its course, Dorothy's pregnancy would have reached thirty weeks' gestational age on the thirty-second day, September 18, a Saturday. As recommended, we'd have returned to the hospital the following Monday or Tuesday to see where we stood. We'll never know what we would have seen.

Does it really matter? Not for my family. Not for me. Not anymore. But it's a story, and a story can lift a struggling heart into the sky, high above math and recommendations and judgment and guilt. I like to think Baby C's story will do just that.

CHAPTER 4

Acceptance and Surrender

Every weakness contains within itself a strength.

—Shūsaku Endō

s my friend Tabby puts it, there is a thin, elusive line between acceptance and surrender. I am walking down Chauncy Street, skating that line. It is April 2003, I'm in my second year of law school, and I am using a walking cane for the visually impaired for the first time.

When I met Chris a few weeks ago, she referred me to Joe, a "mobility coach." Joe and I spent the last two hours together, and he taught me basic cane techniques as we walked Harvard Law School's campus. Then he urged me to practice these basics as much as possible before our next session in a couple weeks, to "get comfortable with the cane." Now I'm walking down Chauncy Street to meet Dorothy in front of our apartment building, practicing, or trying to, at least.

I do not feel comfortable with the cane. I feel very awkward. It is fifty-six inches long, composed of five interlocking graphite segments and covered in a highly reflective, colored coating. The top four segments are a glowing white, while the last, bottom segment is bright red. It has a plastic, teardrop-shaped tip at the end, the best tip for navigating the brick and cobblestone sidewalks of Cambridge, Joe assured me. The grip is that of a putter.

I hold the cane out in front of me in my right hand at waist height. With each step, I swing the tip of the cane from one side to the other, gently tapping the sidewalk at the end of each arc, like a walking metronome. As I step forward with my left foot, I send the cane tip across the sidewalk, just barely above its surface, from my left side over to my right side. As my left foot's stride comes to an end, so, too, does the cane tip reach the end of its arc on my right, and I tap the sidewalk with the teardrop tip. In so doing, I have cleared for obstacles the space my body will occupy as I next step forward with my right foot.

I can now safely take that next step with my right foot, sending the cane tip back across my body out in front of me and tapping it on my left, clearing the space my body will occupy when I step with my left foot again. The cycle begins anew. Step-tap, step-tap, the cane sweeps for obstacles one step ahead of me.

That is the theory. In theory, the cane is a simple, elegant, helpful tool. In reality I am a newborn, sloppy cane swinger, and I am making my life much more difficult by stubbornly assaulting the sidewalk with a graphite stick. Safely walking down the street with my limited sight requires great focus these days. This endeavor to choreograph new, unnatural movements has usurped that focus, and

I am certain that as a result a worse-than-average collision is impending. I am tense.

My sweeps fall out of sync with my steps. The cane tip's supposed glides above the sidewalk are erratic bounces and drags. The teardrop tip is little help. Every twenty yards or so it slips into a crack in the brick sidewalk and jams. My momentum carries me forward, forcing the putter grip into my gut. With the tip stuck in its crack, the handle stuck in my gut and my body stuck in its forward motion, I am levered upward by the cane—the handle digs in and up, lifting me off the ground. The putter grip gut stab is frustrating and painful.

There are other frustrations and pains. I am embarrassed to be seen using this cane. It will undoubtedly be perceived by others—consciously or unconsciously—as a sign of weakness and vulnerability. I do not want to be perceived as weak or vulnerable. I reassure myself: As of a few hours ago, I got along just fine without this cane. I do not need it.

This superficial self-defense only leads to more questions. If I see well enough to get by, if I didn't need the cane yesterday, why am I using it today? Am I weaker than others who cope with vision loss? Am I unable to cope as well as they do?

Am I committing a fraud? I am using a blind man's cane, but I am not blind, not completely, not yet. I will likely be perceived as blind and aided as a blind person, but I can still see a lot, can get by. What will those who know me think when they see me with this cane? This last question is particularly troubling. It is the question I keep coming back to, again and again.

Learning to use this cane was supposed to be a strong man's

proactivity, a form of striving, my taking accountability for a discrete, well-defined problem and implementing a direct solution. I was supposed to express confidence in this walk, to welcome progress, to embody optimism in this moment, even find peace. Why do I feel insecure? Why am I worried that others will think I am weak?

I am confused. In my confusion there is disappointment. There is resentment. *This will take practice*, I tell myself. *Give it time. You will learn to use this cane. For now this is difficult, but soon enough it will be helpful. Be positive, be optimistic. You will integrate this cane into your life, and it will prove a great benefit. Be patient.*

But that is not enough for me. I do not want to integrate this cane into my life. I do not want to need it. Others will find no strength, no confidence, no power in my adapting to blindness. There is no strength in need. Nothing to celebrate in capitulation. They'll see only blindness, and it will define me in their eyes. I do not want to be defined by disability, defined by this cane. I am not a blind man. I am a man who happens to be going blind.

What is my alternative? Ignore my reality? Fight it? Is it better to be blindly stubborn or blind and practical? Should I thrash forward against the tide until I drown? Would that make me look stronger to others?

This is progress. It may not feel like it, but it is. This is eyes wide open. This is what I need to do for myself. It does not matter what others will think. What I think matters. That is my choice. I need to confront my own thoughts about strength and weakness, acceptance and surrender. This is who I am. This is my life.

My internal pep talk taking effect, I take each step-tap with renewed focus. I insist that this cane will do great things for me.

Rounding the bend in Chauncy Street as I walk toward Garden Street, I can now make out Dorothy ahead of me, standing in front of our apartment complex, awaiting my arrival. It is a sight to celebrate, an oasis of emotional support at the end of a desert trek.

I straighten my posture, tighten up my cane swings and taps, and put a bright smile on my face. She returns the favor. I experience a brief moment of energized optimism, and my pace quickens. Then my teardrop tip catches a crack and I am stopped dead in my tracks, lifted slightly off the ground, a shooting pain radiating from my gut. Dorothy sees it all. Tears fill my eyes. I fold up my new cane.

There is a thin, elusive line between acceptance and surrender, between strength and weakness, between confidence and shame. Its contours are complex, its form faint and ethereal. As I walked down Chauncy Street I sought to find that line, but I never did, not that day.

That day I was distracted by bright, bold lines, tempting in their clarity, straight and sharp. Disability is weakness. Dependence is insecurity. Struggle is embarrassment. Those are the lies we tell one another. Those are the lies we tell ourselves. There is no malice in the telling, only negligence or ignorance. Those lines are easy to see and easy to understand. Those lines are simple. They make sense if you don't know any better.

I didn't know any better. It took years for me to forget those lines, to ignore them, to see beyond them. Only then could I begin to discern the true line, to gain confidence, to understand that blindness is not weakness. I accepted my blindness, then embraced it. I learned to find strength in it, even when others saw weakness. *Especially* when others saw weakness.

Looking back, I am amazed by my simplistic, misguided notions of disability, independence, and strength. I am horrified by them. I see that they made me weak, not my blindness. They could have made me a victim, bitter and resentful.

It can be difficult to find that line. You may have to search deep within yourself. You may have to confront others who insist upon very different lines for you. You may have to master the minute details of the disabilities, flaws, or shortcomings you'd rather avoid, master those details, accept them, and embrace them. It can be very difficult.

But to live eyes wide open you must find that line. That line is reality. That line is truth and power, strength and confidence. You must learn to see it. You must choose to see it.

The Three-Ring Circus

I once heard a blind comedian deliver a fantastic line: when you're blind and lazy, people think you're just blind! The observation is both hilarious and true. Like much of great comedy, it also invokes with a simple concept deeper, more complex questions. What assumptions do we make about the capabilities of the blind? What assumptions do we make about disabilities in general? Why? And to what effect—both for the disabled and our society at large?

This chapter is not about disabilities—not in the way you're thinking, at least. But that is a good place to start. What is a disability? That is not a simple question. Scholars, philosophers, religious leaders, lawyers, and legislators have pondered the definition for centuries. Prevailing views vary dramatically across religions, cultures, geographic regions, and socioeconomic classes, and they change over time. How would you define the terms "disability" and "disabled"? Think about your answer for a moment before reading on.

Disabilities can be viewed from three different perspectives. In the first, a disability is a divine punishment for moral sin in this life or another. It is a mark of shame upon the afflicted (and often his family and community as well). The disabled deserve our scorn, our disgust, our condemnation. They should be hidden away, separated from society, denied the opportunity to corrupt the righteous. This view is more prevalent today than you might imagine. It is alive and well in many parts of the world, in many hearts and minds.

In the second view, disability is a medical matter. A disability is a physical or mental impairment; the disabled are "sick." We look to medicine and science to cure, treat, or rehabilitate disability. It is an organic problem, an illness, a condition. The disabled are the afflicted; their disease, the problem. We strive to fix them.

In both of these views, disability begins and ends with the disabled. A disability is a defect; the disabled are defective. Whether the defect warrants punishment or repair, censure or sympathy, guilt or regret, it is a problem with the individual himself. The question for society is: what do we do with him? This common and fundamental characteristic of these first two perspectives is demonstrably flawed.

The third view of disability is broader. It encompasses the roles of environment and societal attitudes. Terminology gets tricky. It is important to be precise with language. The term "disability" refers only to a diminished ability to perform an activity relative to one's peer group. We use another term, such as "disadvantage" or "handicap," to refer to problematic consequences that result from a disability in light of the environment or social attitudes.

Let's consider an example. A person who uses a wheelchair has a disability, a limitation of his ability to use his limbs relative to his peers. Is he disadvantaged? The answer depends on his environment.

The use of a wheelchair is not necessarily a disadvantage in a world that is fully accessible to those who use wheelchairs. Imagine that every building accommodates the use of wheelchairs with elevators, ramps, automatic doors, and suitably wide halls and doorways; every curb has a wheelchair-accessible curb cut; wheelchair-equipped vehicles are readily available for purchase at a reasonable price; all public transportation accommodates wheelchair use. Every bathroom, every store, every hotel room, every restaurant, every public space is constructed to accommodate the practicalities of wheelchair use. In such a world, is the use of a wheelchair a disadvantage? Not when it comes to the physical environment.

But what about societal attitudes in this physically accessible world? Now assume that its inhabitants all share the view that those who use wheelchairs are helpless victims, unsuitable as employees, colleagues, friends, or mates. If you use a wheelchair you will not be educated. You will not be employed. You will be pitied and marginalized. Physical access notwithstanding, the use of a wheelchair is a severe disadvantage in this hypothetical world.

The example is extreme, but it illustrates the fundamental point. Disadvantage does not arise from a disability alone, but from the consequences of that disability in light of the environment and societal attitudes. The real world is never as black and white as our hypothetical example, however. The real world is gray. It is far more complicated. There are no bright lines, only complex contours, faint, ethereal, transient.

What percentage of buildings must be wheelchair accessible for the use of a wheelchair to cease to be a disadvantage? What percentage of employers must harbor biases, and how strong must those biases be for wheelchair use to be considered a disadvantage? If you use a wheelchair, are you disadvantaged one day, in one particular inaccessible building, confronting one particular ignorant store clerk, but not the next day, in another building that is accessible, in another transaction with an enlightened clerk? Do disadvantages come and go even when disabilities and impairments do not?

Can you face disadvantage in the absence of disability? Consider an individual with severe facial scarring that is entirely cosmetic. Does he have a disability? No, he has a physical impairment, not a disability. He is not limited in his ability to perform any activity relative to his peers, not because of his scars, at least. He is nonetheless likely to face substantial disadvantages. Those disadvantages are the product of social construction alone, the creation of misguided minds.

Can you face disadvantage even in the absence of an impairment? Throughout history, many cultures and religions have associated red hair with sin, the devil, or witchcraft. People with red hair, usually *women* with red hair, have been ostracized, forbidden to wed or have children, tortured, and even murdered because of their hair color. For them, red hair was a disadvantage with dire consequences. But does it make any sense to call red hair a physical impairment? What about someone who is just too ugly or too short for society's tastes? Might these attributes rise to the level of disadvantage?

Is disability, like beauty, in the eyes of the beholder? It can be. For example, consider the Americans with Disabilities Act, or ADA. Under the ADA a person is disabled if he (1) has "a physical or mental impairment that substantially limits one or more major life activities," (2) has a "record of such an impairment," or (3) is "regarded as having such an impairment." Read that third definition again. Under federal law, disability can exist in the eye of the beholder, real or imagined.

That is rather remarkable. Think about it. The ADA is federal law that is largely about how we perceive others and how we are perceived by them. It targets discrimination grounded in false assumptions, baseless bias, prejudicial perceptions. It recognizes that the perceiver can deprive the perceived of access to opportunities, to community, to his potential in life by drawing assumptions from his perception. It recognizes that perception alone can yield disadvantage.

At one time or another, each of us has been disadvantaged by another's perceptions, and each of us has disadvantaged another in the same way. Perhaps not by much and not as a matter of law, but without doubt to some degree as a matter of humanity. We make assumptions about others' abilities and disabilities, and others make assumptions about ours. It is an elemental aspect of the human condition, the mind always striving to predict, to forecast, to deduce reality from the preexisting knowledge base.

This is one ring in the mental three-ring circus of self-acceptance. How do we accept the inevitable misperceptions of those around us—accept them without surrendering to them? It is an important question, but the last we will consider. It is the question of Ring Three.

Perception can yield the greatest disadvantages when the perceiver is also the perceived. In your mind you maintain your core concept of who you are, which includes your self-image, the way you view yourself. With that mental image of yourself you can diminish your access to opportunities, to community, to your potential in life. This is where we will begin, where we must begin. It is Ring One in our three-ring circus.

That leaves the center ring, the largest and the locus of the greatest spectacle. In the center ring we see ourselves through others' eyes—that is, we imagine the way they see us. Things can get out of hand in the center ring, and often do. Others see us through the warped lens of their assumptions. In imagining their view, we further warp that image with our insecurities. We see our assumptions about their assumptions about ourselves. It is at best a distorted view.

You've likely guessed it: the boundaries between the rings of our mental circus are complex and fluid. Action in the first, our self-perception, spills over into the center ring, our conception of how others view us. Likewise, action in the third ring, the assumptions others make about our abilities and disabilities, spills into the middle, impacting our assumptions about their assumptions. Just as the act can move inward to the center ring from the smaller side rings, the show in the center ring can bleed into the two outer rings. And because of this, the first and third rings are interconnected as well. Acceptance is quite a circus!

Ring One: Self-Perception

In our minds we all have impairments and disabilities. We catalog our imperfections. That birthmark, the shape of your ears, the size of your nose, your anxiety, the size of your breasts, your depression, the size of your muscles, the amount of your hair, the sound of your voice. We perceive in ourselves "too much" of some things and "not enough" of others. You are too short, too loud, too fat, too shy, too arrogant, too slow, too old, too aggressive, too poor, not funny enough, not patient enough, not smart enough, not pretty enough, not ambitious enough, not good enough. That's what you tell yourself.

How do the faults you perceive in yourself make you feel? Do you ever feel shame or guilt, or think that you are to blame, that you are worthy of condemnation, that you are obliged to apologize for who you are? When you feel that way, you have adopted the first perspective of disability in viewing yourself, disability as condemnation. That perspective is a cancer to excise.

Do you ever think you can be "fixed"? By a nip, a tuck, a pill, a lottery jackpot, a seven-step program to gain confidence and a winning personality? There is something out there that will make you better, repair your defect, correct that which is wrong with you. When you think this way you are ascribing to the second view of disability, disability as a problem to repair. You are misguided, chasing a fallacy. Those things can change your life, but they won't change who you are.

It is not easy to overcome shame, and it is not easy to convince yourself that there is nothing wrong with you, that by definition you are your perfect self. But in both cases the problem is easily recognizable. It is a problem of acceptance. When you feel or think this way, you do not accept yourself for who you are. Your thoughts and emotions serve as warning.

Heed them. They signal the choice you can make openly and intentionally, in every moment: fight who you are or accept who you are. Embrace your life or long for another. Making the right choice may be difficult. But recognizing that you have a choice is not—the choice is always yours.

That leaves the impairments and disabilities you perceive in yourself that you neither condemn nor lament, the ones you understand as part of who you are, nothing more. With these you can do the greatest damage by far. The danger they present is great because it is hidden, masked, unmarked by shame or longing, self-loathing or inferiority.

The danger lies in the self-limiting assumptions you make about yourself, the disadvantages you create. These self-limitations are covert, like fish that swim by backward, unnoticed. When you fail to recognize your self-limiting assumptions, acceptance becomes surrender.

"They want me to do what?" I ask.

"Throw out the first pitch at a Marlins–Cubs baseball game," she says.

"That's what I thought you said," I say.

"That is what I said," she says.

"Do they know that I'm blind?"

"Yes, that is the point," she says. "This is a chance to promote Hope for Vision and our mission to cure blinding diseases."

"Right, I get that. But I can't throw a pitch. I'm blind. This is a horrible idea."

"Well," she says, "is that what you want me to tell them?"

"No, of course not," I say. "Tell them 'yes,' and we'll figure something out."

Then I tried to figure something out. One option was to have a friend, colleague, or family member throw out the pitch for me. We could take the mound together, and I'd just stand next to the pitcher for the pitch. Another option was to scale back the "pitch" required. If I stood only ten or fifteen feet away from the catcher, for example, instead of the roughly sixty-foot distance from the mound to home plate, I could get away with a safe and easy toss. Or I could just stop worrying about it all, show up, and wing the ball. It would be ugly, but what else could they reasonably expect?

I didn't like any of these options. I didn't want it to look ugly, and I didn't want to cop out. I didn't want to do what they would expect, to confirm what they would assume, that a blind person cannot throw a regulation pitch.

But wasn't that the assumption I was making about myself? When that thought struck me, I grew defensive and tried to rationalize some distinction. I thought: *Well, I've never been very athletic. It is not that blind people can't throw a pitch, it is just that I happen to be a bad pick. And I guess in theory I could throw a pitch. It would just take a lot of training and practice. But it has to be possible. I'm just saying it is not something I would do.*

My defense was not convincing. Sure, learning to throw a pitch was "not something I would do" out of the clear blue sky, but was it something I would do now, when asked, as an opportunity to raise awareness of blinding diseases? Did I really believe that this was something I could do? Was I going to choose not to do it because it might take too much time or effort? Had I ever even tried to throw a pitch? Might that be a good place to start?

It was a good place to start. That weekend Dorothy and I walked to Lincoln Park, baseball in hand, our Labrador retriever (named Tainted Evidence) bounding along with us. We marked the mound with a stick, then Dorothy counted off sixty paces to our imaginary home plate and shouted, "Ready!" I took a deep breath and threw my first pitch as a blind man.

It was ugly. The ball sailed way over Dorothy's head, landing far behind her and off to her left. Tainted Evidence tore off after it, running as though our lives depended upon a speedy recovery. As our canine catcher brought the ball back to me, Dorothy provided a debriefing, describing the wild pitch. I made mental adjustments. "Ready!" she shouted again.

As it turns out, it doesn't take all that much time or effort for a blind man to learn to throw a regulation pitch. My first strike came within half an hour. Another hour later I was delivering passable pitches with consistency. It was thrilling and fun—for all of us, not just Tainted Evidence. We practiced a few more times before flying to Miami for the big event. In total we enjoyed three or four hours together in the park, our own version of spring training.

On game day I threw a strike. It was a phenomenal feeling, well worth a few hours in the sun. Walking off the mound, I glowed with pride. But that's not the point of my story.

The point is that when I first got the call and heard the idea I thought it was crazy. I thought it was crazy because I assumed that my blindness made it impossible for me to throw a pitch. I made that assumption without conscious thought. It was something I just "knew," just like you knew Carol was at that party and little Dorothy knew that fish can swim backward. It was my reality, before the call, at least.

The self-limiting assumptions we make about ourselves are buried deep and easily missed. They are born of our ignorance, inherited from our society, learned from those around us. With repetition they are retrenched, anchored deeper, camouflaged.

When I received that call, I was an appellate litigator for the U.S. Justice Department. I traveled the country unaccompanied, arguing cases unaided on behalf of the federal government. I had overcome my fears of Blindness and learned to strive and succeed while embracing my disability. I felt strong, independent, confident.

Yet somehow I believed I could not throw a baseball. I knew about discrete solutions for specific challenges, overcoming obstacles, the triumph of will over adversity. I knew about all of those things in concept. I was familiar with extreme examples, like that of Erik Weihenmayer, a blind man who has climbed the seven summits, the highest mountain on each continent—including Mount Everest, of course. None of that mattered, however, because I also knew myself as someone incapable of throwing a pitch.

The opportunity to promote Hope for Vision was the catalyst for me to change that reality. That's what forced me to recognize my self-limiting assumption, think through it, and choose to see myself eyes wide open, as a man who is capable of throwing a regulation strike if need be. (Necessity is the mother of invention, and good publicity is a nurturing aunt!) But what if I had never received that call? I'd still be living that false reality. Somewhere deep in my mind, I would know that I am incapable of throwing a pitch because I cannot see—one tiny little fish swimming backward unnoticed in my mind. Even one tiny fish can stir the waters, can shift the balance from acceptance to surrender. And when it comes to the way we perceive ourselves, our backward-swimming fish are prolific propagators. Let them breed long enough and they can bend ocean currents.

I walked off the mound with a new determination to root out this invasive scourge, to clear away the lingering toxic remnants of surrender in my mind. I committed myself to vigilance in perceiving my blindness eyes wide open. It is a promise I have kept, though it hasn't always brought me the glory of a major-league strike.

When Dorothy gave birth to our triplets, we faced on our home front an epic barrage of dirty diapers and bottle feedings. Doubly challenged as both male and blind, I could have sought a deferment from Dorothy. Unceasingly understanding, she would have let me off the hook. I could have floated away free of baby care responsibility, upon murky waters that obscured the distinctions between "cannot," will not," and "do not want to." It was tempting. If I didn't think about it too much, I could just slip by.

But those pesky fish thrive and breed in such waters, as I learned when I threw that strike. So instead I looked at myself eyes wide open and insisted upon clarity. I saw that I was in fact capable of changing diapers and feeding babies, no question about it. To be sure, there would be some messy mishaps. But that's par for the course in these matters. And it really wouldn't be all that difficult for me. That is, not much more difficult than it would be for a sighted father.

Seeing myself eyes wide open meant changing thousands of dirty diapers, countless hours feeding our babies, and months with little sleep. The alternative was a minor surrender, perpetuating some vague notion that my blindness was a meaningful limitation, creating a disadvantage from my disability. I accepted myself and surrendered to the diapers and baby bottles.

What have you assumed you cannot do? What goals have you sacrificed? What limitations have you created for yourself? You must keep a vigilant watch for your self-limiting assumptions. Every time you forgo an opportunity, decline an invitation, avoid a situation, decide upon inaction, or settle for less, you face the risk of confusing "cannot" with "choose not to." You must insist upon clarity in that distinction. Ask yourself: "Do I know and believe that I am capable of doing it, but I still choose not to?" Demand absolute honesty in your response. If you're unconvinced, sort out exactly how you would do it if you chose to. If you're still not convinced that you are capable, go ahead and do it. Leave no room for ambiguity. Acceptance erodes into surrender in the tides of that ambiguity. Refuse to surrender.

Ring Two: Distortions Doubled

Bob curses his lawn mower a final time and gives up. Broken, again. He thinks of his wife, Wendy, who has been asking him to mow the lawn for more than a week now. She's just inside the house, enjoying coffee and the Sunday newspaper, no doubt. He doesn't want to face her, so he sets off for his neighbor Gary's house to borrow Gary's lawn mower.

Crossing the lawn, he feels a pang of guilt as he thinks about Gary's wrench. The wrench Bob borrowed about a month ago to fix the sink in the upstairs bathroom. The wrench that somehow disappeared. The wrench that has gone unmentioned since. Not mentioned, not returned, not replaced.

Then Bob remembers the power drill. Gary's power drill. The one Bob borrowed to fix the deck last summer. Bob swears it never worked. He told Gary it never worked when he returned it that same day. You can't blame someone for breaking a power drill that was already broken, right? Bob shakes his head in frustration. That power drill wasn't his fault.

He reaches Gary's door and presses the bell. A question rings in Bob's mind. What about the level? The one I knocked off the rail when Wendy slammed the door. Gary's level, the one that shattered. *Fine, that was my fault,* Bob tells himself, though he really thinks it was Wendy's fault. *I apologized already. What more can I do? That level was old and rusty,* Bob thinks. *I'm not going to buy Gary a brand-new one. Gary's rich anyway. He can buy his own new, fancy level.*

Gary opens the door. "Good morning, neighbor," he says. "What brings you by?" Gary is all warmth and toothy smile.

"Go screw yourself, Gary, you smug bastard!" Bob says. "I don't need your damn lawn mower." Bob turns and storms back to his house.

There is wisdom in this joke, too. Bob is feeling guilty about losing Gary's wrench and breaking Gary's level. He suspects that

Gary blames him for breaking the power drill, which makes Bob angry. Then there is Gary's wealth, the fact that Gary has all of these tools to borrow in the first place. Bob doesn't like having to ask Gary for tools all the time. In his mind it makes him look needy, less successful, like a mooch. In Gary's eyes, Bob imagines.

Bob is also feeling guilty about taking so long to mow the lawn, seeing himself as a lazy deadbeat in Wendy's eyes. He resents her for it, and resents her even more when he thinks of the broken level. All of these emotions bubble and boil together. They all feed and distort Bob's image of himself when he rings the doorbell to ask for the lawn mower.

Gary greets him with kindness, but Bob doesn't see it. Bob sees a Gary who is judgmental, critical, condescending. Bob sees a smug bastard and tells Gary so.

The psychological term for this is projection. We project onto others our own feelings. Because we often project those feelings that are unwanted or threatening to us, projection is described as a defense mechanism. It is anything but.

In Chapter 2 we saw that by awfulizing we distort our realities, often bringing about the very consequences we hope to escape. Fear manifests self-fulfilling prophecies. Projection does much the same with our insecurities. It is hard enough to guard against our insecurities and self-limiting assumptions when we can see them through our own eyes. When we project them upon another, we disguise them further. Worse, we lend them the credibility of external validation. We make them real, and in so doing surrender to them.

Don't bother applying for that promotion, you tell yourself, because your jerk boss will never endorse you. He doesn't think you're good enough. The truth is, however, that you don't feel good enough. It is not about your boss's opinion. It is about your own. Don't bother applying and you can avoid your self-image, blame it all on your boss. You won't have to confront your own feelings. This is an act for Ring One, your perception of yourself. This is surrender projected.

But wait, you say, *I know I'm good enough. And I do want that promotion. My boss really is a jerk, however, and if I apply for that promotion he'll shoot me down and then make my life miserable. It is truly a bad idea for me to apply. This is not about accepting myself. This is about dealing with my boss.* This drama plays out in Ring Three, how others view you.

Which is it? Sometimes there is a clear answer. More often there is not. More often the truth lies somewhere in the middle. When we project, we emphasize, exaggerate, focus selectively. We distort. But we rarely invent wholesale. If you think you're not good enough, your boss might agree. And even if he is just an unsupportive jerk, you might be escaping your own self-doubt by seeing your fate entirely in his hands.

We've arrived at the center ring. The feat to be mastered in this ring is teasing apart where projections begin and end. In Ring Two you must learn to see eyes wide open both the challenges and opportunities that lie in others' perception of you and the manner in which that perception is distorted in your mind. It is an act of mental contortion, art more than science.

Gauge the intensity of your emotional response. Is it justified by the situation or disproportionate? To the extent your reaction is unwarranted, you're likely struggling with your self-image. Similarly, if the troubling perspective raises issues you've wrestled with before, you're likely wrestling with them again. Pay attention to themes that recur in differing situations with different people. The themes you encounter even when you're alone with yourself should sound an alarm in your mind.

Consider the basis upon which your notion of how others perceive you could be formed. What experience does your perceiver have with you? What information does he know about you? On what basis could he form such an opinion of you? Is the opinion reasonably founded, even if it is also incorrect? Or would it be unreasonable for someone to maintain such an opinion on the basis of the facts known? What about this particular person? Can you square this view with what you know about him, the nature of your relationship, and your past experiences together?

Does it even matter? What is at stake? Is this something worth discussing, something to work through? Could it impact your decisions or behavior? Are there any meaningful consequences? If not, should you even bother searching for the "truth"?

Learning to live my life eyes wide open as a blind man afforded me a lot of practice in Ring Two. It was practice I needed. I'll share two stories to illustrate as much.

In the early days of my adaptation to blindness, shortly after I started using my cane, a woman offered me her seat on the T, Boston's underground rail system. "Sir, would you like to sit down?" she asked.

I heard, *You are a weak, needy, pathetic cripple, and you cannot safely ride the T standing up. You'd better sit down.* I heard my own insecurities, vulnerability, confusion, and fear. I heard all of those things in her words, and it made me angry. I lashed out.

"Does it look like there's something wrong with my legs?" I asked. I was loud and aggressive. "Seems to me that you're the one who needs the seat. You must be very confused."

I cringe when I think about that day because I was so rude and foolish, and because I offered up such a miserable Ring Two performance. I was Bob on Gary's doorstep. My emotional reaction was off-the-charts inappropriate. In those days, I wrestled constantly with images of myself as weak and vulnerable, in my eyes and everyone else's. It should have been crystal clear this was my issue, not hers. Plus, was it reasonable to think that a complete stranger would really offer such a thorough indictment, in the guise of offering a seat, no less?

And what did it even matter? What was at stake? Was it the end of the world if I got a seat on a crowded T car? And I could have simply said *no, thanks* if I was so opposed to the idea. Did she make unwarranted assumptions about the capabilities of the blind? Who knows? Maybe. Probably. She was also trying to be nice, no doubt. Was there any sense in objecting, any reason to get into a confrontation or dialogue about the matter? Certainly not.

I can see that now, eyes wide open. As I learned to accept and then embrace my blindness, my Ring Two skills improved, much to my good fortune. My self-image strengthened with acceptance, and the view of myself I imagined in others' eyes followed suit—the choreography of our circus playing out in time. Distortions diminishing, I was able to assess the views of others with rationality and improving clarity.

That leads to the second example, which involves a legal memorandum I prepared for one of the most influential partners at the

New York office of a big, elite, international law firm. I spent two weeks crafting a twenty-page document that was well researched, persuasively presented, and heavily footnoted. It was all-around fantastic. Savoring the moment, I e-mailed it to him and leaned back in my chair with satisfaction.

A few minutes later he bounded into my office. "You can send an e-mail?!" he asked. He was shocked.

I was shocked, too. And frustrated. It seemed to me that if he could hardly believe I was capable of sending an e-mail, he did not understand that I had written the memo attached. Did he assume that as a blind lawyer I relied upon others to use a computer? Just how much help did he think I needed? Did he think my work was not really my own? Should I do something about it? It was time for a Ring Two analysis.

Emotional intensity? Moderate. I was not fired up. True, he'd touched a nerve. I could feel myself grow defensive. But I remained calm and collected, analytical, deliberate.

Frequency level? Very low. This was not a recurring theme. I accepted myself as a highly talented lawyer. My other colleagues did, too. This experience was unusual.

Reasonable basis for my concerns? Yes. He had no prior experience with my work, had never been educated as to my capabilities. Thinking about my prior interactions with him, I realized he had always been very interested in discussing my blindness and never very interested in my legal or educational background. I seemed a novelty to him.

Important and actionable? Yes. This man was an influential

partner in the New York office of the firm. He would evaluate my work and could impact my career trajectory. He definitely needed to understand that my work was my own. And I was confident I could convey the message in an appropriate way. If I had misjudged his perspective, there would be no harm done.

I decided to clear the air. First, I demonstrated my screen-reading software for him with patience. I explained in detail how I am capable of sending and receiving e-mail. Then I said to him, "You know, I used the same technology to write the memo I just sent to you. Nobody else worked on it with me."

"Really?!" he said. The surprise in his voice was unmistakable, as was his doubt.

"Really," I said. "This is the same software I used when I clerked at the U.S. Supreme Court. Nobody helped me with my work there, either."

There was a long pause. He finally got it. "That is amazing," he said.

"Yes, it is great software," I said. "Thanks for stopping by to check it out. I appreciate your interest."

Think twice about perceived slights or offenses. Make an effort to see eyes wide open the intensity of your reactions. Confront that which sets you off, provokes hurt or frustration. Search for that which resonates with your own insecurities, your own assessment of your flaws and shortcomings. Hold yourself accountable to find the bare facts, the unadorned truth of the moment. Recognize that you cannot see yourself clearly through the eyes of another, though you are wired to try.

Once you've done all that, ask yourself if you truly face disadvantage in the misguided assumptions of another. If so, ask whether it matters and whether there is something productive to be done. If you conclude there is both a problem and a solution, do something about it.

Ring Three: How We Perceive One Another

Has this ever happened to you? You are with a group of people and someone mentions a movie you recently saw. You liked the movie. It was okay, not great, nothing special, but entertaining. A bit too long, a bit contrived.

The woman who brought it up loved the film. She explains why, with great passion and excessive detail. Her enthusiasm is charming and convincing. It is endearing. It is contagious. Others join in to laud the movie with her.

Before you know it, you do, too. Perhaps you discovered unrecognized virtues in the film when you considered it through her eyes, and your opinion changed. Maybe you were just trying to make a connection through polite conversation, to "bond," and didn't give it much thought. Or you intentionally misrepresented your thoughts about the movie in an effort to fit in, seem agreeable, be liked.

You might have felt pressure to do so. Imagine that the woman is your boss, that popular parent at your child's school whom everyone adores, the honored guest for the evening, or your desirable date. If you change the facts, you might feel compelled to disagree with her rave review. Is she the curmudgeon from the office whom nobody likes? That movie might have been far worse than you thought. Flash forward a couple days. You're at a friend's house and that same movie comes up. What do you say about it this time? Unless you're a professional critic, it probably isn't all that important.

What you think and feel about yourself, however, is critical to your well-being. Yet your self-image is as susceptible to influence from others as is your opinion about that latest flick. The challenge in Ring Three is to recognize as much eyes wide open.

In myriad and complex ways our interactions with others influence our thoughts, feelings, and behavior. To call that an understatement is an understatement. If you've ever been a teenager in high school, or spent any time with one, you know this to be true. Social pressures can bend steel.

In many ways, this is a good thing. As children, we learn about appropriate emotional responses and acceptable behaviors by fine-tuning ours to the feedback of our parents, teachers, friends, and family. Later, we learn to "read a room" and adjust our message to achieve our objectives. At a more basic level, these skills are central to our ability to communicate, to ensure that we are understood, and to make sense of what we are told in context. It is no surprise, then, that our sensitivity to the cues we receive from others is so natural and instinctive.

This innate human gift is double-edged, however. It is a powerful tool to help you express who you are and effectuate your choices. But it can also spell your surrender to others' view of who you are. Unminded, these cues penetrate and alter your self-conception, undermine your self-acceptance. They can create and fuel the self-limiting assumptions we considered in Ring One.

Imagine the high school class clown. He is hilarious and he knows it. He is always quick with a funny line, loves to goof around, is a master of practical jokes. In the eyes of others, he takes nothing seriously, has thick skin, is always up for a laugh, shrugs off risk and consequences. Others think he is impossible to offend. They are certain he cares little for his studies and extracurricular activities. There's nothing he won't do to amuse. People love to have him around.

There must be more to him, of course. Sensitivities, aspirations, standards, talents. He is self-conscious about his physical appearance. Though he laughs and even joins in when people make fun of his body, it is hurtful to him. He loves to read about history, wants to learn to play the violin, yearns for a deeper sense of connection with friends. He would never admit any of these things. Like every human being, he is complex, multifaceted, nuanced. But he is barraged with direct and indirect cues from others that reinforce his simplistic identity as class clown.

Now imagine that he is your child. You witness a daily struggle within him to conform or resist, to please others or discover himself, to surrender to cliché and expectations or accept and embrace his depth. You know this struggle is difficult and has profound consequences. It will determine the choices he makes—in school, at home, and when he is with his friends. It implicates his health and safety, his happiness, his future. It will shape the man your son becomes. What do you say to him?

Life invites each of us to play certain roles at certain times. We often find great benefit in accepting the invitation—win friends and influence people, as they say. When we do so eyes wide open, while holding firm to who we are, self-acceptance survives unscathed. The danger lies in losing yourself in the part. The boundary between self and character can blur quickly, then fade entirely. Choose to play a part to effectuate who you are, or slip unnoticed into a role you are not. In the difference lies acceptance or surrender.

People form all sorts of ideas about the extent of my capabilities and the quality of my life on the basis of a single attribute, my blindness. Sometimes they share their ideas explicitly and deliberately; other times, implicitly or unintentionally. Often these ideas reflect understandable curiosity coupled with innocent ignorance. Occasionally they can seem condescending or demeaning.

The airline representative might insist, for example, that I will be "safer and more comfortable" if I sit in a wheelchair for the walk to my gate. The salesperson in the store might direct his questions about my purchase to Dorothy even though I'm standing right in front of him. My cabdriver might ask me whether a prescription for glasses could restore my sight, as though I'd simply failed to consider the possibility all these years. Or a reporter might extol the purity of my blind love for Dorothy, assuming in error that I did not see her beauty with my eyes before I lost my sight and that I do not see it now with my hands.

More often than not, powerful feelings accompany others' varied ideas about my blindness. For many the emotional response is anxiety. They ooze awkwardness and tension. Some focus foremost on themselves—how their reaction to my blindness will reflect upon them. They might regret it and feel defensive, pressured. Or welcome it with eagerness, excited to appear and to feel benevolent. Most people cannot avoid the urge to compare, imagining themselves in my shoes. These folks most often exhibit a combination of gratitude and pity.

I feel it all. I feel it when my blindness provokes anxiety in others, when I sense their discomfort, when I hear their eagerness to perform charity for my benefit, and when they want to get away from me at all costs. I'm aware of the assumptions people sometimes make about me, can understand the roles they expect me to play. Ideas and emotions can be infectious.

For years I lost myself in others' images of my blindness. Confronting their anxiety, I felt anxious. Confronting their pity, I felt pitiful. Confronting another's desire to escape, I felt I was a burden. I thought I was responsible for the emotions I stirred in others, responsible to play the part that would make them most comfortable, make it easier for them. I thought I was awkward, needy, burdensome. My surrender was unwitting, but it was surrender nonetheless.

Today I know better. I have chosen to accept and embrace who I am, blindness and all. I have learned that the barrage of cues I receive daily from others is a threat to that acceptance. With vigilance, I keep watch, eyes wide open.

I am confident, not awkward. My blindness does not make me anxious. I am comfortable with it, at peace, content. I regret it when I am a source of anxiety or discomfort for others. Likewise, I regret it when others hope to find in me an outlet for charity, an object for pity, or an exemplar of misery and misfortune. I regret all of these things, but I am not responsible. I bear no obligation to play the roles others have chosen for me.

What role do you play? Do you do so by choice, with deliberation, without surrendering yourself to the part? Or have the cues you get from others swum in backward, distorting your self-image? When it comes to who you are, and your own life, don't let anyone else tell you what to think about the movie. Guard your own review, eyes wide open.

Fishing Trip 4: Supremely Protective

November 2008

"**D**ude, was that your motorcade?"

It is a fair question. I've never contemplated facing that particular conjecture, and I am in no mood to face it now. But it is a fair question. I have, in fact, arrived via motorcade. My arrival wasn't subtle.

You wouldn't expect a motorcade to pull up in front of this place. It is a cigar bar in downtown Philadelphia. A nice one, but still a cigar bar. Not the kind of place that sees a lot of seven-vehicle motorcades, with U.S. Marshals, state police, and city cops in the mix. Not a place that attracts the sort of patrons who require that the police shut down the street before they arrive.

The patrons of this particular cigar bar do not tend to walk in with an escort of law enforcement officials, who aggressively enter the room, survey the scene, choose the table that best satisfies security considerations, and brazenly remove the "reserved" sign from said table, unapologetically claiming it for the object of their protection. Tonight I'm the involuntary object of such protection. I have arrived with such an escort.

It wasn't my intention. It wasn't my desire. I'm in town on a work trip with my boss for a single night. I made plans to reconnect with an old friend—a slow smoke, a drink or two, good conversation. I planned to arrive alone, in a cab. That was the plan.

My neighbor at the next table knows nothing of my plans. He knows what he saw, the abrupt siege of the street out front, the extraordinary multivehicle approach, the dramatic entrance, the expeditious extraction of my advance team, and finally the speedy departure of the motorcade, tires squealing, lights flashing, sirens blaring, one big blur. He knows I'm sitting at the best table in the place, alone, wholly unremarkable but for my arrival. He can be forgiven his confusion.

"Dude, was that your motorcade?"

It is a fair question. I can appreciate that. He must be confused, a school of fish swimming backward in his mind. He is thinking that I must be important. I must be famous. I must be rich. But why did the security detail leave as quickly as it came? I must be eccentric. Did I send them away? They must be nearby. *Who is this guy?* That is what he is thinking. It doesn't make sense.

It doesn't make much sense unless you know the story. Like many stories, this one begins with a betrayal. I was betrayed. By the very woman charged with my well-being, no less. In truth, she is technically responsible for my boss's protection, not mine. I am merely along for the ride, which makes the whole thing worse. But I'm getting ahead of myself.

My boss is Justice O'Connor. As in, Sandra Day O'Connor, who grew up helping out on The Lazy B, her family's cattle ranch in Arizona; graduated third in her class from Stanford Law School; was nonetheless turned down by more than forty law firms when she sought a job, because she is a woman; went on to serve in all three branches of the Arizona state government (assistant attorney general, majority leader of the Senate, and judge on the court of appeals); and became the first woman on the U.S. Supreme Court when she was appointed by President Reagan in 1981. It is November 2008, and I am about four months into my yearlong position as her law clerk. I'm living a dream come true.

Though she has retired as an associate justice of the Supreme Court, Justice O'Connor has in no sense retired. She continues to serve a judicial role, sitting by designation on intermediate appellate courts around the country, traveling to hear arguments, and writing opinions like any other judge. She also writes books, gives dozens of speeches around the world each year, and labors tirelessly on behalf of all sorts of great organizations, like Our Courts America (ourcourts.org), which she founded to help the public appreciate the importance of well-funded, effective, and impartial courts. I am less than half her age, but merely thinking about her commitments and her schedule makes me exhausted. Her energy is endless.

My job is to be helpful to her, primarily with her judicial work, her writing and her speeches, usually from the comfort of my office at the Supreme Court. It requires a lot less energy than her job, thankfully. Justice O'Connor follows the historical tradition of "loaning" her clerk to an active Supreme Court justice. This term, she elected to "loan" me to Justice Ginsburg, so I work for Justice Ginsburg, too. (I can still hear Justice O'Connor asking me on my first day, "Now Isaac, how would you like to help out 'Ruth' this term?")

I currently work for every female justice in the history of the U.S. Supreme Court. It keeps me busy. Today the job brings me to Philadelphia with Justice O'Connor, who will hear oral arguments tomorrow with the U.S. Court of Appeals for the Third Circuit.

I adore Justice O'Connor. Literally. She is an amazing human being—at the same time pragmatic and brilliant, simple and sophisticated, confident and humble, thrifty and generous, tough as nails and endlessly caring. She is a woman of character to her core, in private and in public, a personal role model and a national treasure. I could fill several books with stories about the Justice, the lessons she has taught me, and what she means to my family and me. For now, however, suffice it to say that I love working for her.

All of that said, it can be difficult to sway Justice O'Connor's opinion when she feels strongly about an issue. As written on one of the pillows on her couch in her office, she is "sometimes in error, never in doubt." This holds true even when the issue is someone else's personal decision, particularly her law clerks' personal decisions. She comes from a place of genuine caring, but her path is not easily altered when she knows where she wants to go. And she's taking you with her, like it or not.

For example, because we were traveling from different places, Justice O'Connor and I met up in Philadelphia today. I had planned to grab a cab from the train station to our hotel. I'm capable of accomplishing this humble feat on my own and did not consider an alternative.

Until about a week ago, when Justice O'Connor bounded into my office and asked me to describe my travel plans in detail. It was clear that she had given these plans much thought. Still, I hoped I could breeze through them in summary and avoid debate on the matter. My hope was ill-founded. Justice O'Connor misses nothing.

"What about getting to the hotel from the train station?" she asked when I was done.

I wanted to lie to her and tell her that a friend was going to pick me up. But there's something about lying to your boss that doesn't sit well, especially when that boss is a Supreme Court justice. "Uh, well, I had, uh, I'm going to get a cab," I said. I oozed guilt.

"Ridiculous!" She didn't like the idea.

"No need to worry, Justice, I promise. I do this sort of thing all the time." Though logical, my argument sounded feeble.

"I know you do it all the time. That's impossible! We'll have someone meet you at your train." She wasn't interested in my logic.

I managed to end the conversation with vague assurances that I would "figure something out" and thought that was the end of the matter. I was a fool. We repeated the conversation two or three times in the next few days. Then I got a call from the senior administrator of the court in Philadelphia.

He informed me that he had just received a call from Justice O'Connor personally. At her request, he promised to arrange for one of the law clerks in Philly to meet me at the train station. She asked him to call her back with the name of my escort once these arrangements had been made. Checkmate. There was no way out. In the end, the escort was a great convenience and I made a new friend. I'd never admit that to the Justice, though.

You can understand why I didn't tell the Justice about cigars and drinks with my friend tonight. It doesn't hurt her not to know, and it keeps things simple. Besides, she is not a fan of cigars, or of my smoking them. There's no need to discuss that matter again. She has plenty of other things to think about.

This afternoon we met at the hotel to discuss tomorrow's cases; then she spoke to a crowd at the National Constitution Center; and we're now wrapping up a large banquet in her honor. She has been in hundreds of photographs today and has spoken with dozens of people—judges and janitors; the governor and the mayor; law professors and law students; men, women, and children. She is a hero to many of these people, if not most, and for good reason. Each received her full and unhurried attention today, her genuine interest and her natural kindness. Now it is time to go. She'll do it all again tomorrow, and it is getting late.

As the Justice makes her good-byes at our table of honor, the knowledge that she is departing ripples outward through the crowd. Some of the attendees make their way toward us, hoping to shake her hand or take a picture with her before we leave. These hopefuls increase in number and assertiveness, attracting more of themselves in a snowball effect, producing a competitive urgency to reach Justice O'Connor, to seize the final opportunity to share a moment with her.

Two consequences of these emerging crowd dynamics abruptly become obvious. First, if Justice O'Connor is going to greet each and every attendee heading her way—the sort of thing she would do—we will be trapped here for hours. Second, if she is not, we must make a swift exit or risk an unfortunate scene, people pushing and shoving or worse. In short, it's now or never, and the right choice is now.

The Justice's security detail materializes, forming a protective cordon around us. They have already sized up the situation and sprung into action. It is impressive. A natural as my sighted guide, Justice O'Connor reflexively offers me her elbow. I latch on and we all head briskly toward the door, the sides of our advancing huddle jostled by the crowds as our bow, a large U.S. Marshal, parts the waters ahead.

For me, it is an exhausting end to an exhausting day. I am drained. There's nothing left in the tank. Once again I wonder how Justice O'Connor maintains this pace for days and weeks and months and years. I focus on keeping up with the group. I try to ignore the noise and to disregard the bombardment of my personal space. I imagine a moment of blissful peace after the Justice and I have parted ways back at our hotel. I anticipate taking a deep breath in that moment, enjoying the quiet, calmly making my way to the cigar bar, a normal guy in a normal cab, the intensity of my day evaporating with puffs of cigar smoke, my muscles' tension washed away with the warmth of a whiskey. Just a few more minutes, then freedom and anonymity and peace.

The Justice is unphased. Neither the bedlam of the day nor the mayhem of the moment has exacted from her the slightest toll. "What are your plans?" she asks, shouting over the noise.

A long pause passes before I realize she is addressing me. The realization should sound sirens in my head. Why this question? Why now? This is an odd moment for a chat. But blanketed by exhaustion,

I register only a hint of trouble, the faintest sign something is amiss. I have been careful. She has no reason to suspect anything. Her tone was casual and unknowing. I'm okay here.

"I'm heading back to the hotel with you, Justice," I say. The statement is somewhat misleading, I must confess, but it is also undeniably true. Not even a white lie, it is a grayish fact. I crave my moment of peace.

In one swift move Justice O'Connor stops walking and whips around to face me. "That's not what I heard!" she says.

I'm the kid caught stealing candy, the adulterer discovered in flagrante delicto, and the murderer found standing over the warm corpse, smoking gun in hand, all at the same time. I manage to muster, "Well, Justice, I, uh, I am going to ride with you to the hotel, uh, I am in fact heading to the hotel with you." That's as far as I get before she interrupts me.

"I heard you are going to a bar to smoke cigars!" she says. There's more than a hint of disapproval in her tone.

"Oh," I say, unconvincingly feigning a moment of clarity, as though I misunderstood her question. "You mean *after* the hotel. I see. Well, yes, I did in fact make plans with a friend to—"

"How are you getting to this bar?" she asks, in the manner of a disgusted parent committed to make a bad situation slightly better.

My heart sinks. I want to laugh, cry, and run away. Freedom, anonymity, and peace slip through my fingers. I will accept my fate, but I will not sacrifice my dignity.

"Justice, when we arrive at the hotel I plan to take a cab to the cigar lounge." I nail the delivery. "Lounge" sounds better than "bar," and I've faked an air of calm conviction.

"Nonsense! I'll take you there." A declaratory statement, not a question. She seems not to notice that we're standing in the middle of a banquet hall, surrounded by law enforcement officers, a large and growing crowd pushing in around us. She has drawn a line in the sand. She has all the time in the world.

"Thank you, Justice, that would be great," I say.

Without a word the Justice whips around again and thrusts back her elbow for me to hold. I grab on, and we resume our exit.

The head of the Justice's security detail, a U.S. Marshal we'll call Benedict Arnold, shouts a series of instructions to her team over their walkie-talkies. It is obvious she has already planned this redeployment of her multijurisdictional assets across the city. She knows exactly where we're going. She knows because I told her. She is the only person I told. I swore her to secrecy. I trusted her. She betrayed me.

I'm stunned. Benedict had seemed so friendly, so understanding, so conspiratorial. It was during the cocktail hour. I was taking some time to myself off to the side of the room when she unexpectedly sidled up to chat. She was so interested in hearing about my job, so nice, so sympathetic about my stressful and exhausting day, so quick to pledge absolute secrecy. I trusted her.

"I can't believe you told the Justice," I say to Benedict. We've pulled up in front of the cigar bar, a choreographed frenzy, and she is leading me inside.

Benedict laughs. "You still don't get it," she says. "Justice O'Connor told me to figure out if you were going anywhere tonight."

I feel foolish. I've managed not to do so thus far, but now I wonder what my blindness has to do with the Justice's meddling concerns. The Justice is aggressively protective of all her clerks. I know that. But this feels different. Does she underestimate how capable I am? Does she think I'm helpless? Just how does she see me, exactly?

These questions don't make me angry. They make me sad. I adore Justice O'Connor. I want her to understand my strength, my independence, my confidence and comfort living as a blind man. I want her to admire me, not baby me.

Benedict's response was harsher than she intended. She can tell and she regrets it. She stops and pulls me aside.

"Listen," she says, "there was a threat made against the Justice. Nothing too credible, nothing too serious. But it's the reason for all these precautions. The Justice was worried about you." Benedict adds an afterthought, "The Justice didn't want you to worry."

Benedict's team aggressively enters the room, surveys the scene, chooses the table that best satisfies security considerations, and brazenly removes the "reserved" sign from said table. Benedict leads me to my seat. "You'll be fine leaving here on your own," she says, and they make their exit. I sit for a moment.

"Dude, was that your motorcade?" my neighbor asks.

"No," I say, "the motorcade is for my boss. She is awesome."

As though everything is now clear, he responds with a single word: "Oh." Then he turns back to his friends, our conversation over.

It turns out that I was the only one confused.

CHAPTER 5

Counting Your Luck

Luck is believing you're lucky.

—Tennessee Williams

magine that I'm trying to sell you a new car. I tell you that over time this car is guaranteed to consume more gas than the other model you're looking at. It will require more maintenance and repairs, too. The neat thing about this car, though, is that sometimes a gallon of gas will put as many as one hundred miles under your tires. Other times, however, a full tank might only get you a few blocks from your last fill-up. Likewise, you might go years without a maintenance problem, or see the car in and out of the shop over and over again for weeks. The only thing you know for certain is that this car will cost more in the long run. That's guaranteed.

What do we call this car? The Casino. You'll have good times and bad times as you motor through life in the Casino, guaranteed to lose in the end. Just like blackjack, craps, or roulette. Come on in and give it a spin. No free drinks, alas, but we'll throw in free floor mats if you buy today!

Nobody would want the Casino car, but many people enjoy casino gambling. Why? Among common answers you'll hear: it is entertaining and exciting. In my experience, however, it is only entertaining and exciting when you "win." It is neither entertaining nor exciting to get wiped out early, to lose in your first half hour of play more than you planned to risk all night, to stand around for hours watching your friends gamble while you sulk. Hit a winning streak, however, and you're on top of the world.

Why? We know that every single bet is a losing proposition by meticulous design. Put $100 down on a blackjack table, play with perfect mathematical rigor, and the casino will give you back about $99 on average. Most other games pay even less. That is how it works. Yet many of us feel an urge to place the bet nonetheless. And we invest in the outcome more than the capital at risk. We invest ourselves emotionally.

We hate to lose, hate it when luck is against us. Spend $100 on Cirque du Something tickets and $200 on a fancy dinner with very little food, and you don't think twice about it. But lose $50 at the roulette wheel on the way back to your hotel room, and you'll go to bed miffed. Even if you were "entertained" while you lost it.

We yearn to win, to feel lucky. A fancy lawyer wraps up a two-hour conference call in his Las Vegas hotel room, billing a thousand bucks for each, then complains to his buddies about having to work, spends four hours in the casino, wins a few hundred bucks, and feels like a champion, a titan of good fortune. It is a thrill. He feels lucky.

There's nothing wrong with that, nothing wrong with gambling, as long as you do it responsibly. Casinos artfully exploit the way you perceive luck. They manufacture a thrill you are willing to pay for, and you overpay for it in strict economic terms. Unless you're lucky and you win big, of course, and that's the hook that brings you back. Everyone wants to feel lucky.

Feeling lucky and being lucky are two very different things, however. Casinos prove that beyond doubt. There's nothing wrong with feeling the manufactured thrill of luck in the heat of the moment on the casino floor. That thrill comes naturally to most of us. When you try to understand what it means to be lucky, however, that feeling, that thrill, that illusion is a pernicious fish swimming backward in your mind.

The same is true when you curse your luck.

That is what this chapter is about. This chapter is about seeing your luck eyes wide open. We reach for greater understanding, a metaphysical reckoning, when we question our luck. The inquiry is worthwhile, but the assessment of luck demands far more attention and far greater analytical rigor than it seems. We must open our eyes wide to see the forces that shape our world, understanding that we are not pawns on a cosmic chessboard, and harnessing our luck as proactive creators of our own destinies.

The greatest impact going blind has had on my life is to make me realize how lucky I am. That may sound odd, but it is true. I didn't feel very lucky when I was diagnosed, and when my sight began to deteriorate there were times when I assumed I had very bad luck. But blindness was the blessing that showed me how to live eyes wide open, and eyes wide open I can see that I am lucky beyond measure. I feel grace and gratitude for my good luck, and I strive to put it to productive use every day.

The Cosmic Edge

Let's return to the casino, to the roulette wheel. Visualize yourself standing there, on an epic winning streak. You have one hundred times more money in front of you now than when you started gambling a few hours ago. You're riding the high. Convinced that luck is with you for the moment, you boldly risk it all on one more spin. The little ball races for an eternity, then bounces boldly with flamboyant indifference, makes a few short hops with cold precision, and settles into its shallow metal slot in your destiny. You win. It is thrilling.

A man standing behind the croupier screams in frustration. You recognize him from the casino's marketing materials. He is the casino's largest shareholder and the chairman of its board of directors. He is cursing his luck. "What are the odds?!" he shouts. "I've never been so unlucky!"

The scene is preposterous. Unless you're the elusive "whale" betting multiple millions, your take for the night will not make the slightest impact on the casino's bottom line or the chairman's vast personal fortune. And while its many patrons are gambling with each card or spin or pull, the casino, known as "the House," is not. The House plays in aggregation. It plays millions of hands and rolls and spins and pulls. In aggregation its wagers are a lucrative investment, a business model that promises returns, not gambling. The House has the edge. It wins not because it is lucky, but because the game is rigged in its favor.

If you're reading this book, odds are that in your life you are the House. The cosmos has rigged the game in your favor. You have an undeniable, inescapable edge. What do I mean?

Four hundred million people in the world lack access to essential health services according to a June 2015 report by the World Health Organization and World Bank. The United Nations World Food Programme estimates that 795 million people in the world do not have enough food to lead a healthy, active life. That's approximately one out of every nine people. Poor nutrition stunts the growth of about one out of every four children in the world. And it causes the death of 3.1 million children under the age of five each year, nearly half of all deaths in that age group.

According to Global Issues, more than three billion people— almost half the world's population—live on less than $2.50 per day, and more than 80 percent of the world's population live on less than $10 per day; 1.1 billion people lack adequate access to water; and 2.6 billion lack basic sanitation.

Twenty-nine percent of the world's 2.2 billion children lack adequate shelter, and 18 percent lack access to clean water. "Optimistic" estimates project that seventy-two million children of primary school age in the developing world did not attend school in 2005. A billion people in the world are unable to read or sign their names.

The United States is not immune. For example, according to the

U.S. Census Bureau, 21 percent of American children under the age of eighteen and 15 percent of Americans overall lived in poverty in 2014. The 2014 poverty level was $24,230 in annual income for the average family of four. That's $6,058 per person per year, or $16.60 per person per day. Statistics compiled by StudentsFirst show that in 2013, 66 percent of all U.S. fourth graders scored "below proficient" in reading, and the figure was 80 percent for low-income children. Eighth graders didn't do much better. Only 36 percent of them scored at or above the target level, and 22 percent scored below the "basic" reading level.

Do you have access to essential health services, nutrition, clean water, and sanitation? What about shelter and a quality education? More than $10 per day in income? If you have all of these things, you're playing with a cosmic edge. You're playing a game that is rigged in your favor. You're the House, the chairman of the board. You own the casino.

You own the casino when the House is dealt a winning hand, you own the casino when the House is dealt a losing hand. The edge is always yours, your long-term return on investment guaranteed. If the game is being played, you've already won.

Why, then, do you so often feel unlucky? You feel unlucky when you judge your fortune in this moment, this particular hand, this spin, this pull, this one meaningless wager. You feel unlucky when you see yourself as a player in your casino, not the owner. The real chairman of a real casino pays no attention to one wager on a single, random spin of one roulette wheel on one night. In our lives we do so countless times. When we do so, we misperceive our luck. We play out the preposterous scene earlier imagined, the chairman cursing the House's bad luck on a single roulette spin while the terrific treasure of his corporate coffers compounds all around him.

That's what I did when I was diagnosed with my blinding disease. I cursed my luck. But as I learned to live eyes wide open, I learned to see my luck with clarity, and I realized that my protestations were unfounded, absurd, even offensive.

I was born into a middle-class family in America, to parents who loved me and nurtured me, with three older sisters devoted to my well-being. I've never known hunger, never gone without shelter, never known poverty. I've had the world's best of health care and its best of education. (For readers who studied at Yale, I do mean "the best" quite literally, in light of my time at Harvard.) Talk about a cosmic edge.

Yes, going blind has been a challenge, a tough draw, you might say. But blindness is just one spin of the wheel that didn't go my way. A spin of the wheel in the casino I own, the casino that generates vast returns for me. Would I trade my cosmic edge for sight? Eighty percent of the world lives on less than $10 per day, and 795 million people lack adequate nutrition. Would I trade my cosmic edge for sight? Never. In my casino, blindness is just a meaningless hand that didn't go the House's way.

Is this all just semantics? Do we arrive at a different result if we change the wording of the question? Surely we can assess the impact of one bad hand in our lives, right? For example, instead of asking whether I'm lucky or not, let's just ask whether it was unlucky for me to go blind. Seems simple enough. But it's not. Far from simple, the question is unanswerable.

Bad Hands and Butterflies

You never know what worse luck your bad luck has saved
you from.

—Cormac McCarthy, *No Country for Old Men*

In 1961, Edward Lorenz, an assistant professor in MIT's department
of meteorology, created one of the earliest computer programs to
simulate weather systems mathematically. It used about a dozen
variables to represent atmospheric conditions. While the program
maintained six digits beyond the decimal point for each variable
(e.g., .456789), in printouts it rounded off to only three digits
(e.g., .457).

One day Lorenz wanted to rerun a previous simulation, and to
save time he decided to start it in progress—to play it out from the
middle instead of the beginning. To this end, he used a printout of
data from the middle of the earlier simulation to set the starting
point for his simulation rerun. As a result, he entered the three-digit
approximation of the more precise six-digit values: .506127 became .506, a seemingly insignificant difference.

To his surprise, the difference was quite significant. The extremely minor change in input yielded a major change in output.
That is, the long-term weather prediction generated by his program
was completely different the second time around. He changed an
atmospheric variable by .000127, and his program produced an un-
recognizable result.

In a famous 1972 paper and lecture, Lorenz likened these two
simulations to "two particular weather situations differing by as lit-

tle as the immediate influence of a single butterfly," and he posed the question of whether "a single flap of a butterfly's wing can be instrumental in generating a tornado." His title posed the question more strikingly: "Does the Flap of a Butterfly's Wings in Brazil Set Off a Tornado in Texas?" With that question and his paper, Lorenz popularized the concept of "the butterfly effect" (though the construct of a butterfly's impact on the weather predates him).

As Peter Dizikes observed in a June 2008 *Boston Globe* article two months after Lorenz passed away, "the 'butterfly effect,' the concept that small events can have large, widespread consequences," is "one of the most beguiling and evocative notions ever to leap from the lab into popular culture." However, most mainstream invocations of Lorenz's "deceptively simple" idea "share one major problem: They get his insight precisely backwards." The way in which we get the butterfly effect precisely backward illustrates how we misperceive the force of luck in our lives, and properly understanding it can help us to see that force eyes wide open.

Pop culture answers Lorenz's intriguing question in the affirmative. Yes, it says, the flap of a butterfly's wings in Brazil can set off a tornado in Texas. You know the Hollywood story. The protagonist's life is forever changed because he missed the bus, missed his flight, missed the meeting, missed the shot. It all started with a chance encounter, a random stumble, a bump into a stranger, a spilled cup of coffee. We cringe in our seats as each improbable link is added to the causal chain, the overarching impact growing out of all proportion, yielding unimaginable consequences.

We see it all unfold, from the flap of the butterfly's fragile wings to the violence of the tornado, step by causal step. As Dizikes puts it: "Translated into mass culture, the butterfly effect has become a metaphor for the existence of seemingly insignificant moments that alter history and shape destinies. Typically unrecognized at first, they create threads of cause and effect that appear obvious in retrospect, changing the course of a human life or rippling through the global economy." These obvious threads of causation are entertaining, to be sure, but they have nothing to do with the butterfly effect. They illustrate the domino effect instead, the direct, observable impact of one domino upon another and then another as they fall in sequence.

The true butterfly effect is the domino effect's very opposite. Lorenz's point was that we will never know whether the butterfly's flapping wings caused the tornado. The correct answer to his intriguing question is not *Yes*, but *Who knows?!* As he wrote, "If a single flap of a butterfly's wing can be instrumental in generating a tornado, so also can all the previous and subsequent flaps of its wings, as can the flaps of the wings of millions of other butterflies, not to mention the activities of innumerable more powerful creatures." And "if the flap of a butterfly's wings can be instrumental in generating a tornado, it can equally well be instrumental in preventing a tornado."

In Dizikes's words, "[t]o claim a butterfly's wings can cause a storm...is to raise the question: How can we definitively say what caused any storm, if it could be something as slight as a butterfly?" We cannot. "There are many butterflies out there. A tornado in Texas could be caused by a butterfly in Brazil, Bali, or Budapest. Realistically, we can't know." That is the true butterfly effect, "preventing us from isolating specific causes of later conditions."

The butterfly effect is the foundational principle underlying the field known as "chaos theory." Chaos theory concerns systems that are deterministic, meaning that their future behavior is governed by their current condition, subject only to laws of cause and effect, free from any randomness. In other words, it is about systems that are in theory predictable. Chaos theory describes how the behavior of these theoretically predictable systems cannot be predicted. Chaotic systems are so sensitive to variations in conditions that their behavior is bound to appear random given enough time. Even though they are deterministic, the antithesis of random. As Lorenz put it, chaos occurs "when the present determines the future, but the approximate present does not approximately determine the future."

Dizikes explains that our tendency to misunderstand the significance of the butterfly effect "speaks to our larger expectation that the world should be comprehensible—that everything happens for a reason, and that we can pinpoint all those reasons, however small they may be." We make the same mistake when we consider the question of our luck. We isolate a specific event or circumstance and consider its impact on our lives. We envision the event as a falling domino, assuming that myriad other dominos would have remained standing had only this one held firm, expecting the chaotic millions of other domino cascades in our lives to ripple through our revisionist scenario unchanged. We expect that we can approximately determine our present conditions with a slight variation to our past.

"But nature itself defies this expectation." Our bad hands are mere butterflies before the storm, and butterflies before the rainbow, too. "[S]hould we make even a tiny alteration to nature, 'we shall never know what would have happened if we had not disturbed it,' since subsequent changes are too complex and entangled to restore a previous state." Put another way, you will never know how your life would play out if you change one hand, bad or otherwise. That is the true butterfly effect. It is both elegant and beautiful.

Your life is as complex and expansive as the planet's atmosphere. You are the product of innumerable dynamic forces, the synthesis of countless moments, the summation of events mundane and meaningful alike. You are your wedding day and your daily commute; infant, toddler, and adult; your every pain and every pleasure; dinner alone in front of the television and the guest of honor at the banquet; inspiration and frustration; insight and vice; ignorance and virtue; the risks you took and those you did not; the love you shared and the love you did not; kazoo solo and symphony. You are your friends and your enemies; your wins, losses, ties, and forfeits; that first feeling of drowning and the perfect ocean swim; tax day and Thanksgiving; every tear, every smile; falling; running; sleeping; diving; every breath. You are an indivisible whole composed of minuscule causes and effects, the grain of sand and the beach. You are tsunami and gentle breeze, glacier and desert, mountain and valley, clouds, sky, sunshine, rain, land, and sea. You are all or nothing. You are chaos.

Yet you note the atmospheric agitation of a single butterfly, cheer or lament the disturbance of its wings as it flitters by, count your fortune in its movements. You grasp in an instant a microscopic thread of causation and cling to it as though it were a massive chain, your luck an anchor below the water's surface. You feel lucky or unlucky with the flap of a butterfly's wings, though you are a world in this universe. One with a cosmic edge.

Was I unlucky to inherit my blinding disease? That is like asking whether I am unlucky to exist. I would not exist without my blindness, not in any way I could predict, not in any way I would recognize. Would I be living eyes wide open, married to Dorothy, the father of four healthy children? Would I be happy? Would I be successful? These are questions without answer. It is nonsensical even to ask them. Chaos and its butterflies leave only the question whether I would choose to trade places with a seemingly random version of myself in a seemingly random life. If I did not inherit my blinding disease, I would not be me. That is all I will ever know. It is enough.

Would you toss away the cosmic hand you've been dealt and draw another one? That is the measure of your luck in every instant. The rest is noise. It is chaos.

Free Will, Dice, and Poker

Shallow men believe in luck or in circumstance. Strong men believe in cause and effect.

—Ralph Waldo Emerson

It gets even better. Your life is not deterministic. You have free will, the means to choose how you behave; to choose how you live, lead, and love; even to choose what you think and how you feel. Your life is a frenzied infinity of countless chains of dominos, intertwined, chaotically interdependent, complex, and impossibly long. But you have the power to reach in and redirect the cascades.

Most of the time, at least. Some things in life are predetermined, like a genetic disease, and others are truly random, like a freak accident. You can choose how to respond to such things, but not whether you must. The circumstances beyond our control are the rolls of the dice in the game of life.

It should be noted that not everyone would agree that we live in a world of free will and random rolls of the dice. There are those who hold fast to an extreme belief in determinism. For them, the totality of the universe is a predetermined and unalterable domino cascade. Everything is subject to the laws of nature, they would stress, including the neurons in your brain and the chemistry of your body. In their view, from the very beginning, call it the Big Bang for argument's sake, all matter and energy has proceeded according to the predetermined path dictated by nature. Your every thought, emotion, and decision is a foregone conclusion, as are all rolls of all dice in all casinos for all time. For them, free will is an illusion.

I think they are wrong, their interesting philosophical construct a remnant of a demonstrably flawed understanding of the world. There might be room for strict determinism in a Newtonian world of classical physics, particles moving neatly about in a three-dimensional space, acting upon each other according to definite laws of motion and force. There is no room for it in the modern world of quantum mechanics, however, or in the experience of life. In a sense they are struggling in vain to trace the impact of that pesky butterfly's wings.

But we've ventured too far from the subject at hand, into terrain best charted by other authors in other books. For our purposes it is sufficient to agree that from here on out we will assume our world harbors both free will and random dice, choice and fate, proactive strategy and reactive tactics, skill and luck.

In three words, life is poker. Luck shuffles the deck. We play our cards. This is a well-worn metaphor, I know, but as you've noticed by now, I like metaphors a lot. And when I say life is poker, I don't mean it casually or generally. I've some granular points of comparison in mind. So bear with me, please.

First, it is important to understand that poker is fundamentally different from the "table games" in a casino, games like blackjack, roulette, and craps. As previously considered, these table games are losing propositions by meticulous design. You play against the House, and it has the edge, while you have the disadvantage. The games are rigged against you.

Not so with poker. The players around a poker table play against one another, not the House, and each has the same odds of success. There is no House "bank," either. Competitors play for the chips they collectively bring to their table. Every player can expect $99 for every $100 he risks in blackjack. As a mathematical proposition, the average poker player should expect to leave the table with $100 if he showed up with $100.

True, when you play poker in a casino's poker room, the House takes a "rake," or a small part of every pot. But this is in essence a fee for a service, the casino's compensation for providing the dealer, table, and drinks. It's like throwing in ten bucks for pizza and beer when you play in a home game.

So, every player sits down and puts in $100, and the math says that over time the average player should expect to walk away with $100. Doesn't sound like a lot of fun, does it? Why is the game so wildly popular? Why is it my metaphor for luck and life?

Poker is a game of skill. The average player should expect to break even. But he should also expect to beat bad players and to be beaten by good ones. There's a lot of luck in poker, but there is far more skill involved. It doesn't always feel that way. It is not easy to see. But eyes wide open there is no doubt about it, skill predominates in poker. Just like life.

When I say that skill predominates in poker, I mean the statement with precision. The influence of skill in the outcome of poker is greater than the influence of luck. That is, poker is more than 50 percent skill, less than 50 percent luck. Lest you think this is a frivolous, academic point, this exact question has been litigated in state and federal courts with significant consequences. Years ago I was one of the lawyers litigating it when I worked for Supreme Court advocate Tom Goldstein.

Because illegal "gambling" is often defined as games in which chance "predominates" over skill, criminal convictions involving poker have turned on analyses of luck and skill in the game. For example, in 2012, in United States v. Lawrence DiCristina, Senior Judge Jack Weinstein of the United States District Court for the Eastern District of New York set aside the defendant's conviction for violating the Illegal Gambling Business Act, concluding that the defendant's backroom poker business was not a "gambling" business because skill predominates luck in poker. Unfortunately for Mr. DiCristina, the appellate court reversed Judge Weinstein on other grounds and reinstated the conviction. (The Second Circuit Court of Appeals did not address the degree of skill in poker because it did not have to do so to reach its judgment.)

Fortunately for us, however, Judge Weinstein wrote a thorough opinion on the subject, relying upon the extensive expert analysis of Randal Heeb, an economics PhD from the University of Chicago with an impressive academic résumé including teaching stints at the Yale School of Management, INSEAD (a graduate business school located near Paris), and the University of Chicago Booth School of Business. Dr. Heeb, a poker player himself, analyzed a data set that included 415 million hands of no-limit Texas Hold'Em, the most popular poker game. (In an appendix he explained how his analysis extends to other variants of poker. For simplicity, I'll simply use "poker" to refer to no-limit Hold'Em.) After surveying the "enormous number of complex decisions" players face and the "numerous skills that players can develop to influence the outcome of a poker game," he presented three independent statistical analyses, each of which demonstrated that skill predominates in poker.

First, he asked a clever question: does a player's success with one specific starting hand tell you anything about his success with other starting hands? If luck dominated poker outcomes, success with a particular hand would not be statistically linked to success with other hands. But for each of the 169 possible types of starting hand, players who were successful with that type of hand were also more likely to be successful with the remaining 168 types. Success was about the player, not the hand.

Next, he used statistical analysis to construct a "skill index" for poker play and demonstrated that the index could predict poker success. After identifying 241 statistics to characterize a player's strategy, Dr. Heeb randomly selected half the players from his data set and used a regression analysis to determine the formula to map each player's skill ranking (based on his performance) to his 241 stats. He then showed that this formula for ranking skill reliably predicted success for the remaining half of the players in the data. Players with a higher skill index did better overall, and given the exact same hand, a player with higher skill earned more than a player with less skill—better players played the same hand to better results.

Finally, Dr. Heeb performed a Monte Carlo simulation to determine how the cumulative results of a player with a top 50 percent skill ranking diverge from the cumulative results of a player with a bottom 50 percent skill ranking. In essence, he simulated a ten-thousand-hand competition in which a "good" player and a "bad" player play at two different tables, comparing their overall winnings or losses after each hand. Dr. Heeb ran ten thousand such simulated competitions. These 100 million hands of poker showed that after only thirty hands of play, the good player was ahead of the bad player 60 percent of the time. After 225 hands were played, there was a 75 percent chance that the good player was ahead. After 881 hands, the better player was ahead in 90 percent of Dr. Heeb's simulations.

With 1,399 hands played, the better players were ahead in 95 percent of the simulations. Dr. Heeb showed that a bad player who was behind after these 1,399 hands had only a .36 percent chance of "catching up" to the good player in the next 1,399 hands, or about one-third of 1 percent. Lastly, after 6,384 hands, the better players were ahead 99.99 percent of the time. After 6,384 hands, a bad player would be ahead of a good player less than one time out of every ten thousand.

At this point you might be wondering why I'm blathering on about poker. *I get it*, you think, *the game is 99.99 percent skill with a large enough statistical sample. Great, thanks. What's the point?* The point is that it is easy to miss the skill of poker, to think that luck dominates the outcome, to dismiss the player's role in shaping his destiny, to sit at the table and feel yourself a servant of the shuffle.

Indeed, unlike Judge Weinstein, all other courts that have considered the question have concluded that luck predominates over skill in poker. His eyes wide open view is a legal minority of one. And the majority has its own experts. In the case of United States v. Lawrence DiCristina itself, for example, the government presented the testimony of Dr. David DeRosa, a highly qualified econometrician who concluded that poker is mostly luck.

That's my point. Upon thorough examination success in the game of poker is a matter of skill. Yet if you put aside Judge Weinstein, courts have unanimously concluded that poker is a game of luck. How could this be? How do reasonable people see poker so differently?

To understand how you'll have to humor a bit more poker talk. Keep in mind, though, that I'm talking about your life, too. As in poker, in life it is easy to sit back and watch the hands go by, waiting on luck, without bothering to study the game. But that is a strategy proven to lose. That is why I love to play poker, and why I love poker as a metaphor for luck and life.

If you insist that, as Dr. DeRosa put it, "the relevant frame of reference for determining whether skill or chance predominates is a single hand," you will see luck in every hand and skill in none. But we know that both are always present. The question is to what degree. That question can only be answered over time.

Seeing the right "frame of reference" is rather tricky, however. As poker skill reveals itself over many hands of play, poker skill must also be earned over many hands of play. You have to play a lot to improve and play a lot to see your improvement. It takes skill to see skill. At first you're bound to see only luck.

Moreover, in poker you must learn to see skill without seeing all the cards. A player only shows his cards if he is still in the game at the "showdown," after all rounds of betting. Showdowns are uncommon. Seventy-five percent of poker hands end when all of the players except one have folded, when the winner has driven everyone else off the pot. In these 75 percent of hands, none of the players reveal their cards. The players never know each other's hands.

Thus, poker skill is developed like a baby learning to speak. In the beginning there is raw noise and mimicry in the absence of semantics or syntax. Stop there and you might conclude there is no meaning. But with years of observation and experimentation the power to communicate emerges from babble.

Poker is a rich, complex language. Some people develop basic proficiency, enough to enjoy the occasional social game. Others achieve mastery, the ability to convey sophisticated ideas, fluency in probabilities and uncertainties in thousands of hands played. Most people, however, hear only the noise of one hand at a time, see only an amusing game of luck. Those who speak the language love to play against those who don't.

When there is a showdown, only the players who are still in the pot reveal their cards. In half of these hands, 12.5 percent of all poker hands, the player who winds up with the best cards at the showdown has already folded. That is, the hand that turns out to be the winning hand does not win. Even if the player holding that hand played it perfectly by folding.

When you are that player, that can be hard to see. When you see an opponent win at the showdown and you have folded a better hand, it is easy to conclude (incorrectly) that you made a mistake of some sort. Worse, you may be tempted by an apparition of luck and feel that you need to be more aggressive, to make more bets, to play out more hands, to chase that apparition. Loosen up.

Skill in poker is about tightening up, however. Beginners tend to play far too many hands and to play their hands far longer than they should. Experts disagree on the precise number, but if you're playing poker well at a full table, you should play only 20 to 30 percent of the hands you are dealt. The rest of the times, you fold. You can't lose what you don't put in the middle.

Which leads to another point: you lose what you put in the middle, but win what everyone else has put in. Success in poker is not about the number of hands you win or lose. It is about the number of chips you win or lose. Bad players want to win more pots, good players want to win more money. Good poker players bet on fewer hands, win more with winning hands, and lose less with losing hands. That is the skill of poker.

No amount of skill, however, can alter the shuffle of the deck (not unless you cheat, that is). Even the best poker players fall victim to the "bad beat." What is a bad beat? A bad beat is a highly unlikely loss. It is when you're the statistical favorite by far to win the hand, but luck produces the statistically unlikely result. You've played your hand brilliantly, it is a huge pot, and only one card can save your opponent. That's the card the dealer flips over, and you lose.

A bad beat changes the outcome of the hand, but it doesn't change the level of skill with which the players played it. Bad beats happen. As a ten-to-one favorite, you should expect to lose the hand one time for every ten you win. It is simple math, a question of probabilities. You played the hand well but just happened to lose.

Bad beats don't always feel that way, though. They can be devastating. They can drive even the best players to "go on tilt," to lose discipline, to chase pots, to play erratically, to come undone. One of the most difficult poker skills to master is recovery from a bad beat. It is also one of the most important.

You must learn to recover from your big wins, too. They will tempt you with the feeling that you're "on a roll," on a lucky streak, invincible. A towering stack of chips is a great asset if you wield it properly. It is a great liability if you don't. More chips can get you into more trouble.

Add this all up and it is easy to see why most people see poker as a game of chance. Luck is evident, loud, easy to spot. Skill is subtle, soft-spoken, ambiguous. Luck is unavoidable and obvious. Skill is necessary but easily ignored. Luck is instant explanation, a constant ally. Skill is practiced mastery, sustained effort, and lonely responsibility. Luck is a comprehensive rationale both simple and certain. Skill is difficult to develop and susceptible to doubt.

Luck is the easy choice. But those who count on luck are destined to be disappointed. It is a fact as true in life as it is in poker. I can't prove it using Dr. Heeb's methods, but I'm no less certain.

Think of people you know who are successful, happy, thriving.

Does their well-being seem to track the ups and downs of life, their particular circumstances, their challenges and windfalls? Are they derailed by their failures and successes? By the failures and successes of others? Or do they tend to make the most of life no matter the circumstances? In other words, does their success turn upon the cards they are dealt or do they play all their cards more successfully?

Happy people choose to be happy. Successful people choose to find success. They study the game of life, master their strategy, take responsibility. They're dealt the same cards we're all dealt in the long run. They just play them with greater skill.

You are dealt countless hands—every decision, every interaction, every opportunity, every triumph, every stumble. Focus on your cards and you'll never learn to play them. Blame your bad luck and you'll prove yourself unlucky. But study the probabilities, pick your bets wisely, maximize the value of your wins (and not their number), mitigate your losses, and over time you'll come out ahead. The odds are ten thousand to one.

Lucky Break, Part I

I'm a great believer in luck, and I find the harder I work the more I have of it.

—Thomas Jefferson

After a decade living on the road in cheap motels, bouncing from mediocre venue to mediocre venue while honing her craft and refining her act, a musician scores a lucky break. A man in the audience in

Kansas City is impressed by her set, checks out her Web site, and uses the "spread the word" feature to e-mail his friend from college who lives in Los Angeles and is the producer of a national television show.

Remembering that her old friend from Kansas City was the cool guy in college who always seemed to be ahead of popular trends, Producer visits the site, notices Musician's busy calendar of gigs, reads a couple of Musician's insightful blog posts about popular songs, and then listens to a few of her tracks. Producer likes what she hears and books Musician for her show. Musician's talent is "discovered." She goes viral and soars to the top of the charts.

We focus on the lucky break, not the ten years of effort, and we call her an overnight success. It's a simple, entertaining story about the mystery man in the audience, the superfan who delivered the fairy-tale ending, and we eat it up.

The truth is more complex. She created her lucky break, with countless miles on the road, hundreds of beer-stained fan club e-mail sign-up lists passed around dark bars, hours of practice every day, relentless study of her industry and its players. She worked the probabilities, maximized her odds, extracted value from the hands she was dealt. She fought for her success.

With her gig in Kansas City, in that one hand, she was dealt phenomenal cards, the college buddy of a major television producer sitting up front near the stage. She couldn't lose the hand with those cards, as long as she played them, that is. That part was luck. But holding the winning cards and winning a lot of chips with those cards are not the same.

Ten years ago, Superfan would have liked her show, but he wouldn't have loved it. Her guitar licks were rough and predictable, her lyrics less interesting. She was still doing that "more whine than song" thing with her voice, undeveloped talent augmented with moan. It was augmented with cigarette smoke scratchiness, and it was hangover hoarse, too, as she still smoked back then and partied before "unimportant" performances. It is hard for her to believe it these days. These days she guards her voice, her health, and her sleep. She never plugged her Web site back then because she didn't have one.

Ten years ago she would have won an unremarkable pot with the Superfan hand. He would have liked the show. He might have even mentioned it to Producer in passing. But he wouldn't have bothered to check out her site even if it had existed, and he probably wouldn't remember her name by the time he got home. At best she would have scored some sort of e-mail introduction to Producer that wouldn't have gone anywhere. A neat story, nothing more.

That's not how it happened, though. She didn't just "win" in KC. She made a small fortune, took down a monster pot. She maximized the value of the cards she was dealt. That took skill refined over ten years of play.

She sang her heart out in Kansas City, played the Sunday champagne brunch like she was playing Carnegie Hall, the way she played every gig. Her set was tight and intriguing, her material novel but accessible, market-tested by tens of thousands of patrons in thousands of bars in hundreds of cities. Though it made her cringe, she plugged her Web site four times during her set, keeping the defensive cynicism she felt out of her voice. She even remembered to mention her latest blog post, which took two hours to write the night before the gig in her motel room, when all she wanted to do was sleep. Producer loved that blog post.

Ten years took the stage in Kansas City, long and difficult years. There were bad beats, great gigs that fell through, introductions that went nowhere fast, critics who never showed up, critics who shouldn't have. She wasted a lot of time early on chasing "easy wins" with bad bets, joining bands that were all hype, playing music she didn't like, listening to promoters too often and to herself not at all. She tried not to be jealous when she saw others' luck triumph over her talent, held the bitterness at bay, played through the self-doubt.

She refused to walk away from the table because she loved the game. Others would have walked away long ago, blaming the cards, resigned to fate, bored, broken, or distracted. She loved to play music for people, to perform, and she was making a life of it. That's what mattered to her. She would never give that up. Most of those lucky people weren't playing anymore.

Ten years took the stage in Kansas City, got a lucky break, and became an overnight success. What next? It was a huge win, a monster pot, but it was just one hand. The game went on, the stakes raised. She was ready for it, welcomed it.

She had always played for the game, not for the pot. She understood the game. She understood that luck comes and goes, fans come and go, hands come and go. Luck's highs are high, but its lows are lower. The deal offers cheap thrills, a stab in the back, and everything between. But there is pure joy in the game well played.

One-hit wonder, flameout, sellout. Fluke, floozy, flop, flash in the pan. The deck is reshuffled over and over again. Fortunes easily won are easily lost. Dice and dominos, free will and chaos. Feeling lucky and being lucky. She understood it all.

She still loved the game. She loved to play music for people, to perform. She would make a life of it, famous or not, lucky or not, Carnegie Hall or champagne brunch. She wouldn't let her lucky break throw off her game. She saw through it. Lucky or not, she would play for the game, she would play to win.

Recount

I've mixed, mangled, mashed, and murdered my metaphors, given you an aspiring musician chasing butterflies through the poker room of a casino she owns, giant dice rolling by, dominos cascading, chaos, tornados, and world hunger, too. I've made a mess. Guilty as charged.

Luck is messy. Not on its surface, not the manufactured luck of the casino, not the luck we think we understand. The force of luck in our lives is messy. It is a shifting wind. Close your eyes, hold on tight, and let it blow you about. Or chart your course eyes wide open and harness the wind in your sails. Your choice.

Luck is frame of reference. You create your own reality. You create your luck, too. You can choose to see that, to live eyes wide open, to shape your perspective. That's what this book has been about thus far, choosing to chart your course.

If not a destination, a course implies at least a direction. You cannot chart a course without a goal, a map, and a scale. What does it mean to succeed, to maximize your winnings? How do you measure your skill, assess your performance? Now that you've chosen to chart your course, how do you actually do it? That's the question we'll turn to in Chapter 6.

Fishing Trip 5: Lucky Break, Part II

June 1999

It was lucky timing. I graduated from Harvard in June 1999, at the peak of the dot-com craze, with a degree in math and computer science. My brother-in-law Joe Zawadzki, Harvard class of 1996, was right at that moment gearing up to enter the technology fray. His plan made perfect sense.

Many of our peers had founded start-ups. Most of those who did made outsized success look easy, almost inevitable. They raised war chests of venture capital on hype and hope, their business models measured in "eyeballs"—the number of visitors attracted to their sites. Revenue was simply not a "short-term priority" and profit not the correct "paradigm" in the transformative "new economy." Newly redefined, success rained torrentially. Investment dollars flowed freely, and company valuations soared. Dot-com billionaires were born, mostly on paper.

It was Joe's turn. When he invited me in, I reckoned it was my turn, too. I was only nineteen, but you're never too young to mint money. Besides, I had a great résumé to sell to venture capitalists. Less important, I also had the skills to design and develop software. It made perfect sense. We mounted up and raced to stake our claim in the digital gold rush. What could go wrong?

Our product was a set of cool interactive applications to improve the online shopping experience, and our plan was to sell these applications to online merchants. In those days, that was more than enough to get started. We raised seed capital from friends and family, rented an industrial space in Manhattan's "Silicon Alley," and hired half a dozen employees. A few months later we made the rounds with venture capital firms. We quickly secured a commitment of $6 million in funding at an indefensibly high valuation for our cool ideas and optimistic eyeball projections. Per the numerous terms explicated in a letter of intention memorializing that commitment, Joe and I were paper millionaires, billions only three zeros away. Too easy.

Then the Internet bubble burst. The trajectory of the high-tech stampede reversed overnight. One day the herd saw economic revolution and unbounded fortune in the new economy. Internet start-ups were beacons of the future. Their stratospheric valuations made sense to those visionaries who could see beyond the discredited physics of the old economy.

The next day the herd saw a house of cards balanced on a rocking chair in the breeze. Internet start-ups were scams, frauds, delusions; their founders, charlatans and carnival barkers. Money fled and scores of companies imploded. Paper billions turned to pulp.

It was rotten timing. Joe's and my investors reneged on our deal. Our worries about finding dozens more talented employees became worries about making payroll. Shooting the lights out now meant keeping the lights on, literally. All around us revolutionary companies sought refuge in the old guard's bankruptcy trenches. It seemed the sensible thing to do. It was the only thing to do, really.

A real shame if you thought about it. The Internet was not a passing fad. Millions more people would eventually use it to buy products, access content, and communicate with one another. True, you couldn't just keep pitching companies to spend money for cool applications on Web sites. They weren't spending money on that kind of thing anymore. But there were still plenty of things companies should pay for online—like new customers, completed sales, new subscriptions. In a word, profit. There had to be better ways to generate online profits along with all those eyeballs.

Nobody cared. Investors and entrepreneurs were not looking for Internet opportunities, to put it mildly. They were running away from Internet businesses of any kind. The violent burst of the Internet bubble had everyone focused on triage—cutting losses, dissolving partnerships and business combinations, winding down investment funds, shutting the doors. Who could blame them? It was too late to start over. The damage was done. Rotten timing.

For the survivors, advertising revenue was a glimmer of hope. They were desperate to squeeze every dollar out of every eyeball. The more effective the ads, the more they could charge. Unfortunately, at that time online advertising was woefully ineffective. The prevailing pessimists were betting against rescue via ad revenue.

No surprise there. I was reading news sites and buying all sorts of products online in those days. Like most Internet users in 1999, however, I had never clicked on a banner ad. I couldn't imagine doing so. Online ads were bizarre. They never pitched products or services in which I would have the faintest interest. Definitely a shame.

One day I was perusing a favorite news site, lamenting its certain demise, when a thought occurred to me. If each ad on the page earned only a drop of revenue for the site, in the venture capital drought the site would need a preposterous number of ads to survive. A funny image popped into my head. I imagined the page littered with banner ads, two or three banner ads for every couple lines of text in the article. Funny, but sad, too. What a shame it would be to lose this site.

It got me thinking. I had read about the Internet's promise of "one-to-one advertising"—ads tailored to each particular viewer. At the time the idea was unrealized hype, unfulfilled promise. What might one-to-one advertising look like on this particular site? I imagined ads that were appropriate in context, for products and services of interest to me, with useful, timely information. Then I started thinking about the software algorithms needed to create, target, and deliver such ads.

Many of Joe's and my cool Web site applications could be adapted to the advertising context. Even better, they would enhance a true one-to-one advertising experience. They might even improve the effectiveness of ads, too. If so, we could prove it. I could design technology to track whether we met advertisers' specific goals—whether we generated a lead or sale or e-mail signup—and we could show advertisers their results. In dollars and cents, not eye-balls.

Why stop there? We could charge for success, too, a pricing model called "pay for performance." If an advertiser were charged only when an ad was successful, the advertiser would have nothing to lose and everything to gain. A Web site that displayed such an ad could charge a lot more for it. If our cool applications—reconfigured to deliver one-to-one advertising—made ads successful, they would generate a lot more advertising dollars. Everybody would win.

Tragic timing, too late to start over, plain and simple.

Nothing is plain and simple. Had Joe and I received that $6 million investment, we would have proceeded full speed to build our cool applications without concern for revenue, let alone profit. We would have made the same mistakes our peers made, spending extravagantly on technology infrastructure and "marketing," hiring way too many employees, burning through cash as we raised more and more of it. In that scenario, it would be too late to start over. Good thing the investment fell through. The bubble burst just in time to save us from ourselves.

Were we too early, then? Was that the real tragedy of our timing? It was heartbreaking to launch headlong into the Internet revolution—with money from friends and family—only months before its epic collapse. That hurt. I was exhausted and embarrassed, my confidence shaky at best. Certainly, it would have been better to open our doors after the world pulled the rug out from under the new economy, with our feet planted firmly on the ground. Certainly, we would have started with a very different business plan and with very different promises to friends and family.

Not true. In that scenario we never would have started at all. Joe and I were sucked into the bubble's inflationary vortex, the hype, the excitement, the astronomical opportunity. Had we sat on the sidelines as it popped, we would not have then jumped up and run onto the field to found the next revolutionary start-up amid the debris. That was never our plan. That was nobody's plan.

Nobody was planning to found an Internet advertising technology company. Anyone crazy enough to think about it had better be able to fund it, too, as no sane investor would invest in it. All but a handful of the preexisting Internet advertising technology companies had been wiped out. It was not a promising investment niche.

We weren't too late. We weren't too early. We had the makings of a promising technology business with a barren competitive landscape and monumental barriers to entry for new competitors. Lucky timing.

We again leaned on friends and family for financing and rebuilt our organization. Then we developed and marketed fantastic advertising tools that produced great results—better than we had ever imagined. There were a lot of long hours, and for months Joe and I did not draw salaries from our business. (We made our spending money with weekly poker games, regularly fleecing our wealthier friends in the consulting and banking industries.) Before we knew it, however, we were generating revenue, then profit. It was an old-economy business model, but it sure beat our new-economy alternatives.

Instant riches eluded us, but our venture prospered. Was it luck? It was a frenzied infinity of countless chains of dominos, intertwined, chaotically interdependent, complex, and impossibly long. Was I lucky? I was innumerable dynamic forces, the synthesis of countless moments, the summation of events mundane and meaningful alike. Joe and I played our cards. That's the whole of it.

After a couple grueling years, our company stable, I moved on, returning to Harvard to study law. Joe left five years after me and founded another advertising technology business, once again leading the industry into a new era. Eight years later, the company we founded was acquired. In 2015 it was purchased for $230 million.

Old friends reconnected to extend their congratulations. Acquaintances called to satisfy their curiosities. Strangers of all stripes reached out to sell their wares, from accountants to car salesmen, bankers, brokers, Realtors, and more. All of them assumed, it seemed, that I had made a fortune from the sale.

I burst their bubbles, one by one. I hadn't made a penny, alas. Tough luck.

CHAPTER 6

Measuring Your Success

Try not to become a man of success. Rather become a
man of value.

—Albert Einstein

W hat, precisely, is my problem? That old question again. The
first in the pair I ask when I'm trying to see through my fears
eyes wide open, as I did that day I was lost on Capitol Hill
(in Chapter 2). I've asked myself this question hundreds of times, to
reduce a problem, simplify a situation, expose awful assumptions,
take control.

This time is different, though. I'm already in full control. All is
well. There shouldn't be any problem. The question itself is the
problem, a nagging feeling of discontent I want to ignore, a dull
discomfort, not acute distress. It is a loose thread begging to be
pulled, guaranteed to unravel my clothing, leave me naked. I worry
I'll lose control with my answer. I fear the inevitable second question: what, precisely, can I do about it?

Nothing needs to be done, I tell myself. I've done it already. From my first day of law school in the fall of 2001, I had eight amazing years in law—studying, researching, and publishing; clerking for a judge and two justices; arguing appeals on behalf of the United States as a Department of Justice lawyer. I loved every minute of it, a long, deep drink from the proverbial fire hose of life. Then it was time to settle down and plan for my family's future. I made the obvious choice, the easy choice: accepting a lucrative position with an elite international law firm, earning a full year's salary on my first day in the form of a signing bonus.

Now I'm sitting at my desk about a year later, trying not to pull that thread. I do not enjoy my job. I detest the obligation to keep track of my time in billable six-minute increments and the enormous pressure to work as many of those increments as is humanly possible. Worse, I work as a junior member on teams of lawyers assembled to produce work I used to complete alone in less time. As far as I can tell, this arms-race approach to litigation adds bureaucratic and political complexities while degrading the quality of the work we produce. In all events, my job bears little resemblance to my previous professional experiences, the ones that purportedly made me such an attractive hire. It feels like my eight-year legal joyride earned me a top position as a corporate chauffeur.

Exactly, says maturity. *That's the point*, prudence chimes in. Joyriding is fun, but it isn't safe and it doesn't pay too well. The chauffeur's cap comes with a fat paycheck, dental and vision insurance, and a great 401(k) program. Keep your head down, work hard, climb the ladder. Make partner in two or three years, start taking home seven figures in two or three more years, retire at sixty-five, spend time with the grandchildren. That's success.

By any measure, you're successful, I tell myself. *Appreciate your success, enjoy it—the fancy skyscraper office, the money, the secretary, the nice suits, the status, the money. You've won. The job isn't fun, but what job is fun? It's called work for a reason. Focus on what is important,* I tell myself. *This is a means to provide for your family. Grow up. Make the best of this.*

What, precisely, is my problem? I don't feel successful. Not at all. I wonder whether I am, in fact, successful by any measure. That's the problem. In particular, I wonder whether I'm successful by my own measure. I wonder what my measure of success is, what is important. That is the thread I don't want to pull. Eight years will unravel. I might unravel. That thread could lead to square one, starting over, throwing it all away. I fear I will be lost.

What, precisely, is my problem? I am already lost. I am not in control and never will be. My success is a victory lap swum backward by one of little Dorothy's fish. I am living someone else's success, someone else's life. Sitting at my desk, I feel like an imposter. I feel empty. I don't want to admit it, but denial doesn't make it less true. It is quite a problem, after all.

It is entirely possible for a lawyer to live life eyes wide open and find meaningful success. Some of my colleagues in the firm do just that. I am not suggesting otherwise. I want to be crystal clear on that point. (Please remember it as you read this chapter.) Sitting at my desk, my problem is that I do not.

What, precisely, can I do about it? That's a tougher question. I think about the strong man. What's next? What's the first step? A long, hard look at what "value" and "success" mean to me, eyes wide open. That's next. Businesses rely on time-tested tools to rigorously evaluate these things. I will do the same. Deep breath, then I pull the thread.

Valuation

There is only one success—to be able to spend your life in your own way.

—Christopher Morley

How well do you live? How do you judge your life's success? To answer these questions, you need points of reference, a method of measurement. In the business world we think about "enterprise value," the worth of a business at any moment. You can do the same in life. Eyes wide open, you can take stock of your life with rigor. It starts with your valuation methodology.

In broad strokes, the business world offers us three ways to value an enterprise. When you're endeavoring to make a return investing your capital, each of the three methods is useful. One approach might make more or less sense depending on the specific context, but there's sense in each perspective. When it comes to valuing yourself, however, there's peril in two of the methods and meaning in only one.

The market approach holds that a business is worth precisely what someone is willing to pay for it! This idea underlies public stock markets. One person wants to sell a share of XYZ Company, another wants to buy a share. If they can agree on a price, that's what the share is worth. When more people want to sell than buy, the sellers will have to accept a lower price to get the deal done. When the opposite is true, the buyers will have to pay more to get their hands on the stock. An efficient, liquid market tells us what the company is worth.

The market approach is compelling at a deeper, philosophical level. If your objective is to consummate a transaction, to buy or sell part or all of a business, there's only one relevant question: is there a price at which both you and your counterparty are willing to transact? Supporting your valuation with all the sophisticated financial analysis in the world won't make a lick of difference if there isn't.

We can rule out the market approach for our purposes. When you assess your self-worth with reference to the judgments of others, you make a fundamental and costly mistake. You are selling yourself. Selling yourself short, selling out, selling yourself down the river. You're looking to buy validation, confirmation, or approval, but you're buying only trouble.

You will never find self-esteem in others' eyes. Self-respect is not something for which you can bargain, not something you can trade, borrow, or lend. Your self-worth is nontransferable, nonnegotiable, unmarketable, unassignable, inalienable.

After all the praise and condemnation, after you've been scorned or cheered, after ridicule or adulation, only you can own who you are, your principles, your behavior, and the space between. You might derive value from the input of others, but you will never derive your value. That is something you must own alone.

The second approach pins the worth of an enterprise to the value it will generate. The idea is that a business is worth what you would pay today for the profits you expect from it in the future. With a "discounted cash-flow model," for example, you project the business's profits well into the future, determine what those profits are worth today given the current interest rate, and then further discount that value based on the risk that the projected profits will fail to materialize. In essence, you make your best guess as to what you think you'll get out of it later, then figure out what that is worth today. It is a sensible approach for investment purposes.

It's tempting to think of your life the same way, but that is a temptation you must resist. Ascribe to this view of your value and you too easily justify today's actuality with tomorrow's possibilities. Mask the price of procrastination with optimistic projections of future progress. Credit yourself for your aspirations in the absence of action. Ignore the cost of today's problems with promises of tomorrow's solutions. Borrow against your best-laid plans.

This view of value is the enemy of accountability. It justifies the empty days of dithering or the late nights at the office, the bad habits and harmful vices, the career you resent, the career you lack, the time away from home, the moments missed, the principles you've postponed. *Someday*, you tell yourself, *it will all pay off.* You'll have a meaningful career, you'll have enough money to retire, you'll take the vacations, you'll spend time with your children, you'll kick the habit, you'll get in shape, you'll take up a hobby, you'll read more, you'll reconnect with your spouse. Someday. You just need a little bit more time, a little bit more money, one more promotion, one more success, one more year. A little bit more time.

You can discount for the time value of money, but you cannot discount for the time value of life. Bonds forgotten or forsaken, like those you fail to form, have little present value, no matter what you might invest in them in the future. Children grow up, people grow apart, you grow older every moment. Principles are not easily resurrected. It is difficult to find joy in a good book or a great vacation when you're a stranger to yourself. Bank on a future windfall to create your value in life and you're destined to sustain the heavy losses of regret.

You cannot measure who you are today with promises of who you will become tomorrow. There will never be enough of anything to change that fact, not enough time, not enough money, not enough success, not enough years. And the problem with "there's always tomorrow" is that it's a demonstrable lie. Time passes, doors close, and your final day holds no tomorrow. There's always right now and nothing else.

I do not mean to say that you cannot find value in sacrifice today for benefit tomorrow. I am not advocating hedonism—far from it. The point is that if you are to derive value from sacrifice, it must accrue at the moment it is made. With today's sacrifice for future benefit, you can find great value in yourself. We call that investment. But you'll never find value by sacrificing who you are today for future benefit. That is a phantom gain. We need a valuation methodology that reflects as much.

We have one in the third approach, known as "book value." It is rather simple. Take a business's assets and subtract its liabilities. What is left is its book value, or equity. If a business has $20 in assets and $15 in liabilities, it has a book value of $5 ($20–$15). Whatever has happened in the past, whatever might happen in the future, whether the company's stock trades at an enterprise value of $1 or $100, right now, for this moment, the book value is $5.

This is the eyes wide open approach to assessing your life. Your internal critic will urge the market approach, always judging, comparing, trading, selling you out. And when you lose your footing in the second and third rings of the self-perception circus, you're likely to stumble into the market view. In the warped reality of your fears you take your measure in your future prospects, weigh the dismal present value of the awfulized fate you perceive, borrow trouble. The strong man lives in the moment, marshals resources, confronts obstacles. Assets and liabilities, he takes his measure in his equity.

Book value is often thought of as a measure of "liquidation value." If the company shut its doors, what would its shareholders have to show for it? After suspending operations, selling off the company's assets, paying off the liabilities, what is left? It is the deathbed valuation.

Morbid, perhaps, but also fitting. Consider the platitudes: Live every day like it is your last. You cannot take your possessions with you. Leave unresolved nothing you would regret in your final hour. Live as you'd like to be remembered when you're gone.

These clichés are cliché for a reason. In our human experience we too easily lose sight of the exceptional and focus on the mundane. The practicalities of the means obscure the uncertainty of the end. We see progress without reference to purpose, how without why. We live the ordinary, the routine. Our mortality is a forceful reminder to see life eyes wide open. Death is a context to appreciate life.

To value it, too. How well do you live? How do you measure your life's success? Every moment could be your last, and one is bound to be for certain. How well do you live? How do you measure your life's success? The inquiry is a final reckoning.

Your Balance Sheet

In business, this reckoning is captured in a financial report called a "balance sheet." It is a simple document. The balance sheet reflects the business's assets, liabilities, and equity at one particular moment in time. As noted, "equity" is what is left over when you take all the assets and subtract all the liabilities. Assets − Liabilities = Equity. Rearranging the equation, Assets = Liabilities + Equity.

There are two parts or "sides" to a balance sheet, namely, the two sides of this equation. One side lists all the assets. The other lists all the liabilities, plus the company's equity. By definition, these two sides must be equal. That is, they'd better balance out. If they don't balance, there's an error in the books that needs to be corrected. Hence, the report is called the balance sheet.

Now that we've adopted book value as our valuation methodology, we need to define "assets and liabilities" and consider how to measure them. That is, you need to define assets and liabilities for yourself and you need to determine how you measure them. For the same reasons we rejected the market approach to value, we must reject in principle the idea that there is an external, universal answer. Living eyes wide open is about the internal clarity of your values and holding yourself accountable for those values. It is not about external judgment. It is about *your* right and *your* wrong, not *the* right and *the* wrong. (For example, I made clear that eyes wide open is not an endorsement of hedonism, but eyes wide open is not a condemnation of hedonism, either!)

You might bring to this exercise an external framework, be it a religious faith, a spiritual philosophy, a logical construct, or anything else. That is your choice to make. I have no objection. I'm not questioning that choice, merely suggesting that you should understand that choice eyes wide open and hold yourself accountable for it.

So, what are our assets and liabilities in life? Rather than leave you with the exhortation "figure it out for yourself," let me suggest that they might fall into certain broad categories. You must remember, however, that you are welcome and encouraged to disagree!

For me, life's assets and liabilities fall into three overarching categories: my material wealth, my existence, and my legacy. The first category is clear enough. It includes material possessions and financial interests and obligations. The house, the car, the mortgage, the stock portfolio, the clothes, the loan from a friend.

In the category of my existence I include four subcategories: my health, my memories, my wisdom, and my integrity. I take a broad view of health, including physical, mental, and spiritual health. Memories speak for themselves. By "wisdom," I mean the insights drawn from knowledge and experience, consciously or subconsciously. That leaves integrity.

Merriam-Webster's online dictionary defines "integrity" as: "1. firm adherence to a code of especially moral or artistic values; incorruptibility. 2. an unimpaired condition; soundness. 3. the quality or state of being complete or undivided; completeness." In life, integrity means all three of these things. To have integrity, you must first have principles. They can be simple and broad, as in "do no harm" or "do unto others as you would have them do unto you." They can be rigid and elaborate, requiring strict adherence to religious doctrine, for example, or to a financial plan for budgeting, saving, and charity. They can fall anywhere between. But they must exist. Integrity is the measure by which your behavior conforms to your principles, the degree to which your choices, actions, and words reconcile with your understanding of right and wrong, or what's "best" if that's how you look at the world. The experiences of soundness and completeness derive from your integrity.

Finally, in the category of legacy I include my relationships and my work. Relationships comprise those with family, friends, colleagues, and acquaintances. Work is the product of your efforts, in your career, in your hobbies, in service to others, in school, at home, and in public. Your legacy is the part of your life you share with others—the love, the joy, the hurt, the support, the abuse, the forgiveness, the empathy, your example. It is what you build, physically and otherwise. I value both my living legacy and the one I'll leave behind. That is, in my view my legacy encompasses both the impact I've made during my life and the impact I'll make after I am gone.

The precise categorization of your assets and liabilities is not critical. You get to choose how to structure your balance sheet. Unlike a business, you are not bound by generally accepted conventions or strictly defined terms. You can start with a clean slate. You might decide, for example, to group your assets and liabilities in categories "physical," "spiritual," "emotional," and "intellectual." Or, "personal," "family," and "business." The details should reflect your view of the world and your place in it, but they are not super-important.

Two things are essential when you build your balance sheet, however. First, you need to be comprehensive. Make sure your categories cover everything in your life, however you think about those things. You have to be able to fit it all in somewhere. Call the family dog a "relationship," a "possession," a "nurturing life source," or anything else. Just make sure there's a place for the pooch on your balance sheet—and for everything else in your life.

Second and most important, think about how you value each part of your balance sheet in general, and how you value the specific items you'll list there. In business, this is easy. We reduce everything to dollars and cents (or some other currency), following accepted conventions to assign a value to each asset and each liability. Dollars and cents are universal. In business they provide a precise, standardized measure of value.

In life it is not so simple. There's no regular measure of value, no defined formulas to employ. Each of us embodies a unique array of preferences, priorities, and purposes. We value things differently, even money. There are millionaires who clip coupons, count every penny, and covet their next dollar as much as their first. There are paupers who have no care for money. Some prize character; others, wealth; some, the wisdom born of struggle; others, the stability of risks avoided.

Value is an amorphous concept. What is more important to you, your memories or your wisdom? Is your home worth more to you than the respect of your children? Would you sacrifice some of your physical fitness to avoid a business failure? What value do you place on fidelity to your spouse, if any at all? Does that value lie in your integrity, preserving the relationship, both, neither, something else? Would you trade your memories of your college years for the promotion you want? Your balance sheet is complex and uniquely personal.

I am not suggesting that you can answer these questions with mathematical precision, if you can do so at all. And of course, if you dispense with these questions there's an infinity more. Unlike a business, you cannot prepare a literal balance sheet with values for every entry. That exercise will lead you down the proverbial rabbit hole. Besides, our goal is greater clarity, not obsessive focus, an expansive view of life, not a myopic one.

That said, you should give your balance sheet frequent and serious consideration, starting now. The exercise can be uncomfortable. You might want to avoid it. You might not like what you find. Thinking about your life this way might seem too contrived. But whether you realize it or not, whether you acknowledge it or not, whether you like it or not, you live by your balance sheet, always have, always will.

Your balance sheet calculations define you as an individual. With every choice you make, every action, every word you utter, you implicitly ascribe relative and absolute value to varied and competing aspects of your life. It is easy to see in life's big moments. Do you move the family for a great career opportunity even though the kids love their school and you live near family in a great community? You weigh the pros and cons, consider all the factors, talk it through, make a decision. You run the numbers on your balance sheet.

These calculations are easy to miss in the minutiae of life, however, your day-to-day. Easy to miss, but always there. Do you answer your spouse truthfully when asked if you like the new outfit or haircut? Do you have one more drink before heading home? Do you skip the soccer game, the company retreat, your friend's wedding, the workout, the cigar? Do you scold your child or let it go? Would you like a side salad or french fries with your sandwich? Trade-offs in assets, liabilities, equity.

Life. An endless river of choices, placid and turbulent, pleasant and painful, fraught with perils both hidden and in plain view. Day or night, rain or shine, the current pulls you forward. The trip is yours to captain as you choose. When the river's pull is mellow, the sun bright, and the breeze gentle, you can be tempted to take your hand off the till, to take the rudder out of the water, lulled into a doze. You can be forgiven a minor deviation from your course.

But beware. Navigating the rapids demands vigilance and focus, forethought and care, constant practice and absolute comfort with your craft. When you're upon the fast waters, it is too late to begin. Sleep too long and you might awake lost and unprepared. You might miss the best parts of the trip. You might be condemned to an undesirable destination, beyond your opportunities to change course. Best to keep your hand on the till, rudder in the water.

You can live deliberately or by default, make choices intentionally or haphazardly, hold yourself accountable or abdicate responsibility, decide who you want to be or discover who you've become. You can live eyes wide open, master of the reality you create for yourself, or not. You can give some structure to the balance sheet you live by and think about the value you ascribe to the assets and liabilities it contains, or you can ignore it and hope for the best. Your self-worth is in the balance.

Case Study, Part I

There's a lot to be said for my gig, big law firm practice. There has to be. Most of my Harvard Law School classmates and our peers from similar institutions chose it. Among our common assets each of us counts a powerful intellect honed by an elite education, ambition, and a solid work ethic. We chose to put those assets to work in this position. Why?

The career is lucrative. In general it is stable and reliable if you're willing to put in the long hours. In most circles it conveys prestige, or at least professional respectability. It offers a logical, attractive use for an academic degree bought with years of effort and a small fortune. It is a sensible, safe, conservative choice. And like it or not, lawyers provide a valuable service. As my dad says, everyone hates lawyers until they need one.

What does this all mean in terms of my book value? A lot of it means nothing. That's problematic. The prestige, the respectability, the approval of others. If I hold myself accountable to my valuation methodology, these things have no inherent value. Their value in the market is not value in my life, not unless I can define that value on my balance sheet. A troubling place to start. What about my balance sheet, then?

- **My Material Wealth**

  I value material wealth. I'm not afraid to admit it. I want a nice home for Dorothy and my family. I want to provide our children an exceptional education and to expose them to diverse and enriching experiences like travel and extracurricular pursuits. I want both the security and the flexibility that wealth can offer. These things are important to me. In that respect, my job adds great value.

- **My Existence**

  My job is a liability to my health. The hours are long. There's an intense competitiveness to the work, in terms of both the politics of the firm and the arena of high-stakes litigation. Some of my colleagues seem energized by it, but I find it stressful and draining.

  The work is not contributing much by way of good memories for me, either. I had some fantastic experiences with Tom—the poker litigation I mentioned in the last chapter, a trip to Cuba on a high-profile matter, meaningful responsibility for other interesting cases—but they were few and far between, and in all events he has left the firm. I'm not having a lot of fun, not gaining experiences I value. There's much I can learn as a practitioner in the field by way of knowledge, to be sure, but wisdom is different. Like the old saying goes, knowing that a tomato is a fruit is knowledge, and knowing not to put tomatoes in a fruit salad is wisdom. Too often we aggressively assert the tomato's status as a fruit only to ruin a fruit salad.

I want to offer our clients wise counsel about the fate of the fruit salad, even if they've retained us to fight about the classification of the contested tomato, and even if it results in fewer billings for the firm. My job does not offer me this opportunity. Reasonable people can disagree about the prudence, propriety, and practicalities that might necessitate as much. But my principles are my own, and they are at odds with my work, making my job a substantial liability for my integrity.

Even when the need to fight is clear, I reject the preferred fighting style. By my nature I like to understand both sides of a dispute, recognize and explore both views on legal arguments, advocate a moderate position. This approach to litigation was prevalent in my government practice, and in my estimation it is most effective. In all events, it is consistent with who I am.

My superiors have insisted that I abandon this approach, adopt a more aggressive posture, fight at every turn, take no prisoners. In their eyes my advocacy is insufficiently "zealous" if I even consider yielding ground. They want me to present all available arguments. Worse, they want me to believe them, to be the unquestioning soldier, to drink the Kool-Aid. Some of my colleagues embrace this warrior spirit. It works for them, and I have no problem with that. It doesn't work for me, however. I feel I must either be disingenuous or disappoint the team, act a part or fail to meet the expectations I face. In my work I lack soundness and completeness.

Finally, I'm not by my nature risk-averse. I stagnate with stability, bore with routine, am worn down by the grind. I feel I "should" value the security of this career path, find solace in the trajectory that stretches years ahead of me, yearn to be made a partner some day, for years more of the same. I want to value these things, understand why others do. But they are not me. I crave variety, new experiences, new challenges, unbeaten paths. This is not the professional life I want for decades to come, if there is such a profession.

- **My Legacy**

I want to be part of building something. I want a profession I can explain to my children, one that creates products or services, tangible things, not just words and paper. I want to help clients or customers succeed in the positive, productive aspects of their operations, not share only the ugliness and distraction of their litigation. I want to work with a team that leads a business committed to excellence, to witness others grow and thrive, to learn from them, to make an impact in their lives, to share relationships forged from a common desire to do something special.

I want all these things because above all else I want to live an example for my children. Above all else I value my relationships with them, and with their mother. I want to spend time with them, to teach them, to inspire them, to guide them, to support them. Above all else I value my legacy as a father and husband, while I'm here and when I'm gone.

This tips the scales of my balance sheet, above all else. The long hours demanded of me are not conducive to the family life I desire, or the friendships I cherish. Beyond the inescapable limitations of twenty-four hours in every day and seven days in every week, in the insufficient time I share with others outside of work I am too often exhausted, frustrated, or distracted; too often argumentative, defensive, aggressive. I am a corporate litigator. It doesn't add up.

Profit and Loss

What to do about it? Thus far we've focused on the balance sheet, which is a powerful tool to assess the value of an enterprise in a particular moment. We're now going to shift focus and consider how to evaluate action, choices, plans, performance over time.

For this purpose, the balance sheet isn't very helpful. Let's return to the business world for a simple illustration why. Imagine that your friend Walter launched his new business, Walter's Worldwide Widgets (WWW), on January 1, 2016. In February it produced ten red widgets, boring but practical, for $1 each, spending $10 total. People always need red widgets. There was a shortage in November, and Walter was able to sell his ten for $2 each, $20 total, making a nice $10 profit.

Unfortunately, in February Walter's Worldwide Widgets also produced a single blue widget, fancy and glamorous, for $11. With the world in a panic to find red widgets, in November the blue widgets fell out of fashion. Nobody wanted them anymore. The price plummeted. He sold his for $1, losing $10, wiping out his red widget profit.

In 2017 he asks you to make an investment in WWW. "How was business last year?" you ask. In response he gives you the company's January 1, 2016, balance sheet and its December 31, 2016, balance sheet. He tells you to take a look and see for yourself. What do you learn?

Not much. Those two balance sheets are identical. All of WWW's activities occurred between those two dates. The company began and ended the year with no widgets and it broke even. Comparing those balance sheets yields no insight into its activities during the year. You'll learn that the totality of his efforts did not impact his balance sheet, but not how or why.

For that purpose the business world relies upon a financial report known as an "income statement," also known as a "profit and loss statement" or simply a "P&L." Unlike a balance sheet, a P&L covers a period of time. It has a start date and an end date, and it tells you what happened between. In particular, it lists the enterprise's income and expenses during the period. If you subtract expenses from income, you're left with profit. That calculation is presented on the P&L, too.

So, for example, Walter's Worldwide Widgets's 2016 P&L would look something like this:

Income

Red Widget Sales	$20
Blue Widget Sales	$1
Total Income:	*$21*

Expenses

Cost of Red Widgets Sold	$10
Cost of Blue Widgets Sold	$11
Total Expenses:	*$21*

Profit

Red Widget Profit	$10
Blue Widget Profit	–$10
Total Profit:	*$0*

The P&L tells the 2016 story. It describes the activities that took place between the balance sheets. With a quick glance you see that WWW did very well with the red widgets and terribly with the blue one. The net result was that it broke even. That's information you'll want to consider when weighing your investment.

The balance sheet and the P&L are intertwined in ways both

elegant and powerful. Income and expenses flow from assets and liabilities. For example, consider a factory with expensive manufacturing machinery. The machinery is an asset used to produce income, namely, to manufacture products for sale. It comes at an expense, too. It needs to be maintained and eventually replaced. Some of those costs might come due whether the machinery is churning out products or sitting idle. The trick is to maximize the profit you can generate for the cost of the machinery, the idea businesses refer to when they speak of "leveraging assets" or "asset utilization."

The relationship between assets and liabilities on one hand and revenue and expenses on the other plays out in the links between the balance sheet and the P&L. For example, consider what happens when you pay for gas. That expense on your P&L will generally correspond to either the decrease in the value of an asset on your balance sheet—like a reduction in the amount of cash in your bank account—or an increase in the value of a liability—like your credit card bill. Likewise, income corresponds to the increase in value of an asset—like cash in the bank—or the decrease in value of a liability—like a loan forgiven.

Moreover, the profit (or loss) described on a P&L corresponds to an increase (or decrease) in equity during the relevant period. Put another way, profit on your P&L adds to the value of the enterprise on your balance sheet. Make $100 in a year, and everything else being equal, the book value of the business at the end of that year will be $100 greater.

In summary, a beginning balance sheet and ending balance sheet for a period tell you where the enterprise started and where it wound up, in terms of its assets, liabilities, and equity. The P&L for that period tells the story how, in terms of income, expenses, and profit. When it comes to your life, this is an important story! It is your behavior, your choices, your conversations. It is all the moments big and small. The P&L answers the big questions: How do you leverage your assets and mitigate your liabilities? How do you create or lose value? What is the right business plan for you?

Cash Flow

Before we can answer that last question we need to consider a final wrinkle. We've seen that generating profit increases book value. That's our goal. Is life's optimal business strategy as simple as "maximize profit," then? No.

Profits and Negative Cash Flow

Profit is insufficient for success. A company with a profitable business model can still face financial disaster. Profitable enterprises fail. Let's return to Walter's Worldwide Widgets for an example.

Producing a red widget for $10 and selling it for $20 sounds like a fantastic business. You might be tempted to encourage Walter to make all the red widgets he possibly can. But that advice could spell his doom. How?

Suppose that WWW must pay the $10 to produce a red widget—salaries, the cost of the materials, etc.—precisely one month after completing the widget. It takes four months, however, for the company to sell that widget and collect payment. Put simply, it has to pay its bills three months before it gets paid.

Walter needs at least $10 to get started in business, as a month after he makes his first widget he's going to need to pay out the $10 it cost to make it, and he won't have any money coming in for three more months. No problem, you say, he can borrow the $10 from a bank. Three months after he makes his first widget he can make a second one. By the time the $10 in costs for the second widget comes due, he'll get paid the $20 from his first widget. He can pay back the bank with $10 of that $20 and use the other $10 to pay for his third widget. Life is good, and he's in business.

But what if Walter doesn't want to wait three months before his first and second widget? He's confident in his plan and wants to start off producing one widget per month right away. To do that, he'll need to borrow the cost of his first three widgets, or $30. That's a tougher sell for his bank, but maybe he can pull that off.

The same logic applies if Walter wants to expand his business. If, for example, he wants to go from one widget per month to two widgets per month, he's going to need to have at least $10 in hand to pay for the second widget he makes in the first month he doubles his output. And if he wants to hit two per month and stay there, he's going to need $30.

You get the point. If Walter gets aggressive and tries to make as many widgets as he can right away—tries to grow his company too quickly—he will find himself unable to pay his mounting bills. Even though his business is highly profitable. When money comes due before money comes in, the blessing of success quickly becomes a burden. If Walter follows your advice his widget company will drown in its own success.

The "statement of cash flows" is the financial report that details the flow of money into and out of a business during a given period of time. The term "net cash flow," sometimes simply "cash flow," refers to the net amount of money that flows in. Negative cash flow during a period means more money went out than came in.

The fundamental point illustrated by our example is that a company engaging in profitable activity can generate negative cash flow. In business jargon we would say that Walter's Worldwide Widgets must support three months of negative cash flow for incremental sales. If it plans to increase widget production, it must also plan to pay out money for three months before any money comes in.

Still doesn't sound so bad. Walter is prudent. He's calmer than you are. He can plan ahead to manage his cash flow, work closely with his bank, grow his business within his cash resources. With his 50 percent profit margin he should have no trouble borrowing the money he needs. And soon enough his profits can fund future growth. What could go wrong?

Many things. First of all, to plan ahead for his cash needs your friend must first understand them. Our example is simple. The real world, however, gets complicated quickly. A firm might make dozens of products using hundreds of suppliers, each with different payment terms. Sales through different channels could trigger distinct commission payments on different schedules. We have to factor in rebates, warranty costs, and refunds, too. And that's just the payments directly associated with products sold.

Businesses pay out and take in money in many other ways. They pay overhead costs like rent and salaries. They buy, maintain, repair, and sell machinery, equipment, vehicles, and other fixed assets. They borrow money and pay interest, make investments and pay dividends. And, of course, there are taxes. Always taxes.

There are numerous flows of capital, in and out, some interrelated, dynamics constantly shifting as circumstances change. The first challenge is merely to understand them all. It is a challenge many businesses never undertake and one that more businesses never accomplish.

For businesses that do, at best cash flow can be predicted, or "modeled." It cannot be projected with certainty. Some customers will not pay on time; some will not pay at all. Orders are canceled, goods are damaged in transit, warehouses of inventory are ruined by floods. The availability of capital fluctuates with economic conditions, as does its cost. Most products are produced before they are purchased, not after, with no guarantee that they will ever sell, let alone certainty as to when. Warehouses of unsold inventory gather dust as fashions shift, innovations disrupt, demand fails to materialize. You can prepare for contingencies like lawsuits, theft, forces of nature, forces of the market. You can plan ahead of time, but you will never know ahead of time.

Cash is king, and cash flow is his island kingdom. Profitable businesses find ruin on its rocky shores—through folly, sailing blindly in the dark; or by fate, blown off course by a violent storm. They drown in negative cash flow. It is a cruel end, defeat snatched from the jaws of victory, a rude awakening from dreams naïve or ironic.

As in business, you must understand and manage the cash flow of your life to succeed. Expending time and energy is like burning cash. To improve at work, to stay healthy, to nurture our children and our marriages—for most of us these are highly "profitable" endeavors. They take a lot of energy, commitment, and discipline in the short-term. But, as you engage in these "short-term" expenditures, you're building your balance sheet, increasing the value of your assets. You are growing your life equity, creating value in the love and respect of your family, their success, your health, your career advancement. There's only so much cash you have on hand to spend, however.

No matter how profitable your daily operations are, you can only sustain negative cash flow for so long. We reach our limits. We lose steam. We burn out. Like every business, there is only so much we can invest of ourselves before we must either generate returns, borrow against the future, or fail.

It is a fact well understood by science. For example, numerous studies have demonstrated that we are far more effective at work when we take time to replenish ourselves with frequent breaks. Circumstances demand the grind of an all-nighter from time to time. But when they do we derive diminishing returns from our efforts, and we need some time to recover eventually. Slow and steady wins the race, as the saying goes.

This concept underlies the notion of "balance" in life. Balance between work and play, family and friends, self and others, virtues and vices, obligations and indulgences. There is a rhythm to life well lived, like the seasons, a time to sow and a time to harvest; time for deliberation, action, and patience.

We face myriad demands on our time and energy. Some we can anticipate, like a stressful project at work. Others we cannot, like a sudden family illness. These demands are often complex, often competing. If you are not careful with your cash flow, these demands can jeopardize the success of your enterprise, no matter how profitable it is. Never spread yourself too thin and always save for a rainy day. These are the twin pillars of cash flow management in life.

Positive Cash Flow and Losses

Wreck upon the rocks of negative cash flow is not the worst of King Cash's evils. A worse fate awaits on the other side of the island, where unprofitable enterprises run aground on the inviting shores of positive cash flow. Here King Cash mesmerizes with false promise and holds hostage in bonds of delusion. Some of us unknowingly fall victim to this Siren's call, others intentionally practice its dark art to entrap. In either case the result is the same. All appears well above the waterline, but eventually the tide ebbs, and the stranded ship collapses upon itself, unable to bear its own weight.

Let's call on Walter for a final travesty. We'll change the facts and see how his business plays out. Now Walter's red widgets cost $11 to produce but sell for only $10. WWW will lose $1 on every widget. That loss will take a long time to catch up with its cash, however. WWW gets paid one month after it produces each widget, but it doesn't have to pay its bills for producing that widget for another year thereafter.

In essence, with every widget sale WWW is borrowing $10 for a year, paying $1 for the privilege. One month after production, $10 shows up. WWW gets to keep that $10 for a whole year before paying it back. When WWW pays it back, however, it owes an extra $1. WWW's widgets generate cash quickly and lose money a year later.

If you're wondering why a company would ever do such a thing, you're on the right track. The problem is that many companies do so without even knowing they are doing it. This might be hard to believe, but it's true. In business, accurately accounting for all of your costs is not always simple or easy. It can take a lot of discipline and effort to ensure that you're tracking every penny, putting each in its proper bucket. Often, the best you can do is make your best projection and wait to see how it all shakes out. We covered this earlier. Moreover, companies routinely enter into agreements that carry the risk of future contingencies. A spike in the cost of a commodity, for example, can turn profits into losses if you manufacture a product using that commodity and you have fixed the price of your product well into the future.

The point here is that positive cash flow can work against you. When cash is pouring in, precision in accounting appears less urgent. Cash can obscure inaccuracies and mask inconsistencies. It provides a false sense of security, especially for a growing business with a team that is spread thin. The assumption is made that money is being earned as cash comes in, and no dire need is felt to count precisely how much. Whatever we are doing, the thinking goes, we should do more of it. With every scoop dug, the grave deepens. A burial is inevitable.

The cause of death is either mistake or malice. In the former case we call it a business disaster. In the latter we call it a fraud, a Ponzi scheme. In a Ponzi scheme, the perpetrator pays sham profits to early "investors," using cash flow from new investors to fund payments to old ones. The perpetrator touts these fraudulent returns to promote the scheme, duping his "successful" investors into legitimizing the charade by singing its praises, making them unknowing conspirators as they solicit new victims (and often make additional, larger investments themselves). Positive cash flow masquerades as profit, marks are mesmerized, more cash comes in.

Until it doesn't. Starved of oxygen, the blaze burns out, leaving nothing but ruin. The towers of deceit built by sociopaths like Bernard Madoff rise from explosive foundations of cash flow, foundations that spell their ultimate demise.

In life as in business, positive cash flow can mask your losses. Short-term benefits obscure long-term costs, and it is tempting to sacrifice greater value tomorrow for lesser value today. That is what makes vices so attractive and discipline so unappealing. Sometimes we make these compromises deliberately, eyes wide open. That is okay. We are not perfect, and as recently discussed, life is balance.

Tomorrow you'll pay for staying out with your friends too late tonight and drinking too much. But it might be strictly profitable for you if you gain great memories and strengthen friendships, worth the physical pain and an unproductive day. And even if it is not, as long as you are aware and accountable, you can be forgiven the choice. Sometimes you simply need a night out. What good is profit anyway if you never get to spend any of it?

Too many nights out, too many drinks, too many compromises, however, and the calculus can shift before you know it. Life is balance. Consequences emerge and compound with repetition, consequences for your health, your relationships, your performance at work. They are easily missed, though, trumped by your short-term gains. It can be difficult to see the incremental harm in one more drink or one more night out, but it is always easy to see the good times just ahead. Today's cash flow masks tomorrow's losses, and you perpetuate increasingly unprofitable behavior.

At our worst we endeavor to justify this folly. We lie to ourselves. It is the pathology of the addict who falls off the wagon one more time, making promises worthy of Ponzi. He'll trade anything for one more drink. He trades everything for it.

The idea is easily illustrated with our vices, but it extends far beyond them. Whenever and however you compromise your values, you are destined to generate losses, to burn up your balance sheet, to deplete your assets and accrue liabilities. Cash might come pouring in, but it will never be enough to pay for your unprofitable choices.

Case Study, Part II

Understanding my financials eyes wide open enabled me to create a better business plan for myself. At first, abandoning the practice of law seemed like an indefensible move. Many of my friends and family members told me as much! In their eyes I was going to waste valuable assets. My Harvard Law School degree, the clerkships, the years litigating for the Justice Department—these were costly assets that could be utilized to reliably produce income. I would be a fool to throw them away, some said.

But my financials showed I would be a fool to continue practicing law. Yes, I had money coming in, but my endeavors were highly unprofitable. Positive cash flow masked the deterioration of my book value. Until I saw it eyes wide open. My personality, priorities, and principles, embodied in the values carried on my balance sheet, meant that my liabilities were mounting. I was mortgaging my integrity and my legacy for material wealth. Under the valuations of my personal balance sheet, I was racking up credit card debt, not investing in my future.

How well was I utilizing my assets anyway? Like me, most of my Harvard classmates and our peers from similar institutions chose careers in banking, consulting, or law, in New York or San Francisco. Rather than leverage our academic backgrounds as a powerful advantage, we wasted that advantage by competing against one another in the same industries in the same cities, cities with a very high cost of living to boot. In this respect, my credentials were a liability, not an asset. They led me to walk the path most traveled by those most like me, instead of the path I'd like most.

Moreover, the bright shine of those credentials hid the more valuable asset in their shadow, wisdom. My eight years in the field of law, and all my years before them, comprised an ideal résumé in the law firm world, an obvious asset. Those years embodied far greater value beyond the bullet points, however. I learned to think analytically and to work hard. I learned about challenges facing businesses and government. I learned from practice and by studying great mentors how to relate to and work with all kinds of people. Through experiences diverse and remarkable, I gained a wealth of knowledge and insight, and with that wealth I acquired the treasure of wisdom.

That wisdom was an underutilized asset on my balance sheet. Eyes wide open I saw that by leaving the law behind I was not throwing away my accomplishments, not starting from square one. I had built value in both wisdom and in credentials, the former far more valuable than the latter under the individualized logic of my personal balance sheet. To leverage the former, I would cut myself free of the latter. I'd take the path less traveled by my peers and get further in building my book value.

My mission was clear: find a career consistent with my integrity that would enable me to build the value of my legacy, without sacrificing too much by way of material wealth, hopefully. How to do it? That part was less clear, so I consulted an expert. As I shared in Chapter 3, I retained a career coach to help me discover and evaluate my options. And then I got that call from Zac, my "lucky break." You know how that story turned out.

Do you know how yours will? Take a look at your financials eyes wide open. Is your personal business plan suited to your balance sheet? Do you have more profitable ways to leverage your assets, to create value in your life? Are you managing your cash flow? Don't blindly follow conventions of "achievement" or external standards of "success." Take steps to further your goals, the ones that matter to you. Get off the treadmill and decide where you want to go. Use your personal financials, eyes wide open, to figure out how to get there.

Fishing Trip 6: Super Dad

January 1991

"What's the plan, Pa?" I ask.

Long pause.

"I'm not sure," my father responds slowly. He is staring across the hotel's lobby at the frenzied front desk, observing every detail. "Come on, let's see what happens," he says finally.

We walk over.

My father is a lawyer, the best I know. His office is in Hialeah, Florida, a Cuban-American neighborhood of working-class immigrants, modest homes, and simple strip mall storefronts—bank next to bakery, lawyer next to laundromat. After setting up shop as a solo practitioner straight out of law school, he bought a small single-family home on a postage stamp lot on East Forty-Ninth Street—a heavily trafficked thoroughfare—and made it his office. When his business outgrew its literal first home, my father bought the home next door.

Over a hurried weekend, a guerrilla construction crew long on ingenuity and short on permits connected them, destructing openings in their facing walls, enclosing the area between, creating a space that came to resemble something like a hallway. To match the old one, the newly acquired lawn was planted with asphalt and accented with bright yellow lines of paint—landscape architecture in the style of much-needed parking spots. My father and I visited the job site that weekend. I don't know what he was thinking as he surveyed the ragtag scene. Through my young eyes, however, I saw the global headquarters of his thriving legal empire taking form. It was electrifying, and I was immensely proud.

Before we left he called over one of the workers, who was mixing concrete in an old wheelbarrow. My father respectfully explained what he wanted. The worker formed a square of concrete on top of the asphalt in a prominent spot in front of the building. I removed my shoes and socks.

With childish care, I pressed first my hands and then my feet into the cool, damp grit. I used my finger to sign my initials and to mark the date. ODC Construction, a company I founded and lead, has formed millions of cubic yards of concrete for tens of thousands of homes, including the home in which Dorothy and I live with our children. That day I would have traded every one of those homes for the honor and love my father bestowed upon me, his only son, memorialized in water and earth made solid by cement, a monument for all to witness.

The global headquarters isn't pretty, but it gets the job done. The same can be said of the work it shelters. As a lawyer, my father is a potent mix of tactical genius, street sense, and breathtaking audacity. Not breathtaking in the sense of an awe-inspiring vista, but breathtaking in the way a heavyweight's punch knocks every molecule of air out of an unconditioned body.

With an insurgent force of four or five lawyers and less than a dozen support staff, my father once sued every professional sports team in America, every venue in which those teams play, and dozens more related entities—all to raise the stakes in his class-action litigation against Ticketmaster for its alleged anticompetitive practices. Unsurprisingly, he provoked an army of lawyers from dozens of law firms. When I accompanied my father to a hearing in the case, we found ourselves in an elevator with the general of that army—the lead lawyer in command for the opposition—and a handful of his lackeys.

The general fit the part, with his million-dollar power suit, perfect hair, and brilliant teeth; his voice smoked to a dry-aged growl; his wizened face tanned by sun and drink, smelling of aftershave expensive and astringent. "We're going to bury you, Lidsky, you know that," he said to my father. "We're going to crush you." He spoke with mean eyes and palpable intensity, making me uncomfortable.

My father laughed. The laugh was hearty, booming reverberations in the enclosed space. It was genuine, not feigned bravado. The general's dramatic threat struck my father as hilarious. My father's reaction, in turn, stunned the elevator's other occupants, myself included.

"Are you kidding me?" my father asked, reining in his laughter. "I expected a fruit basket from you when we checked into our hotel. Your law firm is going to bill millions because of me. You should be grateful." This last line was delivered as my father slapped the general's back, chum to chum. The general was not amused. Ticketmaster later filed a bogus $306.8 million defamation suit against my father.

High-profile cases like the Ticketmaster whirlwind are few and far between. The bread and butter of my father's legal practice is plaintiff-side personal injury and insurance matters. His firm primarily represents Hialeah Cubans seeking to force insurance companies to pay up. They come see my father when their auto insurance company won't pay to repair their cars after an accident, when the same insurer won't pay their medical bills, when they are hurt in a restaurant or store and they can't afford to visit a doctor.

Most of his clients are proud, most work hard to make a good life for themselves and their children. They come to my father with reluctance to pursue their last shot for redress, not with enthusiasm to extract an undeserved windfall. They come to see my father because they want to be treated fairly. Most of them have not been treated fairly until they come to see my father.

They come to the right man. My father brings the same mix of tactical genius, street sense, and breathtaking audacity to every case, from the multimillion-dollar class action to the claim for $500 to fix a car so that its owner can travel to his job and earn a living. It might take years of litigation and tens of thousands of dollars in legal fees, but my father will recover that $500, you can be sure of it, and whatever else it takes on top of that $500 to make his client whole. He shows no deference to armies of lawyers or their generals, but he pays respect to his clients, treats them with kindness and humility, guards both their financial interests and their dignity.

I often witness this firsthand at my father's side when I go to work with him—to court for a hearing, to a fancy building downtown for a deposition or settlement negotiation, to his office to visit with clients or staff. He includes me in his day whenever it is appropriate and sometimes when it is not. I know when to keep quiet, know to save my questions for the car.

In the car my father explains everything. He walks me through the case. He covers the procedural history, the legal doctrines, the moves made thus far, the moves yet to come. For a kid of eleven, I have an unusually extensive understanding of civil litigation. His lessons cover far more than litigation, though. My father dissects the practical realities of the dispute. He tells the story behind the story, and often another story further back. On the way to a hearing involving a traffic accident, for example, there is no telling what twists and turns the tale might take.

My father's client's sole concern is avoiding deportation in an unrelated federal proceeding. The judge is running for reelection, facing attacks by his opponent for being "soft on illegals." The insurance company's lawyer is the judge's opponent's former law partner. It is critical that my father's client obtain a favorable state ruling regarding the traffic accident before his hearing in the federal immigration proceeding in a week. But today is Wednesday, the judge doesn't work on Thursdays, Friday is a national holiday, and the judge's secretary will be on vacation next week. She is the only person in the judge's chambers who knows how to use a computer.

She is also an unmitigated grump. When she aims to please, she shoots wide of the target. She rarely aims. She goes to lunch at twelve thirty, come hell or high water, and the judge frequently leaves for the day before she returns. On Wednesdays, he always leaves before she returns. My father must extract a favorable ruling in time to convince the secretary to type up and print out the order before she leaves for lunch, so that the judge can sign it before he takes off to prepare for tomorrow's weekly golf game by hitting some balls and having a few martinis at his club this afternoon, all so that the state ruling is in place before the immigration hearing next week. It is a long shot.

This is the sort of story my father explains in the car. Though they've never discussed the matter with me, my parents have apparently concluded that I have more to learn from these stories than from my public school. Though they've never asked me, I agree. Don't get me wrong, I go to school, too. More than I'd like. Enough to ace all of my classes, which should be sufficient by definition. When given the choice, however, I go to work with my dad.

It is the easy choice. Not because I find run-of-the-mill state trial court hearings fascinating. No eleven-year-old could. It is the easy choice because I find my father fascinating. He is my hero. Let me show you what I mean by playing out the hypothetical challenge I just described.

On our way to the courthouse, my father buys the secretary's favorite pastries from her favorite bakery. When we arrive he asks about her three cats, by name. As we planned in the car, I hand her the pastries and thank her for sharing all her great cat stories with my father, stressing that he tells me every single one and that I love them all. She is a rock, but my father and I both know we've introduced cracks below the surface when she responds with a new cat story, her delivery unnervingly mechanical. We smile and nod. When she's done, my father casually mentions his dire need to obtain a signed order before we leave after the hearing.

Entering the judge's chambers, my father enthusiastically compliments him on this morning's favorable coverage of his judicial campaign in the local paper. The editorial my father has referenced quoted a nasty remark made about the judge by his opponent's retired law partner, who is also the retired law partner of my father's opponent this morning, who is, you'll recall, the judge's opponent's partner. My father's true intention is to bring to the forefront of the judge's mind both the nasty remark and the triangle of opposition, one point of which is currently in the room. The judge's face contorts as though he's bitten into a jalapeno-stuffed lemon. He regards the poor lawyer opposing my father as though the lawyer has just uttered the offending words himself.

The move seems to have worked. The judge quickly rules in my father's favor. Before we can hurry back to the secretary, however, it backfires. Riled up, the judge wants to talk about his race. He holds us hostage while he chews my father's ear off, the minutes ticking by. My father listens with an Oscar-winning performance, playing the part of someone who is interested. Twelve thirty comes and goes, then 12:40. We escape at 12:43, only to find that the secretary is long gone as expected. It appears all hope is lost.

The judge's bailiff walks over, convinced my father has performed a miracle. The secretary prepared an order before heading out to lunch, it turns out. She asked the bailiff to procure the judge's signature on the order at the hearing's conclusion—that is, if my father were to win, of course, as all assumed he would. The bailiff disappears into the judge's office and returns with the signed order. My father has performed a miracle.

That's how the scenario would play out. Victory from the jaws of defeat, run-of-the-mill for my father. He makes miracles happen. I love every minute of it, every time. My father is my hero. He is larger than life.

"What's the plan, Pa?" I ask. Once again I'm by his side as he schemes. We're standing in a hotel, across the lobby from the front desk. This scheme has nothing to do with his work, though. The objective is to obtain a room in the hotel for the weekend. Too earthly an objective for a man of miracles, you say? Not quite.

It is Friday, January 25, 1991. We're in Tampa, Florida, host to Super Bowl XXV, which will take place on Sunday. In two days, the New York Giants and the Buffalo Bills will compete for the NFL Champion title in a stadium about fifteen minutes away from this hotel. The timing is no coincidence. My father and I are in town to attend the game, though we don't have tickets.

As we learned from a few hours' investigation this morning, the Giants are staying at this hotel with their vast entourage. (The identity of the teams' host hotels is a secret that is easily uncovered "on the ground" by a man like my father.) Our hotel choice is no coincidence, either. Miami Dolphins fans, my father and I are rooting against the Bills by rooting for the Giants. We plan to stay with the Giants at this hotel so we can get some pictures and autographs, though we don't have a reservation.

To be clear, we don't have a hotel reservation anywhere. That would violate our self-imposed challenge: 1. Arrive without tickets or a hotel reservation. 2. Figure out how to stay with one of the teams, preferably our favorite. 3. Attend the game. 4. For extra points, attend the official victory party. Those are our rules, always have been. This is our fourth Super Bowl.

I was eight when we attended our first, Super Bowl XXII, Denver Broncos versus Washington Redskins, January 31, 1988, Jack Murphy Stadium in San Diego. We set ourselves the same challenge then, and in the two Super Bowls since. So far we are undefeated. My father is larger than life in Super Bowl trips as in work, and in just about everything else, too.

That's what makes these trips so much fun, watching my father operate, seeing him pull off the impossible time and time again. In truth, I'm not much of a football fan. I try to watch with my father on Sundays. He is riveted all day, but I get bored quickly. I could never tire of my father's Super Bowl feats, however.

Like armies of lawyers and their generals, rules, laws, norms, and all other incarnations of authority earn no deference from my father. We've scalped, bribed, schmoozed, counterfeited, begged, snuck, stretched, bent, and faked our way through three memorable Super Bowl trips. We made it into the San Francisco 49ers' victory party through the kitchen. (A bribed janitor led us most of the way through tunnels in the bowels of the hotel, then left us to follow his detailed instructions when security cameras prevented him from taking us any farther.) Another year we had such success trading in the black market for tickets that we bought and sold multiple pairs, generating a profit. We've manufactured buttons, pins, and passes to gain access to special events. Once we confidently walked right into a catered corporate stadium box and sat ourselves in front-row seats, where we remained undisturbed for the entire game, except to use the private restroom and to grab food and drinks from the impressive free spread. There are many more great stories, many more miraculous moments for an eleven-year-old only son.

"I'm not sure," my father responds slowly. He is staring across the lobby at the frenzied front desk, intently observing every detail. "Come on, let's see what happens," he says finally.

We walk over the only way my father knows how to walk—briskly, with authority, demonstrating to all that we know where we are going, insinuating that we are not to be deterred or detained. We loop around the substantial crowd queued before the desk, marching right up to the end of the counter. It is long, narrow, and made of marble. From our vantage point, we see down its full length, pandemonium on either side—staff to our right, the public to the left, everyone agitated and overwhelmed.

My father looks to the right, catches the eye of an employee, and engages. "Excuse me," he shouts over the crowd. "Are you the manager here?" He is polite but firm, more than a suggestion of entitlement in his voice.

He's going brute force, I think to myself, a natural choice in this situation. I'm guessing we're all about to discover something like a major miscommunication or a mysterious technical failure. Whatever the cause, the consequences are unacceptable and must be remedied promptly, we'll all soon agree.

"No, sir," the first victim shouts back, "he is the manager." Victim One points to a man standing next to him, Victim Two, who is juggling two telephone calls and three conversations on both sides of the desk. Victim One's gesture draws Victim Two's attention, and Victim Two shifts his gaze to my father. Victim Two is not having a good day. My father pounces.

"Sir, we called from—"

That's all it takes.

"Oh, you're the ones who called over from [inaudible]?" Victim Two responds. His tense face yields to comprehension and relief.

"Yes," my father says. No man has ever been more certain of his answer.

Victim Two puts down his two phones, picks up a small envelope from the desk below the counter and walks over. "Enjoy your stay with us," he says. He notices me and smiles. "Enjoy the big game!" he adds. Victim Two hands my father the envelope.

My father betrays not the slightest surprise. Dignified, he nods, offers his thanks, and turns from the counter. We walk away.

The envelope contains two keys to a hotel room. Our room, a corner suite on one of the highest floors, a floor that will also house a bunch of New York Giants for the weekend. We are larger than life, another miracle. It's time to start working on tickets for the big game. My father is my hero.

We've pledged to maintain our Super Bowl tradition forever. As an eleven-year-old I want nothing more. I'm certain we'll do it, too. Just the two of us, no tickets, no hotel reservations, forever. There's gratitude and admiration in my eleven-year-old certainty.

It is not to be, however. We will make our strange pilgrimage a few more times, miss a Super Bowl and blame busy schedules, then try again once or twice. In Atlanta for Super Bowl XXVIII we will decide that attending the game isn't worth the astronomical cost of the tickets. We'll watch it on television at the airport instead so we can catch an earlier flight home. We will make it to Super Bowl XXIX, but that game will be played in our hometown, Miami. We'll arrive in the family car, with tickets in hand and a group of people. Super Bowl XXX will come and go without mention by my father. Relieved, I won't mention it, either. Silence will become our unbroken Super Bowl tradition.

To get quality and durability from concrete requires proper engineering. Without structure to reinforce it, concrete has no tensile strength. It cannot bend without cracking unless it has the strength of steel within. Chemical admixtures that manipulate various properties should be employed to tailor the concrete mix to its intended application. If it is not sealed, concrete will erode and discolor.

Built of whim and bagged concrete, my monument did not endure the years. Deformed by cracks and crumbling edges, marked by stains, the broken molds of tiny hands and feet came to mock, not memorialize; to invoke loss, not love or honor.

With the maturity of adolescence I learned new lessons. Sometimes life is the perfect size and larger than life is too big. Breathtaking audacity is misdirected at waiters and flight attendants, at neighbors, at family, at an only son. Some rules, laws, and norms deserve deference. Mistakes can be larger than life, too, like infidelities, behavior reckless and unhealthy, fortunes made and lost, lies children want desperately to believe. A father can adopt new sons, in words and in his heart, rescinding the title "only son," in words and in his heart.

With these new lessons anger and judgment replaced my fascination. In my father's global headquarters I noticed the cracks, the runs in the carpet, the mismatched furniture, the tiled shower misplaced in a law office bathroom, the unconvincing artificial plants. Countless abnormalities, each an inevitable complication of the conjoined twin homes my father misconceived without license. For years I regarded my father the same way, as a construct of faults and blunders, corrupt at the core, with only himself to blame. I felt duped and betrayed.

I was never his teammate in our Super Bowl challenges. "We" didn't play the game, "he" did; it was "his" contest, not "ours." My role was to watch with admiration. But I did tire of my father's feats after all. I resented him and his games. I resented his brazen hypocrisy, the architect of a class-action lawsuit against an alleged scalper of tickets himself scalping tickets. I resented my complicity in schemes to deny rightful occupants their corner suites. I resented the pressure, real or imagined, to follow in my father's footsteps.

When he didn't mention Super Bowl XXX, it was clear that he knew how I felt. Silence was fine by both of us. Years passed, Super Bowls came and went, my father and I grew apart. I graduated college and law school, married, bought a construction company, built a life for myself. I missed my father. I suppose he missed me, too. We both kept quiet about it.

The New Orleans Saints triumphed in Super Bowl XLIV, the Green Bay Packers in Super Bowl XLV. In the months between I scored two sons of my own—and a daughter. With my parental field goal, I won a new title, father, and with that title the breathtaking responsibility to love, nurture, teach, and protect my children. Not breathtaking in the sense of an awe-inspiring vista, but breathtaking in the way a heavyweight's punch knocks every molecule of air out of an unconditioned body.

With new responsibilities come new lessons. Heroes don't exist. Villains don't, either. Both rise in the eyes of children, destined to fall. We learn the best of love and the worst of pain as parents. Fathers are most equitably assessed by fathers. The maturity of adolescence looks naïve and incomplete in adulthood.

I see that now. As a father, I see my father more clearly. I appreciate the true miracles he worked for my sisters and me, admire his unique humility, recognize that his love has always been endless and unconditional. I can better understand his struggles. I realize that he also felt anger, felt pain, felt loss. I make my own mistakes and regret judging him for his.

My father has aged, too. He has mellowed. There is new patience, new gentleness. He engages his grandchildren with joy, present in the moment. His only way of walking has also changed. Now he uses a cane. Retired, he no longer fights with insurance companies. His struggle is with Parkinson's disease. Though he doesn't complain, it must be painful and frustrating.

Love and respect have replaced my resentment. My father has never apologized, but I have forgiven. He was not a perfect father, but there is no such thing, and in his own way he was a very good one. My father has never asked for an apology, but he could. I was not a perfect son. There is no such thing, but I could have done better.

When my sons get a little older, I plan to take them to a Super Bowl. I'll make a hotel reservation in advance, and I'll buy tickets online. It won't be as exciting as it was when their grandfather took their father, but I know they won't mind. Their grandfather is one-of-a-kind, after all, larger than life. He is my only father, and I love him very much.

CHAPTER 7

Ears Wide Open

When people talk, listen completely.

—Ernest Hemingway

Listening is not merely not talking, though even that is beyond most of our powers; it means taking a vigorous, human interest in what is being told us. You can listen like a blank wall or like a splendid auditorium where every sound comes back fuller and richer.

—Alice Duer Miller

Do your other senses "get better" when you lose one? It is an intriguing and popular idea. The human organism embodies an insuppressible tendency to adapt and an awe-inspiring capacity to do so. Examples abound. We compensate for physical, emotional, and mental trauma dizzying in their character and consequence. We survive, we adapt, we thrive.

Do I hear better because I went blind? I am frequently asked this question. Most often, it is more of a request for confirmation than an inquiry—the questioner clearly assumes that I do, in fact, hear better. It's an understandable assumption, but is it correct?

Let's consider some empirical data. In a recent *Forbes* piece,

Brett Nelson reported that the average adult can read 300 words per minute, the average college student reads 450, and the average "high level executive" reads 575. But I read with my ears, not my eyes. When I use my computer I listen to documents, Web sites, and e-mail with the screen-reading software I first learned about in Chris's office. (The computer synthesizes a human voice that reads to me.) Thus, the rate of speech might provide a more meaningful benchmark in my case. According to the National Center for Voice and Speech, the average English speaker in the United States speaks about 150 words per minute.

I read about 675 to 700 words per minute. If you heard my computer chattering away at this rate, it would likely sound like meaningless babble to you. Most likely, you'd fail to pick out a single word.

The average person speaks at about 22 percent the rate my computer does. Put another way, for every twenty-two words uttered I could listen to an additional seventy-eight. Sometimes I put this underutilized auditory bandwidth to use, listening to more than one thing at a time. Two different conversations in a restaurant, for example, or a book and a newspaper.

So, do I hear better because I'm blind?

No. If an audiologist compared the ability of my ears to perceive sound when I was twelve years old to that ability today, we'd find that I hear worse, not better. Going blind did not improve the functioning of my ears. Aging produced the opposite effect. That's bad news for me, but it's good for you.

I don't hear any better. Because I lost my sight I learned to listen better. That's a critical difference. My ears aren't any better, I just learned to use them more effectively. You can, too. Without going blind, of course.

Are you skeptical? Let's return to our statistics on reading rates. Recall that the average adult reads 300 words per minute, the average college student reads 450, and the average executive reads 575. The average speed-reader, on the other hand, reads 1,500 words per minute, and the fastest, the world speed-reading champion, reads 4,700.

Has every speed-reader undergone a profound biological adaptation? No, of course not. Speed-reading is a technique that is intentionally learned, practiced, and mastered, with time and effort. Does every speed-reader achieve 4,700 words per minute? No, of course not. But 1,500 ain't bad.

The same is true of my listening capability. It didn't happen in the biology of my ears, and it didn't happen overnight. With time, intention, and effort I developed skills to use my ears more effectively. I was highly motivated to do so as my sight deteriorated, and perhaps I achieved above-average success for that reason. (I'm certain I'm not the world record holder, however!) But blindness affords no special claim to the skills I've described. Anyone can develop them.

In fact, some of my sighted friends have done so! Fond of audiobooks and eager to read them more quickly, these friends have followed my lead and nudged up their playback speeds. A little faster here and there, they've trained themselves to speed-listen, with time, intention, and effort. They've been pleasantly surprised by the results. They might even learn to listen to two conversations at the same time.

Listening to audiobooks and newspapers more quickly is a time-saver, and eavesdropping on conversations can be highly entertaining (and informative). I have extensive experience on both fronts! When it comes to listening well, however, far more is at stake. Listening well is the core of human communication.

Communication, in turn, is as indispensable as oxygen. We are social creatures. We need to interact to survive. This is why solitary confinement ranks among the worst of our lawful punishments, and why it is considered cruel and unusual if perpetuated too long.

Each of us is an amalgam of relationships, the cumulative effect of countless interactions with countless people. We accomplish nothing alone. No idea is bred purely by a single mind. There is no impact without its object. No man is self-made.

In business and at home, we manifest our lives through the relationships we share. But we cannot relate without communication. And we cannot communicate without understanding. And we cannot understand without listening. Ergo, we cannot manifest our aspirations without listening to each other.

Unfortunately, we're not very good at it. Often, we don't even try. We are too "busy," too distracted. We refuse to turn off the iPhone for dinner, have to check e-mail while on a conference call, choose a seat in the restaurant with a view of the ball game on television.

"I bought a new red car," you say to your friend.

"You bought a car? Great! What color is it?" he asks, tapping away on his iGadget.

It's maddening. Text messages and tweets, podcasts and broadcasts, Facebook posts of friends and pundits, instant Instagrams, snappy Snapchats. We crave information. We fear missing out. We want so badly to know what is going on that we can't focus on the person who is telling us.

Focus, however, is a prerequisite for basic listening competency. To listen well, you must first intend to listen well. Focus, intention, attention. They're the bare minimum when it comes to listening. The good news is that we can do far better than basic listening competency. With intention we can learn to listen well. As with speed-reading and speed-listening, it is a skill that can be mastered with effort and practice. That's what this chapter is about. Are you listening?

Lawyers and Five-Year-Olds

Most people do not listen with the intent to understand; they listen with the intent to reply.

—Stephen Covey

I've learned to say one thing when I'm thinking about something else, act like I'm listening when I'm not, pretend to be calm and happy when I'm really freaking out. It's one of the skills you perfect as you get older.

—Lauren Oliver

"I'm sorry, but I need you to explain this to me like I'm a five-year-old."

It's one of the most helpful sentences ever uttered. I say it multiple times every week, pretty much every day, sometimes more than once in the same conversation. It usually precedes a moment of clarity or connection, usually engenders care and cooperation. It leads to greater understanding.

The sentence expresses an effective message. It is disarming. It begins with an apology and confesses the speaker's need. *This is my problem, not yours.* It is also a charming message. It conveys both the speaker's humility and the purity of his motives. *I'm coming at this like a young child, sincere and innocent,* it says. *I simply want to understand you. Please help me.*

The sentence's true power flows from the message that is not expressed but is nonetheless inescapable: I need you to speak to me like *you* are a five-year-old. That's the logical implication and the ultimate result sought. Because I need to hear your point in plain and simple terms, you need to deliver your point in those terms. I aim to understand, but you must speak to be understood. That's the power of the sentence.

Like many people, I love to listen to five-year-olds speak. Much of what they say is adorable. There are grammatical flaws, misused and mispronounced words, excerpts overheard and inserted in improper contexts, innocence exposed so sweetly it can break your heart. Lily Louise fell in love with the line "Stop whining, woman up" from Disney's *Big Hero 6,* and for months she was prone to arbitrarily exclaim, "Stop whining, warm it up!" Phin told Dorothy that she is his favorite person in the "uniforce." On the way to his checkup, Thad asked me with intense earnestness: "Will you tell the doctor to turn me into a superhuman?" Kids are inescapably cute.

There's much more to it, though. Young children can speak with breathtaking purity. In sentences short and simple, language plain, they can convey raw, unadorned meaning of surprising depth. Often, they convey this meaning without intention or recognition.

Elated to earn my permission to watch a movie, Phin once offered me a verbal high five, saying, "Daddy, when Mama is not home, you're the boss!" In a discussion about favorite things with family friends, Lily Louise shared that "Daddy's favorite thing to do is nap." Tossing his coin in the fountain, Thad proclaimed without any irony whatsoever: "I wish I lived in a castle and ruled." And when I was their age I asked a woman, "Why are your teeth yellow?" My mother was mortified.

We find in children's speech an unintended wealth of meaning and transparency, treasures of implication and connotation, windfalls of irony and revelation. They provoke thought, spark insight, provide the proverbial mirror in which your image is reflected. All of this because they say what they mean and mean what they say.

All of this because of what they do not do. Young children do not filter their speech. When they exaggerate, embellish, or spin, it is obvious, their motives transparent and basic. Five-year-olds' speech is unmuddled by hedging and disclaimers, packaging, self-doubt and insecurity, ego and vanity, lingo, jargon, misdirection, tact, appeasement, or political correctness. These things characterize adult speech. We learn these things later in life.

As an adult, you strive to manage your image by filtering your speech. Think back to Chapter 4 and our three-ring circus of self-acceptance. Recall that in Ring One you confront your self-image, in Ring Two you see the view of yourself you project onto others, and in Ring Three you face the roles others urge upon you. Not always and not necessarily consciously, but as an adult you often tailor the content and delivery of your speech to alter or advance an image of yourself, as you juggle all three rings. To the contrary, a little kid will for the most part speak from Ring One alone, his self-image likely to be far healthier and more stable than those of his elders.

We manage more than image when we speak. We manage complex and competing means and ends. Primary, secondary, and ulterior motives, short-term versus long-term, personal and professional, tactical or strategic. Delay, deny, deflect, impress, inspire, influence, entice, entrap, entertain. Tangled webs we weave, yarns we spin—stump speeches, sermons, eulogies, toasts, roasts, praise, reprimands, public relations, private promises. Tools of the trade. We construct ornate facades upon the simple structure of truth, shrouding its edges.

Think about a personal moment of unexpected significance in your life. For example, have you ever glimpsed a random image, stirring up a long-forgotten, intense memory? Or overheard part of a private conversation, triggering a realization about yourself? It shouldn't be a major moment of obvious consequence. I'm looking for a casual moment in which you were surprised by the experience of something personal and raw. Do you have something in mind?

How would you describe that moment? Put this book aside for a minute and tell the story in your mind in plain and simple terms. Aim for truth and sincerity.

Now imagine telling the story to your boss and colleagues, to a close friend, to your parents, to your children, on a first date, at a wedding, at a funeral, late at night in a crowded bar, or sitting on a park bench on a sunny day. I'd bet you would tailor the content and delivery to each audience and setting. You'd do so in part out of necessity—different audiences know different things about you, have varying context for your story—and in part to satisfy sensible social norms—raucous humor is great for the bar, but a quiet, contemplative delivery will work better at the funeral. Part of it is the three-ring image management we just considered, too.

But there's more to it. We often communicate to advance objectives independent of the meaning we convey. Passive-aggressiveness is a great example. It is "marked by the expression of negative emotions in passive, indirect ways, as through manipulation or noncooperation" according to Dictionary.com. We've all experienced it, and it can be maddening. The message the speaker is endeavoring to convey is clear, though he refuses to state it. Indeed, he may say the exact opposite.

"Why don't we head over to that little burrito shop and grab some dinner?" she asks.

He feels like she just slapped him. He was looking forward to a long dinner at a nice restaurant with a bottle of wine. He was thinking about that Italian place. It is her turn to treat. Why is she always so cheap? She probably doesn't want to spend time with him anyway. It hurts.

"Oh, the burrito place? Yeah, I guess we could go there," he says. "You know, we don't really have to do anything special. We can just order pizza instead."

It is obvious he is annoyed, which is annoying. Why is everything a big deal with him? She is craving a burrito, she had a long day, and she is exhausted. She just wants to be alone. She hates wasting money on meals anyway. Why won't he ever come out and say what he wants? She takes a deep breath.

"I just thought that since you had that big meeting today you might be exhausted, wanting to do something mellow," she says. "I'm sorry. It is my turn to treat, after all, so you pick the place. I'm up for anything."

She is unconvincing.

"No, no. That burrito place is fine. Let's not make a big deal out of this. It's just dinner," he says.

He sulks, she seethes. Neither is hungry anymore. They wind up ordering pizza. Neither is happy about it.

Five-year-olds do not hesitate to tell you what they want to eat for dinner. Most of the time you don't even need to ask them! I can assure you based on extensive personal experience. Yet for us adults, discerning this information is a pervasive challenge.

Most often, far more than dinner is at stake. Passive-aggression can do you great damage, as its source or its target. Dr. Leon Seltzer put it well in an online post for *Psychology Today*: "Oh, how we manipulate! Like con-artists in training, we look for all the possible ways to address our needs and desires without coming out and requesting them directly. We become masters of indirection and subterfuge."

In myriad more ways we speak to ends beyond conveying the substance of our speech. Let's return to your unexpected moment of personal significance. Remember the way you told it in your mind—simplicity, sincerity, and truth your only objectives. Now consider again the various contexts in which you might share that story, with different audiences and in different settings. Think about how your story changes in the various tellings.

The way you change how you tell the story in each case likely reflects deeper reasons *why* you might tell the story. (Or why you might not share it at all, an idea we'll consider in the next chapter.) That is, the context in which you tell the story changes your purpose for telling it in the first place. Pay attention to what you'd tell your boss versus your spouse, what you'd share at the bar or at the park. Strip away the differences you can explain with social norms or image consciousness. The substantial differences that remain reflect the different objectives you'd endeavor to "accomplish" with your story. By definition, objectives other than simplicity, sincerity, or truth.

Simplicity, sincerity, and truth are rarely our only objectives. We speak to illustrate ideas, to prove points, to advance agendas, to fulfill our purposes, to win our battles. We do so in sacrifice of meaning, at the expense of human connection. This tendency is aptly described as our second nature. The way we speak as five-year-olds is natural, but it is not the way we speak later, as adults. That's our second nature.

Adults speak like lawyers.

"I'm sorry, but I need you to explain this to me like I'm a five-year-old." What you're really saying is: *Please don't speak like a lawyer. Speak like a five-year-old. Tell me what you mean, what you think, what you need, what you want.* You're delivering that message indirectly, with tact and subtlety. You're delivering the message strategically, as a lawyer might.

True, there's some hypocrisy in the approach. It is not the most simple or sincere way to ask someone to speak simply and sincerely. Guilty as charged. But connection pure and true is an end that justifies the means. Sometimes we must fight fire with fire.

While we're on the subject of fighting fire with fire, let's turn from speaking to listening. After all, the title of this chapter is "Ears Wide Open," not "Mouth Wide Open." Sure, we can ask others not to speak like lawyers. But how best to understand them when they do?

Listen like a lawyer.

That suggestion might surprise you. Few people view lawyers as facilitators of sincerity or truth. They are counterintuitive role models in endeavors to foster meaning and connection. But they get a bum rap in this regard. We can and should learn from lawyers as far as listening is concerned. In particular, we should study the way they listen to witnesses.

At my mention of lawyers and witnesses, you likely imagined a dramatic courtroom scene with judge and jury, a brilliant litigator duking it out with a witness he is confronting for the first time. As a statistical proposition, this is the wrong mental image. Most interactions between lawyer and witness occur during a deposition. There's no judge and no jury, no courtroom, either. Most times lawyer and witness meet in a sterile, unremarkable conference room, joined only by a lawyer for the other side and a court reporter.

In most cases, a written transcript of a deposition will be the sole result of the interaction. There's no video. And because most cases settle before trial, the lawyer and the witness are unlikely to meet again after the deposition. In the rare case in which a witness does testify in court, he will almost certainly do so after first being deposed. At trial the lawyers are armed with the written transcript of the deposition, and that transcript narrowly confines what the witness can reasonably say. The damage has been done. The witness will confront the transcript of his previous words early and often. If the witness changes his tune, the results are disastrous for him.

Appellate courts do not hear witness testimony. They deal in transcripts. On appeal, the deposition transcript surfaces again, along with a trial transcript if a trial occurred. Transcripts, transcripts, transcripts.

What's my point? Despite Hollywood's dramatic depictions, legal battles are fought with words on paper. Gestures and facial expressions, the quality and character of speech, subtleties of intonation and emotion—these things do not exist in words on paper. On paper witness testimony is letters, words, phrases, sentences, and paragraphs, permanent and cold. It is nothing more.

A good lawyer knows this. He masters the distillation of text from speech, filtering impurities like subtext and sarcasm. He respects the primacy of the words and also their autonomy. He understands that he is more author than director, his task to line edit, not choreograph.

He labors with his reader in mind. He strips away filters, his own and those of the testifying witness. He is unconcerned with his image, pays no attention to his three-ring circus. His focus is the words. Meaning, he knows, must begin with the words. It is knowledge he can artfully exploit.

In the American legal system, a lawyer represents a client and he is ethically bound to advance a certain position on behalf of that client. Consistent with this obligation, in a deposition a good lawyer endeavors to extract from a witness the words that will best support his case as text on paper. Later he will have the opportunity to argue for his interpretation of those words. His opponent will do the same. Words, after all, are often susceptible to more than one meaning. But the words will lay unadorned before the reader, judge, or jury, plain for all to read, exposed to clinical analysis. Words can only be bent so far before they break, sometimes not at all.

A good lawyer thus manipulates the witness in an effort to generate the most advantageous text for his purposes. Facing a point that contravenes his position, he aims for ambiguity and inconsistency. With helpful testimony he strives for emphasis and clarity. He pokes and prods sore spots, digs for suggestive phrases, protests, pursues, charms, intimidates. He mines for words he can cut and polish. Later, he'll sell them for top dollar. He should be commended when he convinces his buyer, not faulted, for this is his role.

Fine, you say, but what does any of this have to do with our present endeavor, listening to others ears wide open? Our aim is deeper understanding and connection. This doesn't sound like deeper understanding and connection, does it? But what if we charge our lawyer with that end, retain him to solicit the simple and sincere truth, to ensure that the witness is not misunderstood, to extract the text that will most faithfully and completely convey the meaning intended? He can use these same skills to further that objective.

That's what I mean when I say you should listen like a lawyer. You should listen as though you've been retained as counsel for the speaker, charged to ensure that he is understood. Listen with focus, listen with purpose, listen actively. Listen like a good lawyer conducting a deposition.

Your primary focus must be the words. Always the words. We distinguish ourselves as a species with our ability to communicate, an ability that derives from our invention of language. Each word in a language has inherent meaning. It has contextual meaning, too, by virtue of its combination with other words pursuant to the language's rules of grammar. Language provides sufficient precision to convey complex and abstract ideas. At the same time it is flexible enough to embody meaning for Donald Trump and Carrot Top, Stephen King and Martin Luther King, John Stewart and John Grisham, Shakespeare and Shania Twain. Words have infinite power. They are immensely useful.

Language is the bridge between speaker and listener. Each has his own internal three-ring circus, his own insecurities, his own knowledge, his own experiences, his own biases, his own vanities, his own aspirations. Each is a chaotic world unto himself. Each views the other across the chasm, outside the borders, from a unique, limited vantage.

If an idea in one world is to find manifestation in the other, it must traverse a bridge of objective meaning with minimal friction, cross free of substantial distortion or corruption. In its ideal form, human conversation is the cooperative construction of such a bridge. Two people labor together to fashion from the building blocks of words a bridge of language that can support the weight of their communication, a bridge that can facilitate the transfer of their ideas. If intention and effort are aligned, they will find success. They will find connection. That is the miracle of language.

It is also where purpose comes in. Remember your role. Remember that you are charged with stewardship of the words you are hearing. You are building the bridge. Your aim is to make sure that when the conversation is complete, an imaginary transcript would reflect with clarity the speaker's meaning, for any reader intended. You labor in opposition to ambiguity, inaccuracy, and incompleteness. Distance, distrust, mistake, miscommunication, frustration, and hurt are the products of ambiguity, inaccuracy, and incompleteness. Listen ears wide open and use words to build a case against these foes. That's your purpose.

To succeed you must listen actively. Ask clarifying questions, encourage full disclosure. You're a lawyer after all, and this is your deposition. Remember your purpose, however. If you are dismissive or defensive, apathetic or aggressive, inconsiderate or insulting, you will hurt your case. The purity of your objective greatly simplifies your task. "Please explain that a bit more." Good. "I'm not sure I understand exactly what you mean." Good. "Interesting. Do you think that is a good thing, a bad thing, or neither? Why?" Good. "I'm sorry, but I need you to explain this to me like I'm a five-year-old." Excellent.

What about all of the information that gets left out of the transcript, like intonation, gestures, and facial expressions? It is a critical part of active listening. A good lawyer pays close attention to that information, too. A good lawyer can artfully employ this information to craft advantageous text from a witness's speech. He can lull into admission, anger into outburst, shame into revelation, confuse into misstatement, sympathize into confession. The information is just as useful when we listen ears wide open, on behalf of the speaker, in search of sincerity and truth.

A speaker's nonverbal communication is your glimpse of his foreign world beyond the shared bridge under construction. It is a hazy, distant view of an unfamiliar panorama. You should study the scene with care for hazards that might threaten the integrity of your bridge. Storms of emotion, sinking soils of deception, the catastrophic strain of asymmetrical intentions. Your view across the chasm can aid your construction efforts.

Always remember, however, that your view is no substitute for those efforts. Do not confuse the scene you perceive with a reliable depiction of meaning. Do not forget that you are looking outside your borders, at a foreign world you cannot even begin to understand on your own. The scene will mesmerize and deceive. It will distract. You must remember: if an idea in one world is to find manifestation in the other, it must traverse a bridge of language constructed of words.

"Are you pleased with how the project turned out?" he asks his boss.

"For the most part, yes," she replies. Her face suggests the opposite. She furrows her eyebrows and breaks eye contact as she responds, a twinge of annoyance in her voice.

Across the chasm she appears to him frustrated and disappointed. This makes him feel frustrated and disappointed. He worked very hard on the project, and he is proud of that work. That is, he was proud of his work until this moment. Now it seems his work wasn't good enough. Maybe it will never be good enough for her. Maybe he's simply not good enough.

"I guess I'm glad to hear it, for the most part." That is what he wants to say. He feels hurt and defensive. He wants to fire back with something clever and flippant, to appear undisturbed and confident. He wants to walk away, get back to his office, be alone.

Instead he takes a moment to focus on the words. He asked if she was pleased with the project, a project he worked on with several colleagues. He did not ask specifically about his performance. She responded with a five-word phrase: "For the most part, yes."

For the most part she is pleased with how the project turned out. That is all the meaning the words will bear. It is not much. He has heaped great weight upon those words by ascribing meaning to her nonverbal communication. They have collapsed under that weight.

He is right to observe as an active listener the dissonance between her words and her delivery. Her nonverbal communication signals trouble. It indicates they are failing to communicate effectively, that he has yet to understand her. Her nonverbal communication demands more words, better words, clearer words. It is no substitute for words, however. He errs fundamentally if he thinks he can find answers in her eye movements or tone, in her look of concern. He'll find only questions there.

Valuable questions, to be sure. What he really wants to know is whether she is pleased with his work. The impact of her response helps him to see this. He thought he was asking that question, assumed she was addressing it. But the words dispel that idea.

"I guess I'm glad to hear it, for the most part." That is what he wants to say. But to what end? Will that help him to understand what she thinks of his work? What is the purpose of their conversation?

Might he instead work to build with her a bridge of words that can facilitate the transfer of their ideas?

There are many clarifying questions he can ask, like: "Are you pleased with my work in particular?" "How might we have done better?" "Why do you qualify your assessment by saying, 'For the most part?'"

Or he can tackle her nonverbal feedback head-on, with: "It seems to me that you might be frustrated. Am I wrong?" "I sense that you might be disappointed." "Perhaps you don't want to talk about this right now?"

There's no secret recipe, no magic formula. Indeed, it is hard for him to go wrong, so long as he possesses the three key ingredients: focus, purpose, effort. To listen ears wide open requires practiced discipline in these respects, but it requires little more. He knows this.

"Uh, I guess I didn't do a very good job?" he asks. He speaks to her like she is a five-year-old. He speaks like he is a five-year-old. He speaks without filter. He speaks to listen, to share meaning, to connect two worlds.

It is a good thing. As it turns out, his boss was very pleased with his work. Or she had some minor, constructive feedback. Or she mistakenly thought he was responsible for a colleague's error. She looked away with some frustration because her acid reflux was flaring up and she realized that she left her medication at home. Or she was frustrated with herself because of a foolish comment she made during the Q&A. Or something about his question reminded her of her ex-husband, who stopped by the house unannounced yet again this morning.

In the end they laughed about the misunderstanding and reaffirmed how much they enjoy working together. Or they exposed some serious problems she had with his work and parted ways committed to find a solution. Or she shared her wish that he have greater confidence in himself, reminding him that she effusively complimented his work on the project just yesterday. Or he learned something personal and intense about her, productive insight for their next bridge, a subtle gloss upon her words. Whatever happened, he listened ears wide open. He listened, and he understood.

Effective as these techniques are, they are grossly underutilized. We do not tend to listen like lawyers. In conversation we abuse, forsake, ignore, and neglect our words. We are careless when we use them, distracted when we hear them. Too often we listen as spectators in our mental three-ring circus. Our focus internal, we hear what we want to hear, hear what we imagine we are hearing, hear what we feared we might hear. We assume or decipher for ourselves what the speaker means instead of listening to him, instead of asking. We do not listen to the words because we do not focus on them. We focus instead on what we are thinking and feeling. We focus on tone and emotion. We focus on what we are seeing. We focus on ourselves.

Adults listen like five-year-olds.

That's the shame of it. Too often we listen like five-year-olds and speak like lawyers. We get it backward. If we aim to build bridges, to share meaning and connection, we should speak like five-year-olds and listen like lawyers. It would make our uniforce a better place.

Listening and Leading

The art of effective listening is essential to clear communication, and clear communication is necessary to management success.

—James Cash Penney

I don't hear any better because I'm blind, but did going blind help me learn to listen better? I think it did. I think going blind made me a better listener and a better leader. Let me explain how by describing my leadership team meetings at ODC Construction.

I don't receive visual feedback from people. Specifically, I don't see their gestures or facial expressions. This is an important point. And while it may also seem like an obvious one, our tendency to substitute gestures and facial expressions for speech is so strong that people often overlook my blindness when they communicate with me. They might nod, for example, in response to my question. It's amusing, but there's often a lot more going on.

I learned as much in my leadership team meetings. As ODC Construction grew from fewer than a dozen corporate employees working together informally in a strip mall storefront to more than one hundred working in multiple facilities around Florida, amateur micromanagement had to evolve into professional leadership if we were to succeed. Fortunately, from day one the company was blessed with a core team of talented and dedicated managers who were up to the task, and we've been able to add team members of similar caliber over the years.

As for my part, I've always thought my job is to inspire and to coordinate that team. In the former capacity I must tend and effectively express our vision of excellence and ensure that our team embraces it. In the latter I must help the company's leaders work together to realize that vision.

As I see it, the leaders of an organization (or division, etc.) must take collective responsibility for its success. Each might have day-to-day responsibility for particular aspects of the business—e.g., operations, finance, sales—but at the same time the team together bears ultimate responsibility for the company's performance as a whole. If the leadership team is to successfully dispatch this responsibility—and if it is to be held accountable for it—then its members must be fully informed in all spheres and empowered to contribute in all spheres. Everyone has the obligation to understand all the issues, to weigh in, and to work cooperatively to help each other succeed. That's how I see it, at least.

At the core of this approach to management is a weekly leadership team meeting. I've much to say on the form and function of these meetings. For our purposes, however, it is sufficient to summarize. In this meeting, new issues or opportunities are presented and discussed, action items are developed and assigned, and updates are presented on pending matters. The goals are to keep everyone informed, to solicit everyone's perspective, to make new decisions (sometimes by consensus, more often not), and to assess previous decisions.

I'm convinced these meetings are essential, and I'm passionate about their effectiveness in enabling a team to succeed. But I don't think I would have seen any of this if I could see. That's what I want to explain.

Absolutely nothing. It happened a lot in the early days. In a leadership team meeting, someone would propose a course of action, I would ask if the team agreed with the approach, and then... absolutely nothing.

"Folks," I said, "remember that I cannot see you. Are you nodding your heads again?"

Nervous chuckles, then someone mumbled, "Oh, yeah, we were nodding our heads."

In the early days this was frustrating. Because I felt my blindness was an impediment to my leadership, it was disheartening. I thought I was missing out on information from my team, and I wondered what they thought I was missing. There was a simple solution. They'd just have to tell me what they thought. No more nods. We'd all have to get used to it.

"That simply doesn't work. I need to hear you, please. Do you agree? Let's go around the table and answer one by one."

After a long pause, the team member to my right said, "I agree." We went around the table and everyone followed suit. I collected auditory nods and we moved on to another topic. That's what I expected. But it rarely happened that way.

"Uh, yeah, I guess I mainly agree."

That kind of unconvincing response, the kind that begs a further question, came up time and time again.

"Mainly?"

The dam breaks.

"Well, I'm not sure how this or that part might work. And we also have to think about this other thing."

A long, heated discussion ensued. The team did not agree after all. The proverbial devil was lurking in myriad details yet to be contemplated. There's more work to be done on the plan. We'll need to revisit the issue at a later meeting with more information. We'll make a far better decision.

And to think: everyone nodded. How could that be? It is easy to nod. There's ambiguity in a nod. There's safety in it. There's opportunity for clarification, even deniability. A nod means little because it can later be distinguished from what was "really" meant, rationalized with elaboration ex post. Nods can be embellished with other gestures and with facial expressions, watered down even further, qualified. They're too amorphous to pin down.

Reduced to words with meaning, ideas take form, stances are clarified, positions are exposed to examination and discussion. When you tell someone what you think, you become accountable for your thoughts, and there is vulnerability in this accountability. In our tendency to communicate with facial expressions and gestures, we often seek refuge from this vulnerability.

Picture the little kid caught red-handed and told to admit his indiscretion. He lowers his head and glances at the floor, his eyes tear up, his lip quivers, and slowly he nods. He simply can't bear to confess aloud. It's somehow better if he doesn't have to say it.

In the early days I lamented my blindness to my team's facial expressions and gestures. I thought I was missing out on information, and I regretted the awkwardness I seemed to inflict upon them by forcing them to speak up. With time I realized that the awkwardness was a by-product of meaningful communication, not my blindness. It was born of our vulnerability. If we were truly to work together to accomplish our goals, we had to be willing to speak up, vulnerable or not. My problem was our solution.

A beautiful thing happened. The more we shared with each other, the easier it became. There is no trust without vulnerability, there is no team without trust, there is no success without a team. We became a team and found great success together. We learned to avoid ambiguities, communicate at a deeper level, and harness everyone's perspectives and ideas. Most important, my team now knows that what they think truly matters. I don't think I would have seen this if I could see. I would have seen a lot of nods instead. Through my blindness we learned to speak to each other, and to listen.

You've guessed it: you can, too. As it turns out, blindness is easily simulated. Close your eyes, don a blindfold, turn the lights off, or do all of the above. In your next management meeting, your next conversation with your spouse or child, your next tough conversation with a friend, try it. You might feel awkward and vulnerable. But that's a small price to pay to truly listen to one another, isn't it? That's what I hear.

Fishing Trip 7: 98 Days, Part II

September 14, 2010, to November 23, 2010

I t was another universe. So much noise, so many sounds. A constant, shrill, high-pitch monotone that provoked terror. A ding pulsing gently as if to imply a luxurious car's door left ajar. A bizarrely pleasant melody of beeps, the same note repeated three times, then a pause, then the same note once again followed quickly by one a perfect fourth lower—e.g., D-D-D, D-A—like a bird's chirp, a breezy theme repeated ad infinitum, key and volume shifting, in a mechanical orchestra's otherwise jarring, atonal symphony.

Just a few of the sounds generated by the many machines in the room, each machine necessary to care intensively for a baby thrust prematurely into his own new, neonatal universe. For each neonate, one of each type of machine, a dedicated mechanical orchestra performing deaf to all others. The effect was a tessellation of auditory assault, exponential discord, noise. That was just the machines.

The NICU team conducted a continuous performance of miracles—noisy work. Sneakers squeaked on tile, carts crammed with medical clutter clanged, scrubs swished as doctors swiftly strutted, trash cans crashed closed, speakers squawked staccato summonses. Some of the nurses hummed to themselves, others sang to their helpless patients. Their motion was constant and deliberate—more than hustle, not quite hurry—an auditory baseline of efficient atmospheric agitation.

Their speech was clipped and encoded. "Brady over here!" "Where's my blood gas?" "Need a PICC line." "That pulse ox is loose." "Did you order my echo?" "We're going to cannula from CPAP today." "Where's my TPN?"

Parents spoke, too; in their speech the sounds of sadness and worry, helpless frustration, desperate gratitude, sustained exhaustion, aspirational joy, unconditional love expressed in inconceivably trying conditions. The parents were hushed and considerate when they spoke, grasping for privacy and intimacy, careful not to disrupt a rare moment when some simulation of these things was in reach for someone else. Meaning was muffled, but emotion rang through with intensity, gentle vibrations of a violin's string soaring above the orchestra on gusts of resonance, topping even the babies' percussive clamor.

Like their very existence, the babies' cries were both expansive and impossibly small, strength and resilience in the face of complete vulnerability, pain to celebrate as declaration of life. There was an occasional coo or gurgle, sometimes an unnaturally awful cough or wheeze or rasp or gasp. Mainly, though, cries emanated from the isolettes, the cocoons of warm air in which science, medicine, technology, love, and miracles conspired to rob death of precious lives commenced too early and too small. Mainly cries or silence. In the NICU, a silent baby has a deafening sound.

It was another universe. I stood just inside the door, unsure I could survive the suffocating atmosphere, my ears bombarded, my eyes no use. My children, born less than an hour earlier, were trapped somewhere in this soundscape. They could survive, I knew, only in its inhospitable atmosphere. I've never experienced the feeling of drowning, but it must feel like that moment did as I stood and I listened.

For my children I'd gladly flail against the tide and drown exhausted. No current of sound and noise would pull me from them, from the virgin shores of fatherhood I was so determined to reach. I would stay with them and protect them, or sink in the effort. Of this much I was certain. This, at least, was within my control.

A nurse guided me through a couple rows of back-to-back incubators, about a dozen in all, to Baby A, then Baby B. I reached in through oval ports in rigid plastic and felt their skin, held my ear close and heard their beautiful, miniscule sounds. I promised to keep fighting for them, indivisibly and without limitation.

Then to Baby C. I couldn't feel his skin, not that day, his birthday. He was too small, too fragile. I couldn't hear him, either. He was intubated, a tube inserted into his lungs through his mouth, a machine breathing oxygen-enriched air on his behalf. The ports of his incubator remained closed that day.

I took a seat next to him and began to listen like my life depended upon it, like my children's lives depended on it. Not because our lives were in actuality so dependent, but for a reason plain and simple: I am their father. Their father would listen no other way. I listened for hours.

Hours stretched into days, days into weeks. Every morning the doctors and nurses made their rounds, reviewing each patient's progress in the last twenty-four hours and establishing a plan for the next twenty-four. Every morning I joined them as they discussed each of my children. I listened like a lawyer, posing questions, learning the jargon, deciphering meaning and significance with practice. Occasionally I heard an error, like a measurement reported incorrectly, an event from the previous day inaccurately described, or an inconsistency with a previous day's reasoning. When I did, I offered corrections. A few times I even offered a judgment of my own.

Much of what I heard rang dissonant. Our greatest concern at birth was cerebral hemorrhage, but we'd have to wait longer than a week before the children could be tested for brain damage. It is common for a NICU baby to "forget" to breathe or to experience Bradycardia—also known as a "Brady"—a perilous slowing of the heartbeat. A baby's path out of the NICU usually tracks a step backward for every two steps forward. I didn't want to hear these things, but I listened.

I listened to the machines, too, pestering nurses and other parents first to explain and then to confirm what I was hearing. In this way I learned that the ear-piercing shrill of terror came from a machine that slowly pumped precise, tiny volumes (measured in cubic centimeters) of TPN—"total parenteral nutrition," liquid food formulated specifically for each and every feeding—into bellies not much bigger. Its only significance was to mark with inexcusable urgency the uneventful completion of a feeding. The pleasant, bird-like chirping, on the other hand, was emitted by machines breathing for babies, the character of each breezy chirp categorizing the respiratory duress it reported.

Like words, each machine and each sound had its meaning. With hours of listening I learned their language. I also trained my ears to pinpoint each sound's exact location so I could distinguish those that pertained to my children from those that did not, from anywhere in the room. With time I was watching over my children with my ears, informed, aware, and vigilant, looking out for them, speaking up for them. It wasn't necessary, but I am their father.

I lived in the NICU for twelve to fourteen hours each day, or longer. To the NICU team's rounds I added my own, visiting with each of my children in turn, an hour or two at a time. Between visits I holed up in the "family lounge," a small, uncomfortable room that the nurses unofficially renamed "Mr. Lidsky's office" because I practiced law in its claustrophobic quiet (determined to preserve my paternity leave for the distant day when finally my children would live in our home). Baby A, an e-mail or two, Baby B, a conference call, Baby C, finish up a memorandum to the client. In my bed late at night I called the NICU to hear updates before dozing for a few hours. I called again when I awoke.

Dorothy, Brenda, and I crisscrossed paths—coming and going to the NICU; stopping at home to bathe, eat, or sleep; spending time with friends and family who came to support us. Some of our visitors, like my mother, ventured into the NICU. Most, however, could not. For them the NICU remained a world distant and incomprehensible.

It was my world. A world in which the sounds of a baby struggling can coexist with grateful relief when you realize it is someone else's child struggling, not yours—relief, then guilt and shame. A world in which a baby can persevere against all odds unvisited and unloved by its parents, not too sick or too small to be a ward of the state. A world in which a lucky parent can learn to rejoice in a new life while mourning its intolerable prognosis, and an unlucky parent can learn to mourn a baby's death, excruciatingly premature like its birth. I didn't want to hear these things, but I was listening.

I didn't want my children to hear these things, so I spoke to them. I spoke to them so that their father's boundless love would fill their tiny ears and vibrate through their tiny bodies—their hearts, their minds, and their burdened, premature lungs. I hoped they could hear me, hoped they would listen. I prayed they would feel my love, would find comfort and strength in it.

"Just breathe easy, nice and slow. Good boy." For my daughter it was "good girl," of course, but otherwise my simple plea did not change. Eight words repeated slowly and calmly for hours; rolling waves of sound; endless testament to inevitability, forces immutable, motion and momentum, plans not our own. I spoke these words for them, for Dorothy, and for myself, a hundred thousand times and more.

As I did I heard my children forget to breathe. I heard their hearts stop beating. I heard backward steps, weight lost, lungs weakened, unanticipated reintubation, emergency transfusions, the necessity of surgical repair. I heard things a father should not hear, sound and noise that will forever reverberate in me.

With time, however, every chord of dissonance resolved blessedly to consonance. For each step back, two forward, daily NICU miracles. There was no cerebral hemorrhage. Dorothy's and my children's hearts and lungs steadily strengthened. Their nervous systems matured, and they consistently remembered to breathe. Their hearts remembered to beat. The transfusions and surgeries were successful. Our babies grew and gained weight. We escaped the panoply of potential consequences one by one, minor, major, and everything in between.

Our anxious bedside rituals came to approximate the routine of new parenthood. We could touch all of our children, then hold them, change and bathe them, and finally even feed them their bottles, small and numerous. Baby A and Baby B were officially designated "feeders and growers" and moved to a new room with fewer machines, where intensive care was less intensively administered. Gone were the ports of their isolettes. In their new NICU room they shared a crib.

Dorothy and I were two-thirds joy and one-third heartache, elated for the two moving on and devastated for the one left behind without siblings to share his room. It was good practice. On their fiftieth day in the NICU, Baby A and Baby B were discharged. That night they shared a crib in our home while Baby C remained in his NICU isolette. Again their parents' hearts were divided, torn by joy and heartache of far greater dimensions.

Again only Baby C carried the family's burden. For twenty more days he carried it lionhearted, without a stumble. On November 23, 2010, Baby C's seventieth day in the NICU, he was discharged at last. That night three babies shared a crib in our home, triplets, joint venturers in birth and in life. Baby C slept in the middle.

Counting Dorothy's bed rest, we spent ninety-eight days in the hospital. On the ninety-ninth, we shared our first day together at home with our children, all three of them, rolling waves of diapers and bottles and bibs and bouncy seats, private and intimate. The next day, the hundredth, was Thanksgiving.

One of the NICU doctors had stopped me as I carried Baby C out of the hospital for the first time, also the last time, as luck would have it. During the preceding seventy days, I had bonded with this doctor. I wouldn't say that we'd grown close, as we still knew very little about each other and hadn't spent all that much time together. But the intensity of the time we did share, and the nature of the responsibility he undertook to care for my children, had bound me to him in admiration and gratitude eternal and infinite.

He pulled me aside.

"Mr. Lidsky," he said, though I had asked him to call me Isaac a thousand times, "I'm not supposed to say things like this." As always, his manner was mild, his words soft-spoken.

I braced myself.

"Without a doubt," he continued, "in my thirty years of NICU medicine, your family's outcome is the most remarkable I've ever witnessed. You are very blessed. I'm very happy for you."

Very blessed indeed. On Thanksgiving, many thoughtful people will recognize that they've "much to be thankful for." On our children's first Thanksgiving, Dorothy and I had everything to be thankful for, as we have every day since. The Tripskys remind us. They live in celebration of daily NICU miracles. Their parents do, too.

I hear in the sounds of my children echoes of these miracles—in their words, their laughter, their footsteps, their breath. Waves of sound from another universe, in my children these echoes are transposed. They pull me from the shore of fatherhood no longer. Now they carry me back to it, soothe me as I walk along the surf, sustain me in the inevitable storms. The echoes are beautiful, like the sounds of my children, like my children themselves. I suppose the beauty I hear in my children is as common as it is miraculous. I'll keep listening, though, aware and vigilant, never tiring of its sound. I'm their father, after all.

CHAPTER 8

Heart Wide Open

The heart has reasons that reason cannot know.

—Blaise Pascal

The Key Ingredient

was seven when I first heard the cliché "When life gives you lemons, make lemonade." My mother explained it to me. She told me that just as we can do this with real things like lemons, we can also do it with our challenges in life. Turn bad things into good things. Make metaphoric lemonade.

I was intrigued, but not convinced. The concept was attractive. I wouldn't eat a lemon, but I loved to drink lemonade. There was simply no arguing with the fact that you make lemonade from lemons. My mom had taught me how. I was pretty good at it. I had even sold my homemade lemonade in front of my house with my sisters, receiving rave customer reviews. Making lemonade was pretty easy when you got right down to it.

On the other hand, turning pain and unhappiness into joy and contentment, failure into success, or weaknesses into strengths seemed intractable problems. I knew plenty of people who were unhappy, angry, or mean. I often heard folks complain about their challenges, large or small. I had witnessed the pain, fear, and doubt of loved ones, and I had already felt these things for myself. There seemed to be a lot of lemons in the world and very little lemonade.

That's what I didn't like about the saying. "Make lemonade" felt wrong. It stated the obvious—"fix the problem"—without providing any instruction. My mom was clearly talking about a process more difficult and more important than making lemonade. The saying made this great and mysterious feat sound obvious, quick, and easy. That wasn't helpful.

I retreated to my room to encapsulate my mother's lesson in a slogan of my own. After thinking for a while, I wrote one down. For gravitas I drew an accompanying illustration and signed my master-piece. Then I presented it to my mother. It proclaimed: "Life can be wonderful if you know how to squeeze your lemons."

A good start. As I think about my childhood take on the cliché thirty years later, there's a lot I like about it. Emphasis on the "if," it highlights the conditional nature of the promise. To make your life wonderful, you must acquire a necessary ingredient, knowledge. You must bring something to the table. I knew I did not yet possess this knowledge as a kid. That was my biggest problem with the original.

I also like the fact that my version speaks simply of "your lemons." Lemons aren't good or bad; they're just lemons. The lesson is not about the lemons. It's about what you do with them. I think "your lemons" does a better job accommodating this nuance than "when life gives you lemons." The latter seems more pejorative toward lemons, the former more neutral.

Likewise, part of the requisite knowledge is understanding that your lemons are always your own. Life doesn't give them to you. There's nothing and nobody to blame in a wonderful life of home-made lemonade. That's the point.

Whatever can be said in favor of my childhood version, how-ever, it has substantial flaws. First, it lacks conviction. Life can be wonderful "if" a lot of things. Which of those things can we make reality? There's no promise in the others.

As a kid I doubted I'd ever know how to squeeze my metaphoric lemons. I was unsure whether anyone really did. Reflected in my rewrite, these doubts admitted only the possibility of a squeezing technique. Too much emphasis on the "if" after all; diluted citrus, if you will.

Beyond its lacking concentration, my childhood revision fails more critically by omitting the key ingredient. Knowing how to squeeze is not enough. You must also choose to do so. The knowl-edge and the choice are intertwined. To make the choice you must first understand there is a choice to be made, and to obtain the req-uisite knowledge you must first choose to do so.

As between the knowledge and the choice, however, the choice warrants greater emphasis. One can imply in the choice to make lem-onade the knowledge how to do so or the intention to obtain such knowledge. But the converse is untrue. Life is full of obvious choices we understand with conscious clarity and nonetheless forsake. The omission of choice in my childhood formulation is indefensible.

A rewrite is in order. We need a new recipe, with choice the dominant flavor, accented by knowledge and conviction. Here's what I propose: Learn to see lemons, choose to make lemonade.

This book has been about the first part, learning to see lemons. I've explained how you create for yourself the virtual reality you live, and I've shared with you an analytical framework to take control of that reality. This book has also been about the second part, choosing to make lemonade. I've urged you to embrace my eyes wide open vision in your life, not merely to understand it in mine. They are intertwined, of course, this knowledge and this choice. Between the two, however, the choice warrants greater emphasis.

That's the purpose of this final chapter, to emphasize your choice. Learning to live eyes wide open is a matter for the mind. Choosing to do so, however, is a matter for the heart. Accordingly, we'll end this book where your choice to live eyes wide open must begin, heart wide open.

Heart Sight

As with figurative lemons and lemonade, my mother has greatly influenced my thinking about the role of our hearts in our lives. Two of her words in particular have been central in my thoughts. I loathed them at first.

By my preteen years I was a committed über-rationalist. I loved to study math and science, to think analytically, to solve riddles and puzzles, to play chess, to live in my mind. I loved these things, and I was very good at them. On the other hand, I lacked both inclination and expertise on messier matters like emotions and faith, patience and grace. My proverbial square pegs, I forced these undesirables into the neat and tidy round holes of logic and rationality in my mind. I avoided the heart at all costs. I thus detested the name my mother chose for our family's first nonprofit organization, Heart Sight Miami.

Three of her four children recently diagnosed with blinding disease, my mother was determined to help raise the research funding needed to develop a cure. With my father she would ask friends and family in the Miami community for support, in donations, in time, in effort. She would ask those friends and family to turn to their friends and family, and those to theirs, reaching out exponentially, ripples on the pond of philanthropy radiating from a mother's plunge.

"We're asking people to see with their hearts so you can see," she said, explaining "heart sight."

That's nonsensical sentimentality, I thought. What could it possibly mean to "see" with a heart? Nothing. We see with our eyes. Besides, we're only asking people to think logically. The costs we bear as a nation in lost productivity and the provision of services for the blind are orders of magnitude greater than the research funding necessary to cure blindness in the first place. We're asking people to "see" that modest investment in science today will produce tremendous returns tomorrow.

Pure logic. Curing my blindness will be a happy consequence of rational behavior. That's what I thought. I cringed every time I heard "heart sight."

My mother was right, of course. I didn't know it yet, but we don't see with our eyes. We see with our minds. The experience of sight is comprised of far more than data from the eyes. It is also shaped by the emotions of the heart, among other things. Understanding as much was the beginning of eyes wide open, the beginning of this book.

In much the same way, our figurative view of the world is shaped by far more than reason. No matter how hard we try to convince ourselves otherwise, the idea of a purely rational perspective is a pervasive fallacy with disastrous consequences. It is a myth that breeds extremism and polarization, a blight that obscures the nuance of life. We think with our hearts, too. That's why there's so much wisdom in mothers.

Classical economics does not explain Heart Sight Miami. Family, friends, acquaintances, and strangers embraced my mother's mission. They donated a lot of money and countless hours of time, but they gave far more. They gave us their love.

The community that adopted my mother's crusade was not investing to reduce future costs associated with blindness. They were not maximizing the value of their relationships. They were not optimizing utility. They wanted to help my mother save her children from blindness. I just couldn't see it yet.

Heart Seen

"If you can't see the camera, the camera can't see you," the frustrated photographer reminds the uncooperative crowd that is supposed to be posing for a group shot.

"That's not always true!" I respond when I'm in that crowd. More blind-guy humor, my favorite genre.

It's not always true of literal sight, but it is always true of heart sight. To see with your heart you must allow your heart to be seen, by yourself and by others. Heart sight and heart seen are in life like the twin pillars of knowledge and choice are in matters of figurative citrus. They're intertwined, and the latter warrants greater emphasis.

Consider the archetypal example: Husband and wife in the car on the way to a dinner party. They have no navigational technology. The man is driving, they are running late, and they are lost. The woman wants to pull into a gas station and ask for directions. The man does not.

He will figure it out on his own. He is smart, confident, capable. He does not need a random attendant at a random gas station to solve this problem for him. His wife seems to think that he does. He resents her for it.

She abhors tardiness. She cannot understand why her husband is so stubborn that he refuses to get directions from a stranger he'll never even see again. She does not doubt that he could find his way eventually. She does not care. She wants to get to the dinner party as quickly as possible. Her husband seems not to care what she wants. This is hurtful to her.

He cannot see this. Why? He is not seeing her with his heart because he does not see himself in his heart. He does not acknowledge to himself that he is frustrated and disappointed. Frustrated that he got lost, disappointed that he cannot figure his way back to his route.

In his heart he yearns to be a navigational guru, capable of single-handedly plotting journeys for them around the globe. But he knows his directional talents have waned over the years. Is his eyesight fading? Is his mind? In his heart he'll find these questions. He might also find fear, sadness, or embarrassment. He does not want to see these things, so he doesn't look. He keeps his focus in his mind instead, seeing a straightforward, logical challenge that his hysterical wife has exaggerated beyond all proportion.

She does not understand his reality because he has hidden his heart. If she could see his disappointment and frustration, she might understand that his true concern is not the gas station attendant. In a perverse way, what she thinks of him is his concern. What he thinks of himself is his concern. If she could see his heart she might reassure him, or even capitulate and encourage him to figure a route on his own, tardiness be damned. Instead she sees him stubborn, cold, and uncaring.

We can lie to ourselves and to others with our minds, but not with our hearts. Our hearts speak our truth. The truth of the heart is never as bad as the fictions of our fears. We find great and unexpected blessings in the heart. We need only look.

"Honey, I can't believe I got us lost again," he says to his wife. "We used to come over to this part of town all the time."

"Please don't feel bad," she responds to her husband. "It has been years since we've been here, and they've done a ton of construction on the roads."

If they open their hearts they might find blessings in getting lost. They might share a moment of connection, of truth, of sincerity. They might understand each other better. They might feel each other's love.

It is not to be. To her mounting frustration and anger he responds with mounting frustration and anger. When they finally arrive at the party unaided, he concludes he has won. She is disappointed in him and embarrassed for him. She is deeply hurt.

You cannot hide from your heart if you wish to create for yourself the reality you want to live.

You will not see beyond your fears if you refuse to see that you are afraid.

You will not silence your critic by plugging your ears.

You will not test your strength with reason alone.

Without acceptance the disabilities we all possess breed surrender, but with acceptance we can find strength in them.

You will never be lucky if you cannot appreciate your luck.

You cannot succeed if you have not defined your success.

Human conversation takes its ideal form, a bridge of language that can support the weight of ideas, only when intention and effort are aligned.

To feel loved you must love yourself and others.

To live and lead eyes wide open you must live and lead heart wide open. They are one and the same. Twin pillars intertwined.

Heart Wide Open

Going blind opened wide my heart. As I shared in Chapter 2, when I was diagnosed with my blinding disease, a fear raw and intense immersed me in a false, awful reality. Pain fueled my inclination to find retreat in my mind.

Undisturbed in the heart, fear metastasizes. Sadness does, too. In my heart, I was scared and sad, a cancer growing unseen. I refused to see that I was desperate for a cure. I refused to see that I needed help. I refused to open the Pandora's box of chaotic emotions that was my heart. I retrenched in my mind, insisting nonsensically that I would meet Blindness with only rationality.

Because I refused to see these things myself, I did not want to see them through others' eyes. I did not want pity or empathy, charity or aid. I did not want our family and friends to spend hours at our home every week planning elaborate Heart Sight Miami fundraisers because for them, too, it was awful, terrifying, and sad to envision my sisters and me going blind. I did not want their help or their love because I did not want to see that I needed both. I wanted classical economics, a cure to my blindness as the happy consequence of rational behavior.

With Blindness's methodical advance, my needs overcame my wants. When crossing a busy street meant risking my life, for example, I needed to be afraid, even though I didn't want to. I needed to get help, even though I didn't want to. I needed to be vulnerable, heart wide open. There was no alternative. Like the illusion of sight, the dam I erected to contain my emotions broke apart with blindness. My heart flooded my reality.

The truth of the heart is never as bad as the fictions of our fears. We find great and unexpected blessings in the heart. We need only look.

At its best, the human spirit projects compassion and generosity of overwhelming power. It has a force as real as gravity, though we do not understand it as well. We often call it "love," but there's far more to it, and love can take lesser forms. "Humanity" is a poor label for the same reasons and others. My mother calls it "heart sight." I think hers is an excellent name.

When blindness broke open my heart I began to feel the power of heart sight. I felt it in random strangers who helped me. I felt it in friends who labored to understand. I felt it in my sisters, who sought to protect me. I felt it in my parents, whose every breath was a prayer for my eyes. I felt it in the people of Heart Sight Miami.

They taught me to see with my heart, and I fell in love with the view. Joy, grace, beauty, and beneficence are everywhere if you choose to see them. They're at their best in moments of human connection, when two open hearts meet. Feel the magic of such a moment and you're hooked.

I'm hooked. So hooked, in fact, I'll even use blindness to peek into others' hearts. When I was in law school, Professor Charles Nesson suggested that my blindness could be a great asset in a career as a trial lawyer. My blindness would draw in the jury, he explained, capturing their attention and inspiring their empathy. I could use it to form a bond with them, to engender trust, to persuade them.

He was right. The vulnerability others perceive in my blindness catalyzes connection. Confronted with my blindness, people open up, let their emotions in, and overlook barriers of formality and distance. I can feel it, hear it in their voice, recognize it in their manner. They might feel empathy, pity, curiosity, guilt, or gratitude. It doesn't matter. The result is an opportunity to see a heart.

It is a gift I treasure. However brief, the moment of human connection is electric for me, a spark of energy, pure oxygen. I take it whenever I can get it, with a well-timed joke to put someone at ease, with sincere thanks for welcomed help, by never taking myself too seriously, and by refusing to let others do so.

Human connection has its practical advantages, too. While

blindness has never helped me win a trial, it often helps me get a table in a crowded restaurant! I'm usually treated as a longtime regular by my second visit to a business. People tend to remember the funny blind guy with an open heart.

I'm a funny blind guy with an open heart. Sometimes I mismatch my shoes or my clothes. I frequently bump into things. I talk to people who aren't there almost every day. I should see the spills.

What of it? That part is my choice, and I choose to laugh. Humor, too, is everywhere in life—even our struggles, our worries, our setbacks, our disappointments, and our failures. If you choose to see it, your life is funny. (I promise you it is.) For me, it's an easy choice. Laughter is pure joy.

With Dorothy I've seen the heart's brightest. When we fell in love and chose to live our lives together, I sought her partnership in my journey into blindness. She walked with me every step, supporting me in countless ways. The practical value of this partnership was obvious straightaway. Its higher blessings, however, are anything but practical.

Blindness helped me see our marriage clearly. I opened my heart to her, she opened hers to me, and our partnership grew, subsuming our separate lives in a larger life together. I gaze upon her heart every day with mine, and every time I do it is the most beautiful sight I've ever seen. I'd go blind a thousand times for that view.

I am nothing and have nothing that I do not share with Dorothy, my heart wide open. I am better for it. We share four miraculous children. We are better for it. Dorothy and our children are the best of my reality.

Learn to See Lemons

In every moment, we choose how we want to live our lives and who we want to be. This is our ultimate power. Too often we lose sight of it. Most of us never fully understand it. Still, it is always true. There are no exceptions or qualifications. In every moment, we choose how we want to live our lives and who we want to be.

Your life is not happening to you. You are creating it. Every action you take, every thought you have, every word you utter, your every emotion—at the core of it all is choice. Your choice.

With this empowerment comes complete and inescapable responsibility. Ignore your choice and you are choosing not to choose. Tell yourself that others control your choices and you are choosing not to choose. Convince yourself that the irrevocable choices of your past foreordain your present choices and you are choosing not to choose.

You can live unintentionally. You can exist as reaction, as happenstance. Those are choices you can make. Many people do.

Many sleepwalk through their lives. Many are willfully blind to their hearts and the hearts of others. Many see themselves as helpless victims. Many curse luck and lay blame. Far too many tread waters of fear and anger.

Those are choices not to choose. They are choices nonetheless, in every moment.

Choose to Make Lemonade

No one is perfect. I am far from it. I become frustrated. I lose perspective. I make mistakes. I suffer fears and anxieties.

Eyes wide open is my aspiration. It is a discipline, cultivated and practiced. It is effort. It is a faith that demands constant renewal. It is reality as I choose to see it.

I hope you will choose to see what I see. How do you want to live your life? Who do you want to be? Difficult questions you're answering every moment. I encourage you to answer with awareness and accountability, eyes wide open.

I'll conclude by suggesting how you might commence. Samuel Butler said, "The one serious conviction that a man should have is that nothing is to be taken too seriously." That includes you. It's a good place to start.

If you cannot laugh at yourself, you are not living eyes wide open. Graveyards are full of indispensable people. Too few of them enjoyed life. Remind yourself that people have done far more with far less and been much happier doing it.

Precious little of what we do is important. The important things can appear inconsequential, and the unimportant things can appear vital. Others will prioritize your doings in their own lives, their own realities. Don't become confused in yours.

Children are important. Teach them with patience. Understand that they are always learning from your example. Learn from theirs deliberately. The backward-swimming fish in their minds, which are harmless for the most part, show us how to see our own, which are not. On the whole, their vision is a lot clearer.

Love is important. Love children fiercely. As to the romantic type, Lord Tennyson had it right: it is always better to have loved. It is why we are here. With friends, give freely of yourself, expecting no reward. You will reap unexpected rewards, the important kind.

We coexist in quantum nuance. The absolute is unobservable—right and wrong, good and bad, us and them. As Heisenberg taught, when we measure we interfere. Seek to understand, not to judge; to connect, not condemn. Judgment is the exception that proves the rule, the unequivocal wrong.

Be kind to others. Do it for yourself. It makes life easier and more enjoyable. Kindness begets kindness. Do it for them. There but for the grace of God you go.

You manifest what you see in your life. Count your blessings, not your burdens. Live with grace, not greed. Choose to be happy. You might as well. It's only a moment, after all.

Only a moment, and it's all yours.

• • •

Do you see what I see? I've opened my heart to you with this book, and now that you've read it, I want to understand what it means to you. Please visit lidsky.com/eyeswideopen to share your stories and insights, provide feedback, submit your questions, or tell me how eyes wide open has made an impact in your life. Thank you.

ACKNOWLEDGMENTS

learned to live my life eyes wide open and wrote about it. In both endeavors I relied upon and benefited from countless others—family, friends, colleagues, authors, role models. As to the former endeavor, there are simply too many to list and there is too little space for adequate thanks. If you've brought clarity to my vision, helped me to live it well, or encouraged my authorial efforts over the years, you have my enduring gratitude. As to the latter, more discrete endeavor, this book, I'll thank several people in particular.

First and foremost, there's Dorothy. Cous, I could not have written this book without you—without your support, counsel, ideas, understanding, wisdom, or love. This book is as much yours as it is mine. Thank you.

When the calling to share my vision with others grew irrepressible, I sought a mentor to show me the way. I found that mentor in Greg Ray, then a partner and true friend. Greg, I'm grateful you tested me so methodically in the early days, more grateful I somehow passed! Thank you for seeing eyes wide open the heartfelt intentions of a turnaround guy, and for your faith in the potential of those intentions. It has been a privilege and a whole lot of fun to make freshly squeezed citrus with you.

My partners in ODC Construction, Tony Hartsgrove, Zac Merriman, and David Haines—and the entire ODC team—made it possible for me to write this book. Thank you for your support, for the time and space I needed, and for your excellence in managing our business without my full attention. Tony, your insights and advice on process and substance were invaluable to me in this project, as always.

Mike Ward, Chuck Wyre, Ashley Gulbronson, Clint Greenleaf, Henry Wei, John Drury, Tabby George, Erich Wasserman, and The Wolverines were similarly helpful. Thank you for your encouragement, your ideas, and your friendship.

Finally, there's the TarcherPerigee Dream Team, Joanna Ng, Sara Carder, Brianna Yamashita, and Brooke Borneman. Thank you for believing in *Eyes Wide Open* and for making my dream a reality. I look forward to seeing *Hamilton* with you soon…

INDEX